The Economist

POCKET WORLD IN FIGURES

Pocket Asia
Pocket Europe in Figures

Guide to Economic Indicators
Guide to European Union
Numbers Guide
Style Guide
Guide to Analysing Companies
Guide to Business Modelling
Guide to Financial Markets
Guide to Management Ideas

Dictionary of Business
Dictionary of Economics
International Dictionary of Finance

Business Ethics
China's Stockmarket
E-Commerce
E-trends
Globalisation
Successful Innovation
Successful Mergers
Wall Street

Essential Director
Essential Finance
Essential Internet
Essential Investor

The
Economist

═══ POCKET ═══

WORLD IN FIGURES

THE ECONOMIST IN ASSOCIATION WITH
PROFILE BOOKS LTD

Published by Profile Books Ltd,
58A Hatton Garden, London EC1N 8LX

This special paperback edition produced in association with and
exclusively for The Economist

Copyright © The Economist Newspaper Ltd, 1991, 1992,
1993, 1994, 1995, 1996, 1997, 1998, 1999, 2000, 2001, 2002, 2003

Material researched and compiled by
Andrea Burgess, Marianne Comparet, Ulrika Davies, Mark Doyle,
Lisa Foote, Conrad Heine, Carol Howard, Stella Jones,
David McKelvey, Keith Potter, Simon Wright

Typeset in Officina by MacGuru
info@macguru.org.uk

Printed in the United States

A CIP catalogue record for this book is available
from the British Library

ISBN 1 86197 785 9

Contents

CONTENTS

Notes

This 2004 edition of the annual *Economist Pocket World in Figures* includes new rankings on women in parliament, employment costs, CD players and several environmental and health measures. The country profiles cover 63 major countries. The world rankings consider 177: all those with a population of at least 1m or a GDP of at least $1bn; they are listed on page 236. Also included are a profile of the Euro area and, for the first time, the world. The extent and quality of the statistics available varies from country to country. Every care has been taken to specify the broad definitions on which the data are based and to indicate cases where data quality or technical difficulties are such that interpretation of the figures is likely to be seriously affected. Nevertheless, figures from individual countries may differ from standard international statistical definitions. The term "country" can also refer to territories or economic entities.

Some country definitions

Macedonia is officially known as the Former Yugoslav Republic of Macedonia. Data for Cyprus normally refer to Greek Cyprus only. Data for China do not include Hong Kong or Macau. For other countries such as Morocco they exclude disputed areas. Congo refers to the Democratic Republic of Congo, formerly known as Zaire. Congo-Brazzaville refers to the other Congo. Data for the EU refer to its current 15 members. The euro area of 12 EU members came into being on January 1 1999; Greece joined on January 1 2001.

Statistical basis

The all-important factor in a book of this kind is to be able to make reliable comparisons between countries. Although this is never quite possible for the reasons stated above, the best route, which this book takes, is to compare data for the same year or period and to use actual, not estimated, figures wherever possible. Where a country's data is excessively out of date, it is excluded, which is the reason there is no country profile of Iraq in this edition. The research for this edition of *The Economist Pocket World in Figures* was carried out in 2003 using the latest available sources that present data on an internationally comparable basis. Data, therefore, unless otherwise indicated, refer to the year ending December 31 2001.

In the country profiles, life expectancy, crude birth, death and fertility rates are based on 2000–05 averages; human development indices and energy data are for 2000; marriage and divorce data refer to the latest year with available figures. In a number of cases, data are shown for the latest year within a range.

Other definitions
Data shown on country profiles may not always be consistent with those shown on the world rankings because the definitions or years covered can differ. Data may also differ between two different rankings.

Most countries' national accounts are now compiled on a GDP basis so, for simplicity, the term GDP has been used interchangeably with GNP or GNI.

Statistics for principal exports and principal imports are normally based on customs statistics. These are generally compiled on different definitions to the visible exports and imports figures shown in the balance of payments section.

Definitions of the statistics shown are given on the relevant page or in the glossary at the end of the book. Figures may not add exactly to totals, or percentages to 100, because of rounding or, in the case of GDP, statistical adjustment. Sums of money have generally been converted to US dollars at the official exchange rate ruling at the time to which the figures refer.

Energy consumption data are not always reliable, particularly for the major oil producing countries. Consumption per head data may therefore be higher than in reality. Energy exports can exceed production and imports can exceed consumption if transit operations distort trade data or oil is imported for refining and re-exported.

Abbreviations

bn	billion (one thousand million)	GNI	Gross national income
CIS	Commonwealth of Independent States	GNP	Gross national product
		GRT	Gross tonnage
EU	European Union	m	million
kg	kilogram	PPP	Purchasing power parity
km	kilometre	trn	trillion (one thousand billion)
GDP	Gross domestic product	...	not available

World rankings

Countries: *natural facts*

Countries: *the largest*[a]

'000 sq km

1	Russia	17,075	31	Nigeria	924
2	Canada	9,971	32	Venezuela	912
3	China	9,561	33	Namibia	824
4	United States	9,373	34	Pakistan	804
5	Brazil	8,512	35	Mozambique	799
6	Australia	7,682	36	Turkey	779
7	India	3,287	37	Chile	757
8	Argentina	2,767	38	Zambia	753
9	Kazakhstan	2,717	39	Myanmar	677
10	Sudan	2,506	40	Afghanistan	652
11	Algeria	2,382	41	Somalia	638
12	Congo	2,345	42	Central African Rep	622
13	Saudi Arabia	2,200	43	Ukraine	604
14	Mexico	1,973	44	Madagascar	587
15	Indonesia[b]	1,904	45	Kenya	583
16	Libya	1,760	46	Botswana	581
17	Iran	1,648	47	France	544
18	Mongolia	1,565	48	Yemen	528
19	Peru	1,285	49	Thailand	513
20	Chad	1,284	50	Spain	505
21	Niger	1,267	51	Turkmenistan	488
22	Angola	1,247	52	Cameroon	475
23	Mali	1,240	53	Papua New Guinea	463
24	South Africa	1,226	54	Sweden	450
25	Colombia	1,142	55	Morocco	447
26	Ethiopia	1,134		Uzbekistan	447
27	Bolivia	1,099	57	Iraq	438
28	Mauritania	1,031	58	Paraguay	407
29	Egypt	1,000	59	Zimbabwe	391
30	Tanzania	945	60	Japan	378

Mountains: *the highest*[c]

	Name	Location	Height (m)
1	Everest	Nepal-China	8,848
2	K2 (Godwin Austen)	Pakistan	8,611
3	Kangchenjunga	Nepal-Sikkim	8,586
4	Lhotse	Nepal-China	8,516
5	Makalu	Nepal-China	8,463
6	Cho Oyu	Nepal-China	8,201
7	Dhaulagiri	Nepal	8,167
8	Manaslu	Nepal	8,163
9	Nanga Parbat	Pakistan	8,125
10	Annapurna I	Nepal	8,091
11	Gasherbrum I	Pakistan-China	8,068
12	Broad Peak	Pakistan-China	8,047
13	Xixabangma (Gosainthan)	China	8,046
14	Gasherbrum II	Pakistan-China	8,035

a Includes freshwater.
b Excludes East Timor, 14,874 sq km.
c Includes separate peaks which are part of the same massif.

Rivers: *the longest*

	Name	Location	Length (km)
1	Nile	Africa	6,695
2	Amazon	South America	6,516
3	Yangtze	Asia	6,380
4	Mississippi-Missouri	North America	6,019
5	Ob'-Irtysh	Asia	5,570
6	Yenisey-Angara	Asia	5,550
7	Hwang He (Yellow)	Asia	5,464
8	Congo	Africa	4,667
9	Parana	South America	4,500
10	Mekong	Asia	4,425
11	Amur	Asia	4,416
12	Lena	Asia	4,400
13	Mackenzie	North America	4,250
14	Niger	Africa	4,030
15	Missouri	North America	3,969
16	Mississippi	North America	3,779
17	Murray-Darling	Australia	3,750

Deserts: *the largest*

	Name	Location	Area ('000 sq km)
1	Sahara	Northern Africa	8,600
2	Arabia	SW Asia	2,300
3	Gobi	Mongolia/China	1,166
4	Patagonian	Argentina	673
5	Great Victoria	W and S Australia	647
6	Great Basin	SW United States	492
7	Chihuahuan	N Mexico	450
8	Great Sandy	W Australia	400
9	Sonoran	Mexico/US	310
10	Kyzylkum	Central Asia	300

Lakes: *the largest*

	Name	Location	Area ('000 sq km)
1	Caspian Sea	Central Asia	371
2	Superior	Canada/US	82
3	Victoria	E Africa	69
4	Huron	Canada/US	60
5	Michigan	US	58
6	Aral Sea	Central Asia	34
7	Tanganyika	E Africa	33
8	Great Bear	Canada	31
9	Baikal	Russia	30
	Malawi	SE Africa	30

Notes: Estimates of the lengths of different rivers vary widely according to the rules adopted concerning the selection of tributaries to be followed, the path to take through a delta, where different hydrological systems begin and end etc. The Nile is normally taken as the world's longest river but some estimates put the Amazon as longer if a southerly path through its delta leading to the River Para is followed. The level of aridity commonly used to delimit desert areas is a mean annual precipitation value equal to 250ml or less.

Population: *size and growth*

Largest populations, 2001
Millions

1	China	1,285.0		31	Argentina	37.5
2	India	1,025.1		32	Tanzania	36.0
3	United States	285.9		33	Sudan	31.8
4	Indonesia	214.8		34	Kenya	31.3
5	Brazil	172.6		35	Canada	31.0
6	Pakistan	145.0		36	Algeria	30.8
7	Russia	144.7		37	Morocco	30.4
8	Bangladesh	140.4		38	Peru	26.1
9	Japan	127.3		39	Uzbekistan	25.3
10	Nigeria	116.9		40	Venezuela	24.6
11	Mexico	100.4		41	Uganda	24.0
12	Germany	82.0		42	Iraq	23.6
13	Vietnam	79.2			Nepal	23.6
14	Philippines	77.1		44	Malaysia	22.6
15	Iran	71.4		45	Afghanistan	22.5
16	Egypt	69.1		46	North Korea	22.4
17	Turkey	67.6			Romania	22.4
18	Ethiopia	64.5		48	Taiwan	22.3
19	Thailand	63.6		49	Saudi Arabia	21.0
20	France	59.5		50	Ghana	19.7
	United Kingdom	59.5		51	Australia	19.3
22	Italy	57.5		52	Sri Lanka	19.1
23	Congo	52.5			Yemen	19.1
24	Ukraine	49.1		54	Mozambique	18.6
25	Myanmar	48.4		55	Syria	16.6
26	South Korea	47.1		56	Madagascar	16.4
27	South Africa	43.8		57	Côte d'Ivoire	16.3
28	Colombia	42.8		58	Kazakhstan	16.1
29	Spain	39.9		59	Netherlands	15.9
30	Poland	38.6		60	Chile	15.4

Largest populations, 2050
Millions

1	India	1,531.4		18	Russia	101.5
2	China	1,395.2		19	Turkey	97.8
3	United States	408.7		20	Yemen	84.4
4	Pakistan	348.7		21	Germany	79.1
5	Indonesia	293.8		22	Thailand	77.1
6	Nigeria	258.5		23	Afghanistan	69.5
7	Bangladesh	254.6		24	Tanzania	69.1
8	Brazil	233.1		25	Colombia	67.5
9	Ethiopia	171.0		26	United Kingdom	66.2
10	Congo	151.6		27	Myanmar	64.5
11	Mexico	140.2		28	France	64.2
12	Egypt	127.4		29	Sudan	60.1
13	Philippines	127.0		30	Iraq	57.9
14	Vietnam	118.0		31	Saudi Arabia	54.7
15	Japan	109.7		32	Nigeria	53.0
16	Iran	105.5		33	Argentina	52.8
17	Uganda	103.2		34	Nepal	50.8

Fastest growing populations, 2000–05
Average annual growth, %

1	Somalia	4.17	11	Angola	3.20
2	Liberia	4.05	12	Burundi	3.10
3	Afghanistan	3.88	13	Mali	3.00
4	Sierra Leone	3.80	14	Mauritania	2.98
5	Eritrea	3.65	15	Bhutan	2.96
6	Niger	3.62		Chad	2.96
7	West Bank and Gaza	3.57	17	Burkina Faso	2.95
8	Yemen	3.52		Guinea-Bissau	2.95
9	Kuwait	3.46	19	Oman	2.93
10	Uganda	3.24	20	Saudi Arabia	2.92

Slowest growing populations, 2000–05
Average annual growth, %

1	Estonia	-1.10	11	Kazakhstan	-0.36
2	Latvia	-0.93	12	Romania	-0.23
3	Georgia	-0.92	13	Croatia	-0.19
4	Bulgaria	-0.85	14	Moldova	-0.11
5	Ukraine	-0.78		Slovenia	-0.11
6	Lithuania	-0.58	16	Czech Republic	-0.10
7	Russia	-0.57		Italy	-0.10
8	Hungary	-0.46	18	Philippines	-0.08
9	Armenia	-0.45		Serbia & Montenegro	-0.08
	Belarus	-0.45			

Fastest growing populations, 2045–50
Average annual growth, %

1	Niger	2.40	11	West Bank and Gaza	1.51
2	Yemen	2.19	12	Chad	1.50
3	Somalia	2.05	13	Congo	1.45
4	Uganda	2.04	14	Afghanistan	1.42
5	Mali	1.81	15	Congo-Brazzaville	1.40
6	Burkina Faso	1.78		Madagascar	1.40
7	Angola	1.74	17	Mauritania	1.33
	Guinea-Bissau	1.74	18	Ethiopia	1.30
9	Liberia	1.59	19	Malawi	1.19
10	Burundi	1.54	20	Eritrea	1.18

Slowest growing populations, 2045–50
Average annual growth, %

1	Estonia	-2.04		Cuba	-0.80
2	Latvia	-1.51		Italy	-0.80
3	Georgia	-1.17		Lithuania	-0.80
4	Ukraine	-1.11	14	Switzerland	-0.72
5	Armenia	-1.09	15	Romania	-0.70
6	Bulgaria	-1.00	16	Hungary	-0.68
7	Russia	-0.86	17	Barbados	-0.67
8	Slovenia	-0.84	18	Kazakhstan	-0.66
9	Belarus	-0.80		Moldova	-0.66
	Bosnia	-0.80	20	Czech Republic	-0.65

Population: *matters of breeding*

Highest fertility rates
Average no. of children per woman, 2000–05

1	Niger	8.00	21	Madagascar	5.70
2	Somalia	7.25	22	Benin	5.66
3	Angola	7.20	23	Zambia	5.64
4	Guinea-Bissau	7.10	24	Mozambique	5.63
	Uganda	7.10	25	West Bank and Gaza	5.57
6	Yemen	7.01	26	Eritrea	5.43
7	Mali	7.00	27	Nigeria	5.42
8	Afghanistan	6.80	28	Togo	5.33
	Burundi	6.80	29	Tanzania	5.11
	Liberia	6.80	30	Pakistan	5.08
11	Congo	6.70	31	Bhutan	5.02
12	Burkina Faso	6.68	32	Senegal	4.97
13	Chad	6.65	33	Oman	4.96
14	Sierra Leone	6.50	34	Central African Rep	4.92
15	Congo-Brazzaville	6.29	35	Laos	4.78
16	Ethiopia	6.14	36	Cambodia	4.77
17	Malawi	6.10		Iraq	4.77
18	Guinea	5.82	38	Côte d'Ivoire	4.73
19	Mauritania	5.79	39	Gambia, The	4.70
20	Rwanda	5.74	40	Cameroon	4.61

Lowest fertility rates
Average no. of children per woman, 2000–05

1	Hong Kong	1.00	26	Georgia	1.40
2	Bulgaria	1.10		Moldova	1.40
	Latvia	1.10	28	South Korea	1.41
	Macau	1.10		Switzerland	1.41
5	Russia	1.14	30	Portugal	1.45
	Slovenia	1.14	31	Canada	1.48
7	Armenia	1.15	32	Barbados	1.50
	Spain	1.15	33	Cuba	1.55
	Ukraine	1.15		Trinidad & Tobago	1.55
10	Czech Republic	1.16	35	Taiwan[a]	1.60
11	Andorra[a]	1.20		United Kingdom	1.60
	Belarus	1.20	37	Sweden	1.64
	Hungary	1.20	38	Croatia	1.65
14	Estonia	1.22		Serbia & Montenegro	1.65
15	Italy	1.23	40	Belgium	1.66
16	Lithuania	1.25	41	Australia	1.70
17	Poland	1.26	42	Netherlands	1.72
18	Greece	1.27	43	Finland	1.73
19	Austria	1.28		Luxembourg	1.73
	Slovakia	1.28	45	Denmark	1.77
21	Bosnia	1.30		Malta	1.77
22	Japan	1.32	47	Aruba[a]	1.80
	Romania	1.32		Norway	1.80
24	Germany	1.35	49	China	1.83
25	Singapore	1.36	50	France	1.89

a 2000

Fertility rates
Average no. of children per woman, 2020–25

Highest			Lowest		
1	Niger	6.49	1	Singapore	1.46
2	Somalia	5.66		Slovenia	1.46
3	Angola	5.60	3	Hong Kong	1.47
4	Yemen	5.55		Macau	1.47
5	Mali	5.44	5	Moldova	1.48
6	Uganda	5.43	6	Estonia	1.49
7	Guinea-Bissau	5.35		Japan	1.49
8	Burkina Faso	5.18		Lithuania	1.49

Crude birth rates
Average no. of live births per 1,000 population, 2000–05

Highest			Lowest		
1	Liberia	55.5	1	Latvia	7.8
2	Niger	55.2	2	Bulgaria	7.9
3	Somalia	51.8	3	Ukraine	8.1
4	Angola	51.3	4	Germany	8.2
5	Uganda	50.6		Slovenia	8.2
6	Mali	49.6		Sweden	8.2
7	Sierra Leone	49.1	7	Austria	8.3
8	Yemen	48.8			
9	Chad	48.5			

Teenage birth rates
Average no. of births per 1,000 women aged 15–19, 2000–05

Highest			Lowest		
1	Niger	233	1	North Korea	2
2	Congo	230	2	South Korea	3
	Liberia	230	3	Japan	4
4	Angola	229		Netherlands	4
5	Somalia	213	5	China	5
6	Sierra Leone	212		Sweden	5
7	Uganda	211		Switzerland	5
8	Chad	195	8	Italy	6
	Guinea-Bissau	195		Spain	6
	Mali	195	10	Denmark	7
11	Guinea	168		Finland	7
12	Gabon	161		Singapore	7
13	Malawi	152	13	Belgium	8
14	Burkina Faso	151		Slovenia	8
15	Mauritania	147	15	France	9
16	Congo-Brazzaville	146		Luxembourg	9
	Zambia	146	17	Cyprus	10
18	Central African Rep	141		Greece	10
19	Gambia, The	139		Norway	10
20	Nicaragua	138	20	Germany	11
21	Madagascar	136	21	Austria	12
22	Mozambique	129		Malta	12
23	Cameroon	127			

Population: *age*

Highest median age[a]
Years, 2000

1	Japan	41.3
2	Italy	40.2
	Switzerland	40.2
4	Germany	39.9
5	Sweden	39.6
6	Finland	39.4
7	Belgium	39.1
	Bulgaria	39.1
	Greece	39.1
10	Croatia	38.9
11	Denmark	38.7
12	Austria	38.3
13	Hungary	38.1
	Slovenia	38.1
15	Estonia	37.9
16	Latvia	37.8
17	United Kingdom	37.7
18	Czech Republic	37.6
	France	37.6
	Netherlands	37.6
21	Spain	37.4
22	Ukraine	37.3
23	Norway	37.2

Lowest median age[a]
Years, 2000

1	Niger	15.1
	Uganda	15.1
3	Mali	15.4
	Yemen	15.4
5	Burkina Faso	15.5
6	Burundi	15.8
7	Somalia	16.0
8	Angola	16.3
9	Congo	16.5
10	Benin	16.6
	Guinea-Bissau	16.6
	Liberia	16.6
13	Chad	16.7
	Congo-Brazzaville	16.7
	Zambia	16.7
16	Tanzania	16.8
	West Bank and Gaza	16.8
18	Eritrea	16.9
	Ethiopia	16.9
20	Rwanda	17.0
21	Malawi	17.1
22	Nigeria	17.3
23	Swaziland	17.4

Highest median age[a]
Years, 2050

1	Japan	53.2
2	Slovenia	53.1
3	Latvia	53.0
4	Italy	52.4
5	Estonia	52.3
6	Singapore	52.0
7	Spain	51.9
8	Czech Republic	51.7
9	Armenia	51.5
10	Greece	51.3
11	Ukraine	50.7
12	Bulgaria	50.6
	Switzerland	50.6
14	Austria	50.3
15	South Korea	50.2
16	Belarus	50.0
17	Hungary	49.6
18	Bosnia	49.4
19	Macau	49.2
20	Poland	48.9

Lowest median age[a]
Years, 2050

1	Niger	20.0
2	Angola	22.0
3	Somalia	22.1
4	Yemen	22.3
5	Uganda	22.5
6	Mali	22.6
7	Burkina Faso	22.7
8	Guinea-Bissau	23.1
9	Liberia	23.3
10	Burundi	23.4
11	Malawi	23.8
12	Congo	24.1
	Lesotho	24.1
	Zambia	24.1
15	Chad	24.5
	Swaziland	24.5
17	Congo-Brazzaville	24.6
18	Zimbabwe	24.7
19	Botswana	25.6
	Sierra Leone	25.6

a Age at which there are an equal number of people above and below.

Highest population aged 0–14

%, 2000			%, 2050		
1	Uganda	49.9	1	Niger	38.9
2	Niger	49.8	2	Somalia	35.1
3	Mali	49.1	3	Angola	35.0
	Yemen	49.1		Yemen	35.0
5	Burkina Faso	48.9	5	Uganda	34.3
6	Burundi	48.0	6	Burkina Faso	34.0
7	Somalia	47.8	7	Mali	33.9
8	Angola	47.3	8	Guinea-Bissau	33.3
9	Congo	46.8	9	Burundi	33.2
10	Guinea-Bissau	46.7	10	Liberia	32.9
11	Liberia	46.6	11	Malawi	31.9
12	Chad	46.5	12	Congo	31.6
13	Congo-Brazzaville	46.4	13	Zambia	31.3
14	Zambia	46.3	14	Chad	31.1
15	Benin	46.2	15	Congo-Brazzaville	30.8
16	Ethiopia	45.9	16	Lesotho	30.5
17	Eritrea	45.8	17	Ethiopia	29.6
	Tanzania	45.8	18	Swaziland	29.6
19	Malawi	45.6	19	Zimbabwe	29.5
20	Rwanda	45.4	20	Afghanistan	29.3
21	Nigeria	45.0		Sierra Leone	29.3

Highest population aged 60 and over

%, 2000			%, 2050		
1	Italy	24.1	1	Japan	42.4
2	Greece	23.4	2	Slovenia	41.5
3	Japan	23.3	3	Estonia	41.4
4	Germany	23.2	4	Latvia	40.9
5	Sweden	22.3		Spain	40.9
6	Belgium	22.1	6	Italy	40.6
7	Bulgaria	21.7	7	Greece	39.6
8	Croatia	21.6	8	Czech Republic	39.5
9	Switzerland	21.3	9	Bulgaria	38.1
10	Estonia	21.2	10	Belarus	37.9
	Latvia	21.2	11	Ukraine	37.7
	Spain	21.2	12	Armenia	37.6
13	Portugal	20.8	13	Switzerland	37.5
14	Austria	20.7	14	Singapore	37.4
	United Kingdom	20.7	15	Austria	37.2
16	Ukraine	20.6	16	South Korea	36.9
17	France	20.5	17	Bosnia	36.6
18	Denmark	20.0	18	Cuba	36.4
19	Finland	19.9	19	Poland	36.2
20	Hungary	19.7	20	Barbados	36.1
21	Norway	19.5		Macau	36.1

City living

Biggest cities[a]
Population m, 2000

1	Tokyo, Japan	26.4
2	Mexico City, Mexico	18.1
3	São Paulo, Brazil	18.0
4	New York, USA	16.7
5	Mumbai, India	16.1
6	Los Angeles, USA	13.2
7	Kolkata, India	13.1
8	Shanghai, China	12.9
9	Dhaka, Bangladesh	12.5
10	Delhi, India	12.4
11	Buenos Aires, Argentina	12.0
12	Jakarta, Indonesia	11.0
	Osaka, Japan	11.0
14	Beijing, China	10.8
15	Rio de Janeiro, Brazil	10.7
16	Karachi, Pakistan	10.0
	Manila, Philippines	10.0
18	Seoul, South Korea	9.9
19	Paris, France	9.6
20	Cairo, Egypt	9.5
21	Tianjin, China	9.2
22	Istanbul, Turkey	9.0
23	Lagos, Nigeria	8.9
24	Moscow, Russia	8.4
25	London, United Kingdom	7.6
26	Lima, Peru	7.4
	Bangkok, Thailand	7.4
28	Chicago, United States	7.0
	Tehran, Iran	7.0
30	Hong Kong	6.9

Fastest growing cities[b]
Average annual growth, 2000–05, %

1	Ansan, South Korea	9.2
2	Ghaziabad, India	6.4
3	Surat, India	6.2
	Toluca, Mexico	6.2
5	Sanaa, Yemen	5.8
6	Niamey, Niger	5.7
7	P'ohang, South Korea	5.4
	Songnam, South Korea	5.4
	Faridabad, India	5.4
10	Rajshahi, Bangladesh	5.3
11	Kabul, Afghanistan	5.1
	Campo Grande, Brazil	5.1
	Antananarivo, Madagas.	5.1
14	Kampala, Uganda	5.0
	Lagos, Nigeria	5.0
	Mogadishu, Somalia	5.0
17	Freetown, Sierra Leone	4.9
	Dar es Salaam, Tanzania	4.9
19	Dhaka, Bangladesh	4.8
20	Nairobi, Kenya	4.7

Highest quality of life index[c]
New York=100, November 2002

1	Zurich, Switzerland	106.5
2	Geneva, Switzerland	106.0
	Vancouver, Canada	106.0
	Vienna, Austria	106.0
5	Auckland, New Zealand	105.0
	Bern, Switzerland	105.0
	Copenhagen, Denmark	105.0
	Frankfurt, Germany	105.0
	Sydney, Australia	105.0
10	Amsterdam, Neth.	104.5
	Munich, Germany	104.5
12	Brussels, Belgium	104.0
	Dusseldorf, Germany	104.0
	Toronto, Canada	104.0

Lowest quality of life index[c]
New York=100, November 2002

1	Brazzaville, Congo-Braz.	28.5
2	Bangui, CAR	30.0
3	Baghdad, Iraq	30.5
4	Pointe Noire, Congo-Braz.	32.5
5	Khartoum, Sudan	33.5
6	Ouagadougou, Burk. Faso	38.0
7	N'Djamena, Chad	38.5
	Sanaa, Yemen	38.5
9	Luanda, Angola	39.0
	Nouakchott, Mauritania	39.0
11	Kinshasa, Congo	40.0
	Bamako, Mali	40.0
	Niamey, Niger	40.0
	Antananarivo, Madag.	40.0

a Urban agglomerations. Estimates of cities' populations vary according to where geographical boundaries are defined.
b Cities with a population of at least 750,000
c Based on 39 factors ranging from recreation to political stability.

Highest urban population
% population living in urban areas, 2001

1	Bermuda	100.0		Malta	91.2
	Hong Kong	100.0	17	Lebanon	90.1
	Singapore	100.0	18	Netherlands	89.6
4	Guadeloupe	99.6	19	United Kingdom	89.5
5	Macau	98.9	20	Bahamas	88.9
6	Belgium	97.4	21	Argentina	88.3
7	Kuwait	96.1	22	Libya	88.0
8	Qatar	92.9	23	Germany	87.7
9	Iceland	92.7	24	United Arab Emirates	87.2
10	Bahrain	92.5		Venezuela	87.2
11	Andorra	92.2	26	Saudi Arabia	86.7
12	Uruguay	92.1	27	Chile	86.1
13	Luxembourg	91.9	28	New Zealand	85.9
14	Israel	91.8	29	Denmark	85.1
15	Australia	91.2	30	Sweden	83.3

Lowest urban population
% population living in urban areas, 2001

1	Rwanda	6.3	16	Sri Lanka	23.1
2	Bhutan	7.4	17	Chad	24.1
3	Burundi	9.3	18	Vietnam	24.5
4	Nepal	12.2	19	Yemen	25.0
5	Uganda	14.5	20	Bangladesh	25.6
6	Malawi	15.1	21	Swaziland	26.7
7	Ethiopia	15.9	22	Tajikistan	27.7
8	Burkina Faso	16.9	23	Guinea	27.9
9	Cambodia	17.5		India	27.9
10	Papua New Guinea	17.6		Somalia	27.9
11	Eritrea	19.1	26	Myanmar	28.1
12	Laos	19.7	27	Lesotho	28.8
13	Thailand	20.0	28	Madagascar	30.1
14	Niger	21.1	29	Congo	30.7
15	Afghanistan	22.3	30	Mali	30.9

Percentage of the total pop. residing in a single city[a]
%, 2000

1	Beirut, Lebanon	59.2	12	Tripoli, Libya	32.8
2	Kuwait City, Kuwait	45.9	13	Buenos Aires, Argentina	32.5
3	Brazzaville, Congo-Braz.	43.3	14	Riga, Latvia	31.4
4	Panama City, Panama	41.1	15	Santo Domingo, Dominican Republic	30.6
5	Montevideo, Uruguay	39.7			
6	Lisbon, Portugal	38.5	16	Ulan Bator, Mongolia	30.2
7	Yerevan, Armenia	37.1	17	Athens, Greece	29.4
8	Santiago, Chile	35.9	18	Auckland, New Zealand	29.2
9	San Juan, Puerto Rico	35.4	19	Lima, Peru	29.0
10	Dubai, UAE	34.0	20	Guatemala City, Guatemala	28.5
11	Tel Aviv, Israel	33.1			

Men and women

Most male populations
Number of males per 100 females[a]

1	United Arab Emirates	186
2	Qatar	173
3	Kuwait	151
4	Bahrain	135
	Oman	135
6	Saudi Arabia	116
7	Guam	109
	Jordan	109
9	Brunei	108
10	Afghanistan	107
	Libya	107
	Sri Lanka	107
13	China	106
	India	106
	Papua New Guinea	106
16	Bangladesh	105
	Pakistan	105
18	Albania	104
	Côte d'Ivoire	104
	Fiji	104
	Nepal	104
	Taiwan	104
23	Costa Rica	103
	Dominican Republic	103
	Iran	103
	Iraq	103
	Malaysia	103
	West Bank and Gaza	103
	Yemen	103

Most female populations
Number of males per 100 females

1	Estonia	85
	Latvia	85
3	Lesotho	87
	Lithuania	87
	Ukraine	87
6	Belarus	88
	Russia	88
8	Georgia	91
	Hungary	91
	Macau	91
	Rwanda	91
	Swaziland	91
	Virgin Islands	91
14	Kazakhstan	92
	Martinique	92
	Moldova	92
	Puerto Rico	92
18	Croatia	93
	Guadeloupe	93
	Mozambique	93
	Netherlands Antilles	93
	Portugal	93
23	Armenia	94
	Bulgaria	94
	Italy	94
	Poland	94
	Slovakia	94
	Uruguay	94

Women in parliament
% of seats held by women[b]

1	Sweden	45.3	16	Vietnam	27.3
2	Denmark	38.0	17	Namibia	26.4
3	Finland	37.5	18	Bulgaria	26.2
4	Netherlands	36.7	19	Turkmenistan	26.0
5	Norway	36.4	20	Rwanda	25.7
6	Cuba	36.0	21	Australia	25.3
7	Costa Rica	35.1	22	Uganda	24.7
8	Iceland	34.9	23	Belgium	23.3
9	Austria	33.9	24	Switzerland	23.0
10	Germany	32.2	25	Laos	22.9
11	Argentina	30.7	26	Tanzania	22.3
12	Mozambique	30.0	27	Eritrea	22.0
13	South Africa	29.8	28	China	21.8
14	New Zealand	28.3	29	Pakistan	21.6
	Spain	28.3	30	Latvia	21.0

a Large numbers of immigrant workers, mostly men, result in the high male ratios of
  several Middle Eastern countries.
b Lower house.

Refugees and asylum

Largest refugee nationalities
'000, 2001

1	Afghanistan	3,809.6	11	Eritrea	333.1
2	Burundi	554.0	12	Croatia	288.6
3	Iraq	530.1	13	Azerbaijan	268.7
4	Sudan	489.5	14	Liberia	244.6
5	Angola	470.6	15	Myanmar	191.0
6	Somalia	439.9	16	Sierra Leone	179.0
7	Bosnia	426.0	17	Serbia & Montenegro	138.7
8	Congo	392.1	18	Sri Lanka	122.4
9	Vietnam	353.2	19	China	117.3
10	West Bank and Gaza	349.1	20	Bhutan	110.8

Countries with largest refugee populations
'000, 2001

1	Pakistan	2,198.8	11	Armenia	264.4
2	Iran	1,868.0	12	Saudi Arabia	245.3
3	Germany	903.0	13	Kenya	239.2
4	Tanzania	668.1	14	Uganda	199.7
5	United States	515.9	15	Guinea	178.4
6	Serbia & Montenegro	400.3	16	India	169.5
7	Congo	362.0	17	Algeria	169.4
8	Sudan	349.2	18	Ethiopia	152.6
9	China	295.3	19	Netherlands	152.3
10	Zambia	284.2	20	United Kingdom	148.6

Nationality of asylum applications in industrialised countries
'000, 2001

1	Afghanistan	52.8	11	Colombia	12.9
2	Iraq	50.4	12	Mexico	11.4
3	Turkey	32.0	13	Algeria	11.0
4	Serbia & Montenegro	28.7		Bosnia	11.0
5	China	21.1	15	Sierra Leone	10.8
6	Russia	18.3	16	Pakistan	10.7
7	Iran	15.8	17	Congo	10.6
8	India	14.7		Ukraine	10.6
9	Sri Lanka	14.4	19	Nigeria	10.0
10	Somalia	14.3	20	Armenia	8.6

Asylum applications in industrialised countries
'000, 2001

1	United Kingdom	92.0	11	Czech Republic	18.1
2	Germany	88.3	12	Norway	14.8
3	United States	86.4	13	Denmark	12.5
4	France	47.3	14	Australia	12.4
5	Canada	42.7	15	Ireland	10.3
6	Netherlands	32.6	16	Hungary	9.6
7	Austria	30.1		Italy	9.6
8	Belgium	24.5	18	Spain	9.5
9	Sweden	23.5	19	Slovakia	8.2
10	Switzerland	20.6	20	Greece	5.5

The world economy

Biggest economies
GDP, $bn

1	United States	10,065.3	26	Hong Kong	161.9
2	Japan	4,141.4	27	Denmark	161.5
3	Germany	1,846.1	28	Turkey	147.7
4	United Kingdom	1,424.1	29	Indonesia	145.3
5	France[a]	1,309.8	30	Venezuela	124.9
6	China	1,159.0	31	Finland	120.9
7	Italy	1,088.8	32	Greece	117.2
8	Canada	694.5	33	Thailand	114.7
9	Mexico	617.8	34	Iran	114.1
10	Spain	581.8	35	South Africa	113.3
11	Brazil	502.5	36	Portugal	109.8
12	India	477.3	37	Israel	108.3
13	South Korea	422.2	38	Ireland	103.3
14	Netherlands	380.1	39	Egypt	98.5
15	Australia	368.7	40	Malaysia	88.0
16	Russia	310.0	41	Singapore	85.6
17	Taiwan	282.3	42	Colombia	82.4
18	Argentina	268.6	43	Philippines	71.4
19	Switzerland	247.1	44	Puerto Rico	67.9
20	Belgium	229.6	45	United Arab Emirates	67.6
21	Sweden	209.8	46	Chile	66.5
22	Austria	188.5	47	Pakistan	58.7
23	Saudi Arabia	186.5	48	Czech Republic	56.8
24	Poland	176.3	49	Algeria	54.7
25	Norway	166.1	50	Peru	54.0

Biggest economies by purchasing power
GDP PPP, $bn

1	United States	9,792	21	Turkey	390
2	China	5,111	22	Iran	387
3	Japan	3,193	23	Taiwan[b]	386
4	India	2,930	24	Poland	365
5	Germany	2,087	25	Colombia	303
6	Italy	1,430	26	Philippines	301
7	France	1,420	27	Saudi Arabia	285
	United Kingdom	1,420	28	Pakistan	267
9	Brazil	1,269	29	Belgium	262
10	Russia	1,028	30	Egypt	229
11	Canada	843	31	Austria	217
12	Mexico	838	32	Sweden	215
13	Spain	828	33	Bangladesh	214
14	South Korea	714	34	Ukraine	213
15	Indonesia	615	35	Malaysia	208
16	Australia	492	36	Switzerland	203
17	South Africa	488	37	Algeria	188
18	Netherlands	436	38	Greece	185
19	Argentina	424	39	Portugal	182
20	Thailand	392	40	Hong Kong	167

a Includes overseas departments.   b Estimate.
For list of all countries with their GDP see pages 236–239.

Regional GDP

$bn, 2001		*% annual growth 1996–2001*	
World	31,110	World	3.5
Advanced economies	24,700	Advanced economies	2.8
G7	20,570	G7	2.6
EU15	7,890	EU15	2.7
Asia[a]	2,300	Asia[a]	5.8
Latin America	2,000	Latin America	2.4
Eastern Europe[b]	860	Eastern Europe[b]	3.3
Middle East[c]	820	Middle East[c]	3.7
Africa	430	Africa	3.1

Regional purchasing power

GDP in PPP, % of total		*$ per head*	
World	100.0	World	7,400
Advanced economies	55.7	Advanced economies	26,860
G7	44.0	G7	28,720
EU15	19.7	EU15	24,170
Asi a[a]	22.9	Asia[a]	3,260
Latin America	7.9	Latin America	7,210
Eastern Europe[b]	6.3	Eastern Europe[b]	6,520
Middle East[c]	4.0	Middle East[c]	5,170
Africa	3.2	Africa	2,160

Regional population

% of total (6.1bn)		*No. of countries[d]*	
Advanced economies	15.4	Advanced economies	29
G7	11.5	G7	7
EU15	6.2	EU15	15
Asia[a]	52.4	Asia[a]	25
Latin America	8.3	Latin America	33
Eastern Europe[b]	6.4	Eastern Europe[b]	28
Middle East[c]	5.0	Middle East[c]	16
Africa	12.4	Africa	51

Regional international trade

Exports of goods and services, % of tot.		*Current account balances, $bn*	
Advanced economies	74.6	Advanced economies	-187.3
G7	45.3	G7	-282.6
EU15	38.6	EU15	-19.0
Asia[a]	10.0	Asia[a]	34.5
Latin America	4.5	Latin America	-53.3
Eastern Europe[b]	4.9	Eastern Europe[b]	12.0
Middle East[c]	4.1	Middle East[c]	50.3
Africa	1.9	Africa	-0.4

a Excludes Hong Kong, Japan, Singapore, South Korea and Taiwan.
b Includes Russia and other CIS.
c Includes Malta and Turkey.
d IMF definition.

Living standards

Highest GDP per head

$

1	Luxembourg	41,950	36	Martinique	14,250
2	Norway	37,020	37	New Caledonia[b]	13,900
3	United States	35,200	38	Macau	13,810
4	Bermuda[a]	34,920	39	New Zealand	13,240
5	Switzerland	34,460	40	Taiwan	12,660
6	Japan	32,520	41	Guadeloupe	12,300
7	Denmark	30,290	42	Bahrain	12,170
8	Qatar[b]	28,620	43	Cyprus	11,560
9	Iceland	27,410	44	Netherlands Antilles	11,060
10	Ireland	26,890	45	Greece	11,030
11	United Arab Emirates	25,470	46	Portugal	10,940
12	United Kingdom	23,920	47	Réunion	10,660
13	Netherlands	23,860	48	Barbados	10,290
14	Sweden	23,750	49	Slovenia	9,480
15	Austria	23,350	50	Malta	9,240
16	Finland	23,340	51	South Korea	8,970
17	Hong Kong	23,260	52	Saudi Arabia	8,870
18	Germany	22,510	53	Oman[b]	7,560
19	Canada	22,390	54	Argentina	7,170
20	Belgium	22,370	55	Trinidad & Tobago	6,800
21	France	22,030	56	Libya[b]	6,310
22	Singapore	20,850	57	Mexico	6,150
23	Guam	20,250	58	Uruguay	5,550
24	Australia	19,070	59	Czech Republic	5,530
25	Italy	18,930	60	Hungary	5,240
26	Brunei	18,510	61	Venezuela	5,070
27	Aruba	18,270	62	Lebanon	4,700
28	Israel	17,550	63	Poland	4,570
29	Puerto Rico	17,180	64	Croatia	4,350
30	Kuwait	16,640	65	Chile	4,310
31	French Polynesia[b]	16,580	66	Estonia	4,010
32	Bahamas[b]	15,640	67	Costa Rica	3,920
33	Virgin Islands	14,750	68	Malaysia	3,890
34	Spain	14,570	69	Mauritius	3,840
35	Andorra	14,440	70	Slovakia	3,790

Lowest GDP per head

$

1	Congo	100	11	Eritrea	180
	Ethiopia	100	12	Mozambique	190
	Myanmar	100	13	Chad	200
4	Burundi	110	14	Burkina Faso	210
5	Malawi	150		Rwanda	210
6	Guinea-Bissau	160	16	Mali	230
	Sierra Leone	160	17	Nepal	240
8	Liberia	170		Uganda	240
	Niger	170	19	Bhutan	250
	Tajikistan	170		Cambodia	250

a Estimate.   b 2000

Highest purchasing power
GDP per head in PPP (USA = 100)

1	Luxembourg	141.7	36	Brunei[a]	52.5
2	Bermuda[a]	101.5	37	Portugal	51.7
3	United States	100.0	38	Greece	51.1
4	Switzerland	90.3	39	Taiwan[a]	50.2
5	Norway	85.6	40	Slovenia	49.8
6	Iceland	84.2	41	Bahamas	45.7
7	Denmark	83.1	42	Bahrain	44.9
8	Aruba[ab]	81.7	43	Barbados	44.1
	French Polynesia[b]	81.7	44	South Korea	43.9
10	Netherlands	79.9	45	Virgin Islands[ab]	43.8
11	Ireland	79.3	46	Andorra[ab]	42.0
12	Canada	77.4	47	Czech Republic	41.8
13	Austria	77.0	48	Martinique[b]	40.9
14	Belgium	76.3	49	Saudi Arabia	38.8
15	Hong Kong	74.6	50	Malta	38.3
16	Japan	74.5	51	Guadeloupe[b]	35.0
17	Germany	73.6		Hungary	35.0
18	New Caledonia	73.5	53	Slovakia	34.4
19	Australia	71.8	54	Netherlands Antilles[ab]	33.3
20	Italy	71.6	55	Argentina	32.0
21	United Kingdom	71.0	56	South Africa	31.8
22	France	70.2	57	Oman	31.3
23	Finland	70.1	58	Réunion[b]	30.6
24	Sweden	69.4	59	Mauritius	28.8
25	Singapore	66.7	60	Estonia	28.2
26	Macau	63.1	61	Poland	27.3
27	Kuwait	62.8	62	Costa Rica	27.0
28	Qatar[a]	61.8	63	Croatia	26.1
29	Cyprus	61.6	64	Chile	25.8
	United Arab Emirates[a]	61.6	65	Trinidad & Tobago	25.1
31	Guam[ab]	61.3	66	Lithuania	24.4
32	Spain	57.9	67	Uruguay	24.1
33	Israel	57.3	68	Mexico	24.0
34	New Zealand	53.2	69	Malaysia	23.1
35	Puerto Rico	52.8	70	Latvia	22.6

Lowest purchasing power
GDP per head in PPP (USA = 100)

1	Sierra Leone	1.3	11	Ethiopia	2.3
2	Tanzania	1.5		Nigeria	2.3
3	Malawi	1.6	13	Madagascar	2.4
	Somalia[a]	1.6	14	Guinea-Bissau	2.6
5	Congo	1.8		Niger	2.6
6	Burundi	2.0	16	Afghanistan[ab]	2.7
	Congo-Brazzaville	2.0	17	Benin	2.8
8	Yemen	2.1		Kenya	2.8
9	Mali	2.2	19	North Korea[ab]	2.9
	Zambia	2.2		West Bank and Gaza[a]	2.9

Note: for definition of purchasing power parity see page 235.

The quality of life

Human development index[a]

1	Norway	94.2
2	Sweden	94.1
3	Canada	94.0
4	Australia	93.9
	Belgium	93.9
	United States	93.9
7	Iceland	93.6
8	Netherlands	93.5
9	Japan	93.3
10	Finland	93.0
11	France	92.8
	Switzerland	92.8
	United Kingdom	92.8
14	Austria	92.6
	Denmark	92.6
16	Germany	92.5
	Ireland	92.5
	Luxembourg	92.5
19	New Zealand	91.7
20	Italy	91.3
	Spain	91.3
22	Israel	89.6
23	Hong Kong	88.8
24	Greece	88.5
	Singapore	88.5
26	Cyprus	88.3
27	South Korea	88.2
28	Portugal	88.0
29	Slovenia	87.9
30	Malta	87.5
31	Barbados	87.1
32	Brunei	85.6
33	Czech Republic	84.9
34	Argentina	84.4
35	Hungary	83.5
	Slovakia	83.5
37	Poland	83.3
38	Bahrain	83.1
	Chile	83.1
	Uruguay	83.1
41	Bahamas	82.6
	Estonia	82.6
43	Costa Rica	82.0
44	Kuwait	81.3
45	United Arab Emirates	81.2
46	Croatia	80.9
47	Lithuania	80.8
48	Trinidad & Tobago	80.5
49	Qatar	80.3
50	Latvia	80.0
51	Mexico	79.6
52	Cuba	79.5
53	Belarus	78.8
54	Panama	78.7
55	Malaysia	78.2
56	Russia	78.1
57	Bulgaria	77.9
58	Romania	77.5
59	Libya	77.3
60	Colombia	77.2
	Macedonia	77.2
	Mauritius	77.2
63	Venezuela	77.0
64	Thailand	76.2
65	Saudi Arabia	75.9
66	Fiji	75.8
67	Brazil	75.7
68	Suriname	75.6
69	Lebanon	75.5
70	Armenia	75.4
	Philippines	75.4
72	Oman	75.1
73	Kazakhstan	75.0
74	Georgia	74.8
	Ukraine	74.8
76	Peru	74.7
77	Jamaica	74.2
	Turkey	74.2
79	Azerbaijan	74.1
	Sri Lanka	74.1
	Turkmenistan	74.1
82	Paraguay	74.0
83	Albania	73.3
84	Ecuador	73.2
85	Dominican Republic	72.7
	Uzbekistan	72.7

a GDP or GDP per head is often taken as a measure of how developed a country is, but its usefulness is limited as it refers only to economic welfare. In 1990 the UN Development Programme published its first estimate of a Human Development Index, which combined statistics on two other indicators – adult literacy and life expectancy – with income levels to give a better, though still far from perfect, indicator of human development. In 1991 average years of schooling was combined with adult literacy to give a knowledge variable. The HDI is shown here scaled from 0 to 100; countries scoring over 80 are considered to have high human development, those scoring from 50 to 79 medium and those under 50 low.

Economic freedom index[a]

#	Country	Score	#	Country	Score
1	Hong Kong	1.45		Germany	2.10
2	Singapore	1.50	22	Bahamas	2.15
3	Luxembourg	1.70		Cyprus	2.15
	New Zealand	1.70	24	Barbados	2.20
5	Ireland	1.75		United Arab Emirates	2.20
6	Denmark	1.80	26	El Salvador	2.25
	Estonia	1.80	27	Norway	2.30
	United States	1.80		Taiwan	2.30
9	Australia	1.85	29	Italy	2.35
	United Kingdom	1.85		Lithuania	2.35
11	Finland	1.90		Spain	2.35
	Iceland	1.90	32	Portugal	2.40
	Netherlands	1.90	33	Israel	2.45
	Sweden	1.90		Latvia	2.45
15	Switzerland	1.95	35	Botswana	2.50
16	Bahrain	2.00		Cambodia	2.50
	Chile	2.00		Czech Republic	2.50
18	Canada	2.05		Japan	2.50
19	Austria	2.10		Uruguay	2.50
	Belgium	2.10			

Gender-related development index[b]

#	Country	Score	#	Country	Score
1	Australia	95.6	21	Spain	90.6
2	Belgium	94.3	22	Israel	89.1
3	Norway	94.1	23	Hong Kong	88.6
4	Sweden	94.0	24	Singapore	88.0
5	Canada	93.8	25	Cyprus	87.9
6	United States	93.7		Greece	87.9
7	Iceland	93.4	27	Slovenia	87.7
8	Finland	93.3	28	Portugal	87.6
	Netherlands	93.3	29	South Korea	87.5
10	United Kingdom	93.2	30	Malta	86.0
11	Japan	92.7	31	Brunei	85.1
12	France	92.6	32	Czech Republic	84.6
13	Denmark	92.5	33	Argentina	83.6
14	Switzerland	92.3	34	Hungary	83.3
15	Austria	92.1		Slovakia	83.3
16	Germany	92.0	36	Poland	83.1
17	Ireland	91.7	37	Uruguay	82.8
18	New Zealand	91.5	38	Bahamas	82.5
19	Luxembourg	91.4	39	Chile	82.4
20	Italy	90.7	40	Bahrain	82.2

a Ranks countries on the basis of ten indicators of how government intervention can restrict the economic relations between individuals. The economic indicators, published by the Heritage Foundation, are trade policy, taxation, monetary policy, the banking system, foreign-investment rules, property rights, the amount of economic output consumed by the government, regulation policy, the size of the black market and the extent of wage and price controls. A country can score between 1 and 5 in each category, 1 being the most free and 5 being the least free.
b Combines similar data to the HDI (and also published by the UNDP) to give an indicator of the disparities in human development between men and women in individual countries. The lower the index, the greater the disparity.

Economic growth

Highest economic growth, 1991–2001

Average annual % increase in real GDP

1	Bosnia[a]	22.6		Jordan	5.0
2	China	9.8		Nepal	5.0
3	Vietnam	7.7		Oman	5.0
4	Ireland	7.1	30	Syria	4.9
5	Singapore	6.9	31	Bangladesh	4.8
6	Lebanon	6.6		Benin	4.8
7	Bhutan	6.4		Costa Rica	4.8
	Malaysia	6.4		Tunisia	4.8
	Myanmar	6.4	35	Burkina Faso	4.7
	Uganda	6.4	36	Israel	4.6
11	Mozambique	6.3		Sri Lanka	4.6
12	Chile	6.2	38	El Salvador	4.4
	Laos	6.2		Malta	4.4
14	South Korea	5.9		Namibia	4.4
15	Eritrea	5.8		United Arab Emirates	4.4
	Kuwait[b]	5.8	42	Ghana	4.3
	Sudan	5.8	43	Egypt	4.2
18	Yemen	5.7		Iran	4.2
19	Dominican Republic	5.6		Puerto Rico	4.2
	Taiwan	5.6		Thailand	4.2
21	Botswana	5.4	47	Cyprus	4.1
	India	5.4		Indonesia	4.1
	Luxembourg	5.4		Mauritania	4.1
24	Cambodia	5.3		Panama	4.1
25	Mauritius	5.2	51	Ethiopia	4.0
26	Bahrain	5.0		Papua New Guinea	4.0

Lowest economic growth, 1991–2001

Average annual % change in real GDP

1	Moldova	-8.5	20	Belarus	-0.7
2	Georgia	-8.2		Haiti	-0.7
3	Tajikistan	-7.6	22	Macedonia	-0.5
4	Ukraine	-6.6	23	West Bank and Gaza[d]	-0.4
5	Congo	-5.4	24	Mongolia	0.1
6	Sierra Leone	-3.7		Zimbabwe	0.1
7	Latvia	-3.6	26	Uzbekistan	0.3
8	Russia	-3.3	27	Czech Republic	0.4
9	Kirgizstan	-3.2	28	Jamaica	0.5
10	Lithuania	-2.9	29	Slovakia	0.6
11	Armenia	-2.7	30	Rwanda	0.7
12	Kazakhstan	-2.2	31	Switzerland	0.9
13	Azerbaijan[c]	-1.9	32	Angola	1.0
14	Burundi	-1.3		Hungary	1.0
15	Bulgaria	-1.2	34	Japan	1.2
	Romania	-1.2		Zambia	1.2
17	Croatia	-0.9	36	Togo	1.3
	Estonia	-0.9		Venezuela	1.3
19	Turkmenistan	-0.8	38	Guinea-Bissau	1.4

a 1995–2001 b 1993–2001 c 1992–2001 d 1995–2001

Highest economic growth, 1981–91

Average annual % increase in real GDP

1	Botswana	10.6	12	Malaysia	6.3
2	China	9.3	13	Pakistan	6.2
3	Oman	8.9	14	Cambodia[b]	6.0
4	South Korea	8.7		Swaziland	6.0
5	Taiwan	7.9	16	Mauritius	5.8
	Thailand	7.9	17	Cyprus	5.7
7	Macau[a]	7.6		New Caledonia	5.7
8	Singapore	7.3	19	Chad	5.5
9	Bhutan	7.1	20	India	5.3
10	Indonesia	6.6	21	Egypt	5.1
11	Hong Kong	6.4	22	Guinea-Bissau	5.0

Lowest economic growth, 1981–91

Average annual % increase in real GDP

1	Liberia	-11.3		Suriname	-0.1
2	Georgia	-2.5	14	Congo	0.0
3	Albania	-1.8		El Salvador	0.0
4	Nicaragua	-1.3		Haiti	0.0
5	Brunei	-1.1	17	Niger	0.1
6	Slovakia[c]	-0.8		Tajikistan[e]	0.1
7	Romania[d]	-0.7	19	Trinidad & Tobago	0.2
8	Peru	-0.5	20	Uruguay	0.3
9	Argentina	-0.3	21	Bolivia	0.6
10	United Arab Emirates	-0.2		Kuwait[f]	0.6
11	Hungary	-0.1		Mozambique	0.6
	Madagascar	-0.1			

Highest services growth, 1991–2001

Average annual % increase in real terms

1	Bosnia[g]	35.9	9	India	7.4
2	Georgia[g]	19.0		Uganda	7.4
3	China	8.9	11	Slovakia	7.3
4	Botswana	7.9	12	Vietnam	7.1
	Iran	7.9	13	Malaysia	6.8
6	Taiwan	7.8	14	South Korea	6.7
7	Azerbaijan[h]	7.6	15	Nepal	6.4
8	Armenia	7.5	16	Mauritius	6.3

Lowest services growth, 1991–2001

Average annual % increase in real terms

1	Congo	-11.4	7	Moldova[k]	-2.2
2	Liberia[i]	-6.5	8	Tajikistan	-2.1
3	Kirgizstan	-3.6	9	Central African Rep	-2.0
4	Bulgaria	-3.2	10	Singapore	-1.5
5	Angola	-2.4	11	Sierra Leone	-1.2
6	Romania[j]	-2.3	12	Turkmenistan	-0.8

a 1983–91 b 1988–91 c 1985–91 d 1982–91 e 1986–91 f 1981–89
g 1995–2000 h 1993–2001 i 1991–99 j 1991–2000 k 1992–2001
Note: Rankings of highest industrial growth 1991–2001 can be found on page 42 and
highest agricultural growth on page 45.

Trading places

Biggest traders

% of total world exports (visible & invisible)

1	Euro area	16.80	23	Malaysia	1.20
2	United States	14.70	24	Denmark	1.02
3	Germany	8.75	25	Australia	1.01
4	United Kingdom	6.74	26	Norway	0.98
5	Japan	6.32	27	Saudi Arabia	0.94
6	France	5.18	28	Luxembourg	0.93
7	Italy	3.88	29	Thailand	0.92
8	Canada	3.75	30	Brazil	0.81
9	China	3.54	31	India	0.78
10	Netherlands	3.37	32	Indonesia	0.74
11	Belgium	3.36	33	Finland	0.66
12	Spain	2.24	34	Poland	0.62
13	South Korea	2.16	35	Turkey	0.61
14	Mexico	2.02	36	Israel	0.50
15	Switzerland	1.99	37	Czech Republic	0.49
16	Taiwan	1.74		United Arab Emirates	0.49
17	Ireland	1.46	39	Philippines	0.48
18	Russia	1.37	40	Portugal	0.46
19	Sweden	1.33	41	South Africa	0.43
20	Austria	1.29	42	Argentina	0.42
21	Hong Kong	1.26		Hungary	0.42
22	Singapore	1.23	44	Greece	0.37

Most trade dependent

Trade as % of GDP[a]

1	Liberia	527.1
2	Aruba	126.2
3	Syria	105.8
4	Malaysia	89.5
5	Singapore	73.9
6	Belgium	70.4
7	Estonia	67.8
8	Swaziland	67.7
9	Slovakia	66.8
10	Tajikistan	63.2
11	Belarus	62.8
12	United Arab Emirates	62.6
13	Malta	62.4
14	Panama	61.9
15	Czech Republic	61.5
16	Ireland	61.3
17	Congo-Brazzaville	61.0
18	Lesotho	60.6
19	Bahrain	60.5
20	Gabon	59.7
21	Mozambique	58.3

Least trade dependent

Trade as % of GDP[a]

1	Madagascar	2.5
2	Somalia	5.5
3	North Korea	7.0
4	Japan	8.4
5	Argentina	8.5
6	Bangladesh	8.8
	Cuba	8.8
8	United States	9.3
9	Rwanda	10.0
10	Egypt	10.7
	India	10.7
12	Brazil	11.3
13	Sudan	12.4
14	Central African Rep	12.7
15	Burundi	12.9
	Uganda	12.9
17	Guam	13.2
	Peru	13.2
19	Tanzania	13.4
20	Uruguay	13.5
21	Burkina Faso	14.5

Notes: The figures are drawn from balance of payment statistics and, therefore, have differing technical definitions from trade statistics taken from customs or similar sources. The invisible trade figures do not show some countries due to unavailable data. For Hong Kong and Singapore, domestic exports and retained imports only are used.

Biggest visible traders

% of world visible exports

1	United States	15.76	24	Thailand	0.99
2	Euro area	15.04	25	Brazil	0.96
3	Germany	8.87	26	India	0.86
4	Japan	5.88		Saudi Arabia	0.86
5	United Kingdom	5.07	28	Denmark	0.80
6	France	4.90	29	Norway	0.79
7	China	4.20	30	Indonesia	0.78
8	Canada	4.17	31	Poland	0.77
9	Italy	3.96	32	United Arab Emirates	0.71
10	Netherlands	3.26	33	Puerto Rico	0.64
11	Mexico	2.76	34	Finland	0.62
12	Belgium	2.73		Turkey	0.62
13	South Korea	2.44	36	Czech Republic	0.59
14	Spain	2.25	37	Portugal	0.54
15	Taiwan	1.89	38	Philippines	0.50
16	Switzerland	1.60	39	Hungary	0.49
17	Malaysia	1.33		Israel	0.49
18	Russia	1.31	41	South Africa	0.48
19	Sweden	1.17	42	Hong Kong	0.43
20	Austria	1.14	43	Argentina	0.39
21	Ireland	1.07	44	Venezuela	0.37
	Singapore	1.07	45	Iran	0.35
23	Australia	1.06		Syria	0.35

Biggest invisible traders

% of world invisible exports

1	United States	19.63	24	Australia	0.85
2	Euro area	18.93	25	India	0.83
3	United Kingdom	10.91	26	Greece	0.75
4	Germany	6.76	27	Turkey	0.66
5	Japan	5.88	28	Mexico	0.62
6	France	5.61		Russia	0.62
7	Belgium	4.53	30	Thailand	0.59
8	Italy	3.37	31	Malaysia	0.57
9	Netherlands	3.19	32	Israel	0.54
10	Hong Kong	3.14	33	Finland	0.50
11	Spain	2.72	34	Portugal	0.49
	Switzerland	2.72	35	Brazil	0.44
13	Luxembourg	2.53	36	Poland	0.43
14	Canada	2.08	37	Egypt	0.37
15	Ireland	1.71		Philippines	0.37
16	Austria	1.58	39	Argentina	0.35
17	China	1.50	40	Saudi Arabia	0.33
18	Singapore	1.44	41	Czech Republic	0.32
19	Sweden	1.40	42	Hungary	0.31
20	Denmark	1.33	43	Indonesia	0.26
21	South Korea	1.28	44	Kuwait	0.25
22	Taiwan	1.05	45	South Africa	0.24
23	Norway	0.90			

a Average of imports and exports of goods as % of GDP.

Current account

Largest surpluses
$m

1	Japan	87,800	26	Venezuela	3,931
2	Russia	34,621	27	Netherlands	3,743
3	Norway	25,960	28	Turkey	3,396
4	Switzerland	22,624	29	Germany	2,440
5	France	21,360	30	Oman	2,315
6	Canada	19,479	31	Libya[a]	1,984
7	Taiwan	19,028	32	Pakistan	1,880
8	Singapore	17,884	33	Luxembourg	1,674
9	China	17,401	34	Morocco	1,606
10	Saudi Arabia	14,502	35	Ukraine	1,402
11	Hong Kong	11,736	36	Yemen	1,107
12	Belgium	9,392	37	Syria[b]	1,062
13	United Arab Emirates	8,860	38	Vietnam	682
14	Finland	8,631	39	Nigeria[a]	506
15	South Korea	8,617	40	Botswana	438
16	Kuwait	8,562	41	Aruba	425
17	Malaysia	7,287	42	Congo-Brazzaville[b]	324
18	Indonesia	6,899	43	Papua New Guinea	282
19	Algeria	6,800	44	Mauritius	247
20	Sweden	6,696	45	Bahrain	157
21	Thailand	6,221	46	Bermuda	145
22	Iran	5,256	47	Namibia	64
23	Philippines	4,503	48	Slovenia	31
24	Qatar	4,256	49	Fiji	26
25	Denmark	4,142	50	Central African Rep	16

Largest deficits
$m

1	United States	-393,390	21	New Zealand	-1,403
2	United Kingdom	-23,490	22	Bosnia	-1,365
3	Brazil	-23,211	23	Chile	-1,243
4	Mexico	-17,708	24	Kazakhstan	-1,240
5	Spain	-15,082	25	Guatemala	-1,238
6	Euro area	-12,320	26	Peru	-1,098
7	Portugal	-9,959	27	Hungary	-1,097
8	Greece	-9,400	28	Ireland	-1,043
9	Australia	-8,876	29	Tunisia	-863
10	Poland	-5,357	30	Bulgaria	-847
11	Argentina	-4,554	31	Dominican Republic	-839
12	Austria	-4,103	32	Uganda	-802
13	Lebanon	-3,984	33	Ecuador	-800
14	Czech Republic	-2,624	34	Jamaica	-788
15	Romania	-2,317	35	Tanzania	-738
16	Israel	-1,852	36	Latvia	-734
17	Slovakia	-1,800	37	Costa Rica	-702
18	Colombia	-1,789	38	Honduras	-670
19	Mozambique	-1,604	39	Chad	-660
20	Angola	-1,431	40	Trinidad & Tobago[c]	-644

a 1999   b 2000   c 1998

Largest surpluses as % of GDP

%

#	Country	%		#	Country	%
1	Qatar	26.3			Thailand	5.4
2	Kuwait	26.1		27	Indonesia	4.7
3	Aruba	22.3			Morocco	4.7
4	Singapore	20.9		29	Iran	4.6
5	Norway	15.6		30	Belgium	4.1
6	United Arab Emirates	13.1		31	Ukraine	3.7
7	Algeria	12.4		32	Pakistan	3.2
8	Yemen	11.9			Sweden	3.2
9	Congo-Brazzaville[b]	11.8		34	Venezuela	3.1
10	Oman	11.6		35	Canada	2.8
11	Russia	11.2		36	Denmark	2.6
12	Papua New Guinea	9.5		37	Turkey	2.3
13	Switzerland	9.2		38	Japan	2.1
14	Luxembourg	9.0			Namibia	2.1
15	Botswana	8.4			Vietnam	2.1
16	Malaysia	8.3		41	Bahrain	2.0
17	Saudi Arabia	7.8			South Korea	2.0
18	Hong Kong	7.2		43	Central African Rep	1.6
19	Finland	7.1			France	1.6
20	Taiwan	6.7		45	China	1.5
21	Bermuda	6.6			Fiji	1.5
22	Philippines	6.3		47	Nigeria[a]	1.2
23	Libya[a]	5.8		48	Netherlands	1.0
24	Mauritius	5.5		49	Slovenia	0.2
25	Syria[b]	5.4		50	Germany	0.1

Largest deficits as % of GDP

%

#	Country	%		#	Country	%
1	Mozambique	-45.1		22	Armenia	-9.5
2	Chad	-41.3		23	Macedonia	-9.4
3	Eritrea	-30.3		24	Mali[b]	-9.2
4	Bosnia	-28.6		25	Portugal	-9.1
5	Lebanon	-23.8		26	Slovakia	-8.8
6	Nicaragua	-22.4		27	Greece	-8.0
7	Bhutan	-20.4		28	Tanzania	-7.9
8	Sierra Leone[b]	-16.4		29	Ethiopia	-7.7
9	Angola	-15.1		30	Malawi	-7.5
	Mongolia	-15.1		31	Bahamas	-7.3
11	Liberia[b]	-15.0			Trinidad & Tobago[c]	-7.3
12	Uganda	-14.1		33	Tajikistan	-7.0
13	Burkina Faso	-13.5		34	Moldova	-6.9
14	Gambia, The	-12.9			Rwanda	-6.9
15	Zambia	-12.7		36	Georgia	-6.7
16	Lesotho	-12.0		37	Niger	-6.6
17	Suriname	-11.1		38	Myanmar	-6.5
	Togo[b]	-11.1		39	Senegal	-6.4
19	Honduras	-10.5		40	Bulgaria	-6.2
20	Jamaica	-10.1			Estonia	-6.2
21	Latvia	-9.8				

Inflation

Highest inflation, 2001–02

% consumer price inflation

1	Zimbabwe	134.5		Guatemala	8.1
2	Angola	110.0	33	Mongolia[b]	8.0
3	Suriname[a]	98.9	34	Honduras	7.7
4	Turkey	45.0	35	Slovenia	7.5
5	Congo	31.5	36	Jamaica	7.1
6	Malawi[b]	27.2	37	Bhutan[a]	6.8
7	Argentina	25.9	38	Sudan[b]	6.4
8	Uzbekistan[c]	24.9	39	Colombia	6.3
9	Romania	22.5	40	Swaziland[b]	5.9
10	Venezuela	22.4	41	Bulgaria	5.8
11	Zambia	22.2		Kazakhstan	5.8
12	Mozambique	16.8	43	Kenya[b]	5.7
13	Madagascar	15.9	44	Israel	5.6
14	Russia	15.8	45	Albania	5.5
15	Ghana	14.8	46	Mauritius[b]	5.4
16	Iran	14.3	47	Hungary	5.3
17	Uruguay	14.0	48	Chad	5.2
18	Nigeria	12.9		Dominican Republic	5.2
19	Ecuador	12.5		Iceland	5.2
20	Indonesia	11.9		Moldova	5.2
21	Papua New Guinea	11.7	52	Mexico	5.1
22	Myanmar	11.4	53	Mali	5.0
	Namibia	11.4	53	Kirgizstan	4.8
24	Laos	10.6	55	Georgia[b]	4.7
	South Africa	10.6		Ireland	4.7
26	Paraguay	10.5		Mauritania[b]	4.7
27	Haiti	9.9	58	Tanzania[b]	4.6
28	Sri Lanka	9.7		Cameroon[b]	4.6
29	Costa Rica	9.2	60	Congo-Brazzaville	4.3
30	Brazil	8.4		India	4.3
31	Botswana	8.1			

Highest inflation, 1996–2002

% average annual consumer price inflation

1	Angola	198.2	17	Sudan[f]	19.3
2	Congo	182.5	18	Myanmar	19.0
3	Belarus	77.9	19	Indonesia	17.4
4	Turkey	64.2	20	Moldova	16.9
5	Bulgaria	61.4	21	Iran	16.2
6	Zimbabwe	58.4		Kirgizstan	16.2
7	Romania	55.6	23	Ukraine	14.7
8	Laos	42.3	24	Mongolia[f]	14.1
9	Ecuador	42.1	25	Haiti	12.9
10	Suriname[d]	36.4	26	Burundi	12.7
11	Uzbekistan[e]	31.8		Sierra Leone	12.7
12	Russia	29.1	28	Colombia	12.4
13	Malawi[f]	27.6	29	Honduras	12.3
14	Venezuela	26.1	30	Mexico	12.2
15	Zambia	24.3	31	Papua New Guinea	11.4
16	Ghana	21.1			

Lowest inflation, 2001–02
% consumer price inflation

1	Lesotho[b]	-9.6		Qatar[b]	1.4
2	Sierra Leone	-3.3	28	Ethiopia	1.5
3	Hong Kong	-3.0		United States	1.5
4	Burundi	-1.3	30	Belgium	1.6
5	Bahrain[b]	-1.2		United Kingdom	1.6
6	Japan	-1.0	32	Austria	1.8
7	China	-0.8		Czech Republic	1.8
8	Saudi Arabia	-0.5		El Salvador	1.8
9	Singapore	-0.4		Finland	1.8
10	Uganda	-0.3	36	France	1.9
11	Taiwan	-0.2		Jordan	1.9
12	Macedonia	0.0		Latvia	1.9
13	Peru	0.1		Malaysia	1.9
14	Lithuania	0.3		Poland	1.9
15	Panama[b]	0.4	41	Croatia	2.0
16	Syria[b]	0.5		Rwanda	2.0
17	Thailand	0.6	43	Bangladesh	2.1
18	Switzerland	0.7		Gabon[b]	2.1
19	Gambia, The[c]	0.8		Luxembourg	2.1
	Ukraine	0.8	46	Bahamas	2.2
21	Bolivia	0.9		Burkina Faso	2.2
22	Armenia	1.1		Canada	2.2
23	Germany	1.3		Sweden	2.2
	Kuwait	1.3	50	Denmark	2.7
	Norway	1.3		Egypt	2.7
26	Algeria	1.4		Senegal	2.7

Lowest inflation, 1996–2002
% average annual consumer price inflation

1	Hong Kong	-0.7		France	1.3
2	Saudi Arabia	-0.6	18	Kuwait	1.4
3	Bahrain[f]	-0.2	19	Bahamas	1.5
	Syria[f]	-0.2		Congo-Brazzaville	1.5
5	Japan	-0.1		Germany	1.5
6	Azerbaijan	0.0	22	Austria	1.6
	Macedonia	0.0	23	Belgium	1.7
8	China	0.1		New Zealand	1.7
9	Taiwan	0.6		Senegal	1.7
10	Singapore	0.7	26	Morocco	1.8
11	Switzerland	0.8	27	Finland	1.9
12	Panama[f]	1.0		Luxembourg	1.9
13	Gabon[f]	1.2		Mali	1.9
	Lesotho[g]	1.2	30	Canada	2.0
	Sweden	1.2		Ethiopia	2.0
16	Central African Rep	1.3			

a 1998–99   b 2000–01   c 1999–2000   d 1996–99   e 1996–2000   f 1996–2001
g 1999–2001
Notes: Inflation is measured as the % increase in the consumer price index between two dates. The figures shown are based on the average level of the index during the relevant years.

Debt

Highest foreign debt[a]

$m

1	Brazil	226,362	25	Morocco	16,692
2	China	170,110	26	Sudan	15,348
3	Mexico	158,290	27	Bangladesh	15,215
4	Russia	152,649	28	Kazakhstan	14,372
5	Argentina	136,709	29	Ecuador	13,910
6	Indonesia	135,704	30	Ukraine	12,811
7	Turkey	115,118	31	Vietnam	12,578
8	India	97,320	32	Lebanon	12,450
9	Thailand	67,384	33	Serbia & Montenegro	11,740
10	Poland	62,393	34	Romania	11,653
11	Philippines	52,356	35	Côte d'Ivoire	11,582
12	Malaysia	43,351	36	Congo	11,392
13	Chile	38,360	37	Slovakia	11,121
14	Colombia	36,699	38	Tunisia	10,884
15	Venezuela	34,660	39	Croatia	10,742
16	Pakistan	32,020	40	Uruguay	9,706
17	Nigeria	31,119	41	Bulgaria	9,615
18	Hungary	30,289	42	Angola	9,600
19	Egypt	29,234	43	Sri Lanka	8,529
20	Peru	27,512	44	Cameroon	8,338
21	South Africa	24,050	45	Panama	8,245
22	Algeria	22,503	46	Iran	7,483
23	Czech Republic	21,691	47	Jordan	7,480
24	Syria	21,305	48	Ghana	6,759

Highest foreign debt

As % of exports of goods and services

1	Burundi	1,790	21	Chad	462
2	Liberia	1,731	22	Benin	456
3	Congo	1,121	23	Lebanon	428
4	Sierra Leone	1,100	24	Guinea	426
5	Guinea-Bissau	1,096	25	Gambia, The	415
6	Rwanda	910	26	Mali	384
7	Central African Rep	766	27	Serbia & Montenegro	379
8	Sudan	710	28	Argentina	375
9	Nicaragua	702	29	Brazil	337
10	Zambia	626	30	Bolivia	327
11	Ethiopia	598	31	Cameroon	324
12	Mozambique	569	32	Syria	307
13	Mauritania	568	33	Pakistan	299
14	Burkina Faso	567	34	Kirgizstan	292
15	Malawi	556	35	Togo	288
	Uganda	556	36	Peru	284
17	Madagascar	544	37	Ghana	277
18	Niger	540	38	Senegal	252
19	Laos	507	39	Myanmar	245
20	Tanzania	500	40	Côte d'Ivoire	240

a Foreign debt is debt owed to non-residents and repayable in foreign currency; the figures shown include liabilities of government, public and private sectors. Developed countries have been excluded.

Highest foreign debt burden
Foreign debt as % of GDP

1	Liberia	487	23	Tajikistan	109
2	Guinea-Bissau	336	24	Guinea	105
3	Nicaragua	306	25	Madagascar	104
4	Congo	257	26	Ecuador	102
5	Congo-Brazzaville	231	27	Cameroon	99
6	Mauritania	222		Indonesia	99
7	Sierra Leone	178	29	Mongolia	92
	Zambia	178	30	Ethiopia	91
9	Laos	157	31	Jordan	89
10	Burundi	156		Panama	89
	Sudan	156	33	Honduras	88
12	Malawi	151		Moldova	88
13	Angola	147		Nigeria	88
14	Kirgizstan	131	36	Gabon	87
15	Mozambique	125	37	Cambodia	85
	Syria	125	38	Central African Rep	84
17	Serbia & Montenegro	123	39	Niger	82
18	Gambia, The	120	40	Latvia	80
19	Ghana	116		Papua New Guinea	80
20	Mali	114	42	Kazakhstan	79
21	Côte d'Ivoire	111	43	Myanmar	78
	Togo	111	44	Senegal	77

Highest debt service ratios[b]
%

1	Sierra Leone	89	23	Thailand	25
2	Brazil	81		Venezuela	25
3	Argentina	67	25	Indonesia	23
4	Lebanon	50		Mauritania	23
5	Hungary	42		Peru	23
6	Turkey	40	28	Algeria	22
7	Burundi	39		Ecuador	22
8	Bolivia	38		Moldova	22
	Guinea-Bissau	38		Romania	22
10	Colombia	37	32	Morocco	20
	Lithuania	37	33	Bulgaria	19
	Nicaragua	37		Ethiopia	19
13	Kazakhstan	35		Slovakia	19
	Uruguay	35	36	Bosnia	18
15	Poland	32	37	Philippines	17
16	Croatia	31	38	Kenya	16
17	Kirgizstan	30		Oman	16
18	Chile	28		Russia	16
	Pakistan	28		Senegal	16
20	Angola	27	42	Gabon	15
	Mexico	27		Latvia	15
22	Uzbekistan	26			

b Debt service is the sum of interest and principal repayments (amortisation) due on outstanding foreign debt. The debt service ratio is debt service expressed as a percentage of the country's exports of goods and services.

Aid

Largest bilateral and multilateral donors[a]

$m

1	United States	11,429	13	Switzerland	908
2	Japan	9,847	14	Australia	873
3	Germany	4,990	15	Belgium	867
4	United Kingdom	4,579	16	Austria	533
5	France	4,198	17	Saudi Arabia	490
6	Netherlands	3,172	18	Finland	389
7	Spain	1,737	19	Ireland	287
8	Sweden	1,666	20	Portugal	268
9	Denmark	1,634	21	South Korea	265
10	Italy	1,627	22	Greece	202
11	Canada	1,533	23	Luxembourg	141
12	Norway	1,346	24	United Arab Emirates	127

Largest recipients of bilateral and multilateral aid

$m

1	Pakistan	1,938		Malawi	402
2	India	1,705	35	Cameroon	398
3	Indonesia	1,501	36	Burkina Faso	389
4	China	1,460	37	French Polynesia	388
5	Vietnam	1,435		Nepal	388
6	Serbia & Montenegro	1,306	39	Colombia	380
7	Egypt	1,255	40	Tunisia	378
8	Tanzania	1,233	41	Zambia	374
9	Russia	1,110	42	Madagascar	354
10	Ethiopia	1,080	43	Mali	350
11	Bangladesh	1,024		New Caledonia[b]	350
12	Poland	966	45	Brazil	349
13	Mozambique	935	46	Bulgaria	346
14	Nicaragua	928	47	Sierra Leone	334
15	West Bank and Gaza	865	48	Sri Lanka	330
16	Uganda	783	49	Czech Republic	314
17	Bolivia	729	50	Rwanda	291
18	Honduras	678	51	Georgia	290
19	Ghana	652	52	Thailand	281
20	Romania	648	53	Eritrea	280
21	Bosnia	639	54	Benin	273
22	Philippines	577	55	Guinea	272
23	Ukraine	519	56	Albania	269
24	Morocco	517	57	Angola	268
25	Kenya	453	58	Mauritania	262
26	Peru	451	59	Congo	251
27	Jordan	432	60	Niger	249
28	South Africa	428	61	Macedonia	248
29	Yemen	426	62	Laos	243
30	Senegal	419	63	Lebanon	241
31	Hungary	418	64	El Salvador	234
32	Cambodia	409	65	Azerbaijan	226
33	Afghanistan	402	66	Guatemala	225

Largest bilateral and multilateral donors[a]
% of GDP

1	Denmark	1.03	13	Spain	0.30
2	Norway	0.83	14	Austria	0.29
3	Luxembourg	0.82	15	Germany	0.27
	Netherlands	0.82		Kuwait	0.27
5	Sweden	0.81	17	Australia	0.25
6	Belgium	0.37		New Zealand	0.25
7	Saudi Arabia	0.35		Portugal	0.25
8	Switzerland	0.34	20	Japan	0.23
9	Ireland	0.33		United Arab Emirates	0.23
10	Finland	0.32	22	Canada	0.22
	France	0.32	23	Greece	0.17
	United Kingdom	0.32	24	Italy	0.15

Largest recipients of bilateral and multilateral aid
$ per head

1	New Caledonia[b]	1,667	34	Tunisia	39
2	French Polynesia	1,617	35	Kirgizstan	38
3	Netherlands Antilles	295	36	El Salvador	37
4	West Bank and Gaza	262		Rwanda	37
5	Nicaragua	179	38	Gambia, The	36
6	Bosnia	156	39	Lithuania	35
7	Macedonia	124		Malawi	35
	Serbia & Montenegro	124		Zambia	35
9	Honduras	103	42	Tanzania	34
10	Mauritania	97	43	Burkina Faso	33
11	Albania	87		Ghana	33
12	Bolivia	86		Guinea	33
13	Jordan	85		Uganda	33
14	Mongolia	82	47	Fiji	32
15	Eritrea	74	48	Bahrain	30
16	Sierra Leone	73		Cambodia	30
17	Lebanon	67		Czech Republic	30
18	Cyprus	63		Mali	30
	Slovenia	63		Slovakia	30
20	Namibia	61	53	Romania	29
21	Suriname	58	54	Azerbaijan	28
22	Armenia	56		Bhutan	28
	Georgia	56		Israel	28
24	Mozambique	50		Moldova	28
25	Estonia	49	58	Bahamas	27
	Guinea-Bissau	49		Swaziland	27
27	Laos	45	60	Cameroon	26
28	Bulgaria	44		Lesotho	26
	Latvia	44		Tajikistan	26
30	Benin	43	63	Poland	25
	Senegal	43	64	Congo-Brazzaville	24
32	Hungary	42		Croatia	24
33	Papua New Guinea	41	66	Yemen	22

a China also provides aid, but does not disclose amounts.   b 2000

Industry and services

Largest industrial output
$bn

1	United States	2,227		Belgium	56
2	Japan	1,433	27	Sweden	51
3	China	593		Thailand	51
4	Germany	514	29	Malaysia	43
5	United Kingdom	345	30	Israel	40
6	France	300	31	Ireland	39
7	Italy	282	32	Iran	37
8	Canada	200		United Arab Emirates	37
9	South Korea	175	34	Denmark	36
10	Spain	159	35	Finland	35
11	Brazil	151	36	Turkey	33
12	Mexico	150	37	South Africa	31
13	India	114	38	Egypt	30
14	Russia	102	39	Puerto Rico	29
15	Australia	95	40	Algeria	28
	Netherlands	95		Portugal	28
17	Saudi Arabia	91	42	Singapore	27
18	Taiwan	87	43	Colombia	23
19	Switzerland	77		Greece	23
20	Argentina	68	45	Philippines	22
	Indonesia	68	46	Czech Republic	21
22	Norway	63		Hong Kong	21
23	Venezuela	61		Hungary	21
24	Poland	58	49	Chile	20
25	Austria	56	50	New Zealand	18

Highest growth in industrial output
Average annual real % growth, 1991–2001[a]

1	Eritrea	44.0	11	Laos	10.1
2	Bosnia	26.0	12	Sudan	8.8
3	Mozambique	15.0	13	Syria	8.5
4	China	13.0	14	Mali	8.4
5	Ireland	12.1	15	Lesotho	8.0
6	Cambodia	11.6	16	Malaysia	7.3
	Vietnam	11.6	17	Bangladesh	7.2
8	Myanmar	11.3	18	Serbia & Montenegro	7.0
9	Uganda	11.0	19	Dominican Republic	6.9
10	Bhutan	10.6	20	Nepal	6.8

Lowest growth in industrial output
Average annual real % growth, 1991–2001[a]

1	Tajikistan	-10.7	11	Russia	-5.2
2	Moldova	-9.8	12	Azerbaijan	-5.0
3	Armenia	-8.8	13	Slovakia	-3.0
4	Kirgizstan	-8.2		Uzbekistan	-3.0
5	Latvia	-8.1	15	Burundi	-2.7
6	Ukraine	-7.9	16	Bulgaria	-2.5
7	Congo	-7.2		Estonia	-2.5
8	Liberia	-6.2	18	Zambia	-2.3
9	Turkmenistan	-6.1	19	Guinea-Bissau	-2.2
10	Kazakhstan	-5.7	20	Macedonia	-2.1

Largest manufacturing output
$bn

1	United States	1,422	21	Argentina	43
2	Japan	854	22	Thailand	40
3	China	411	23	Austria	38
4	Germany	405		Indonesia	38
5	United Kingdom	229	25	Poland	31
6	France	215	26	Israel	29
7	Italy	205	27	Ireland	28
8	Russia[b]	153	28	Finland	27
9	South Korea	127		Malaysia	27
10	Canada	111		Puerto Rico	27
11	Mexico	108	31	Denmark	24
12	Spain	95		Portugal	24
13	Brazil	94		Venezuela	24
14	Taiwan	71	34	Saudi Arabia	20
15	India	67		Singapore	20
16	Switzerland	65		Turkey	20
17	Netherlands	63	37	Iran	19
18	Sweden	56		South Africa	19
19	Australia	47	39	Egypt	18
	Belgium	47		Norway	18

Largest services output
$bn

1	United States	6,975	26	Norway	83
2	Japan	2,828	27	Saudi Arabia	81
3	Germany	1,124	28	Turkey	77
4	United Kingdom	903	29	Greece	76
5	France	839	30	Israel	69
6	Italy	664	31	Finland	66
7	Canada	419	32	South Africa	65
8	China	390	33	Portugal	63
9	Mexico	385	34	Singapore	59
10	Spain	349	35	Ireland	56
11	Brazil	253	36	Iran	55
12	Australia	240	37	Indonesia	54
13	Netherlands	239		Venezuela	54
14	South Korea	229	39	Thailand	51
15	India	209	40	Egypt	46
16	Taiwan	190	41	Colombia	43
17	Switzerland	182	42	Philippines	38
18	Argentina	175		Puerto Rico	38
19	Russia	153	44	Malaysia	37
20	Belgium	146	45	New Zealand	34
21	Sweden	133	46	Chile	33
22	Hong Kong	130	47	Hungary	32
23	Austria	109	48	Peru	30
24	Denmark	99	49	Czech Republic	28
25	Poland	92		Pakistan	28

a Or nearest available years.
b 1998

Agriculture

Most economically dependent on agriculture
% of GDP from agriculture

1	Myanmar	57		Ghana	36
2	Congo	56		Uganda	36
	Guinea-Bissau	56	27	Uzbekistan	35
4	Central African Rep	55	28	Bhutan	34
5	Ethiopia	52		Malawi	34
6	Laos	51	30	Nicaragua	32
7	Albania	50	31	Madagascar	30
	Burundi	50		Mongolia	30
	Sierra Leone	50	33	Tajikistan	29
10	Tanzania	45		Turkmenistan	29
11	Cameroon	43	35	Armenia	28
12	Nigeria	41	36	Moldova	26
13	Gambia, The	40		Papua New Guinea	26
	Niger	40	38	India	25
	Rwanda	40	39	Pakistan	25
16	Chad	39	40	Côte d'Ivoire	24
	Nepal	39		Guinea	24
	Sudan	39		Vietnam	24
	Togo	39	43	Bangladesh	23
20	Burkina Faso	38		Guatemala	23
	Kirgizstan	38	45	Mozambique	22
	Mali	38		Syria	22
23	Cambodia	37		Zambia	22
24	Benin	36	48	Mauritania	21

Least economically dependent on agriculture
% of GDP from agriculture

1	Hong Kong	0.1	23	Denmark	2.8
	Singapore	0.1		Italy	2.8
3	Luxembourg	0.7	25	France	2.9
	Puerto Rico	0.7	26	Oman	3.2
5	Bahrain	0.8		Slovenia	3.2
6	United Kingdom	1.0		South Africa	3.2
7	Germany	1.3	29	Australia	3.5
8	Japan	1.4		Finland	3.5
	United States	1.4	31	Poland	3.6
10	Belgium	1.5		Spain	3.6
11	Switzerland[a]	1.6	33	New Caledonia[c]	3.7
	Trinidad & Tobago	1.6	34	Portugal	3.8
13	Sweden	1.7	35	Ireland	3.9
14	Haiti[b]	1.9	36	Cyprus	4.0
	Norway[b]	1.9	37	Slovakia	4.1
	Taiwan	1.9	38	Czech Republic	4.3
17	Jordan	2.1	39	Mexico	4.4
18	Canada	2.2		South Korea	4.4
19	Austria	2.3	41	Latvia	4.5
20	Botswana	2.4	42	French Polynesia[b]	4.7
21	Brunei	2.6	43	Argentina	4.8
22	Netherlands	2.7	44	Hungary	4.9

a 1998   b 2000   c 1997

Highest growth
Average annual real % growth, 1991–2001[a]

1	United Arab Emirates	13.7	10	Myanmar	5.5
2	Sudan	10.5	11	Benin	5.3
3	Eritrea	7.0	12	Laos	5.2
4	Albania	6.7	13	Bosnia	5.0
	Liberia	6.7		Peru	5.0
6	Yemen	6.4	15	Syria	4.7
7	Nicaragua	6.1	16	Malawi	4.6
8	Gambia, The	6.0	17	Mauritania	4.5
9	Cameroon	5.7	18	Oman	4.4

Lowest growth
Average annual real % growth, 1991–2001[a]

1	Moldova	-10.3	9	Belarus	-2.9
2	Hong Kong	-6.9	10	Kazakhstan	-2.8
3	West Bank and Gaza	-6.7	11	Estonia	-2.6
4	Latvia	-6.4	12	Morocco	-2.4
5	Tajikistan	-4.9		Singapore	-2.4
6	Sierra Leone	-4.2	14	Japan	-2.2
7	Russia	-3.3	15	Macedonia	-2.1
8	Ukraine	-3.1	16	United Kingdom	-1.9

Biggest producers
'000 tonnes

Cereals

1	China	398,394	6	Indonesia	59,261
2	United States	325,288	7	Brazil	56,478
3	India	240,026	8	Germany	49,711
4	Russia	83,202	9	Canada	43,298
5	France	60,331	10	Bangladesh	40,237

Meat

1	China	65,482	6	Spain	5,049
2	United States	37,807	7	India	4,917
3	Brazil	15,161	8	Mexico	4,636
4	France	6,527	9	Russia	4,474
5	Germany	6,472	10	Italy	4,163

Fruit

1	China	68,738	6	Spain	14,921
2	India	48,571	7	Mexico	14,217
3	Brazil	31,795	8	Iran	11,769
4	United States	30,100	9	Philippines	11,122
5	Italy	18,275	10	France	11,038

Vegetables

1	China	350,372	6	Russia	13,735
2	India	68,059	7	Egypt	13,683
3	United States	35,513	8	Japan	12,484
4	Turkey	24,165	9	South Korea	12,413
5	Italy	15,361	10	Spain	11,926

a Or nearest available years.

Commodities

Wheat

Top 10 producers			*Top 10 consumers*	
'000 tonnes			*'000 tonnes*	
1	China	94,000	1 China	109,600
2	EU15	90,500	2 EU15	90,500
3	India	68,800	3 India	64,300
4	United States	53,300	4 Russia	38,300
5	Russia	46,900	5 United States	32,800
6	Australia	24,900	6 Pakistan	19,800
7	Ukraine	21,000	7 Turkey	16,200
8	Canada	20,600	8 Egypt	13,400
9	Pakistan	19,100	Iran	13,400
10	Turkey	15,500	10 Ukraine	12,400

Rice[a]

Top 10 producers			*Top 10 consumers*	
'000 tonnes			*'000 tonnes*	
1	China	124,306	1 China	134,581
2	India	91,600	2 India	87,351
3	Indonesia	33,089	3 Indonesia	36,358
4	Bangladesh	24,310	4 Bangladesh	25,553
5	Vietnam	21,036	5 Vietnam	17,400
6	Thailand	17,499	6 Myanmar	9,900
7	Myanmar	10,440	7 Thailand	9,767
8	Philippines	8,450	8 Japan	9,000
9	Japan	8,242	9 Philippines	8,900
10	Brazil	7,137	10 Brazil	8,075

Sugar[b]

Top 10 producers			*Top 10 consumers*	
'000 tonnes			*'000 tonnes*	
1	Brazil	20,300	1 India	17,300
2	India	19,900	2 EU15	13,600
3	EU15	15,500	3 Brazil	9,800
4	United States	7,800	4 United States	9,100
5	China	7,200	5 China	8,900
6	Mexico	5,600	6 Russia	5,800
7	Thailand	5,400	7 Mexico	4,900
8	Australia	4,800	8 Indonesia	3,400
9	Cuba	3,700	Pakistan	3,400
10	Pakistan	2,700	10 Japan	2,300

Coarse grains[c]

Top 5 producers			*Top 5 consumers*	
'000 tonnes			*'000 tonnes*	
1	United States	262,000	1 United States	217,600
2	China	123,600	2 China	133,200
3	EU15	107,700	3 EU15	102,200
4	Brazil	36,900	4 Brazil	37,100
5	Russia	36,800	5 Mexico	36,500

Tea

Top 10 producers '000 tonnes		*Top 10 consumers* '000 tonnes	
1 India	854	1 India	673
2 China	702	2 China	452
3 Sri Lanka	296	3 Japan	149
4 Kenya	295	4 Russia	144
5 Indonesia	161	5 Turkey	138
6 Turkey	143	6 United Kingdom	137
7 Japan	90	7 Pakistan	107
8 Vietnam	80	8 United States	97
9 Argentina	59	9 Iran	82
10 Bangladesh	57	10 Egypt	56

Coffee

Top 10 producers '000 tonnes		*Top 10 consumers* '000 tonnes	
1 Brazil	2,058	1 United States	1,125
2 Vietnam	735	2 Brazil	816
3 Colombia	717	3 Germany	522
4 Indonesia	459	4 Japan	422
5 India	297	5 France	315
6 Mexico	260	Italy	315
7 Ethiopia	225	7 Spain	178
8 Guatemala	216	8 United Kingdom	125
9 Côte d'Ivoire	207	9 Ethiopia	110
10 Uganda	195	10 Indonesia	100

Cocoa

Top 10 producers '000 tonnes		*Top 10 consumers* '000 tonnes	
1 Côte d'Ivoire	1,212	1 United States	691
2 Ghana	395	2 Germany	296
3 Indonesia	385	3 France	205
4 Nigeria	180	4 United Kingdom	200
5 Brazil	163	5 Russia	173
6 Cameroon	133	6 Japan	147
7 Ecuador	89	7 Brazil	114
8 Dominican Republic	45	8 Italy	101
9 Papua New Guinea	39	9 Spain	71
10 Colombia	37	10 Canada	69

a Milled.
b Raw.
c Includes: maize (corn), barley, sorghum, rye, oats and millet.

Copper

Top 10 producers[a] '000 tonnes		*Top 10 consumers[b]* '000 tonnes	
1 Chile	4,739	1 United States	2,594
2 United States	1,360	2 China	2,207
3 Indonesia	1,047	3 Japan	1,145
4 Australia	896	4 Germany	1,092
5 Peru	722	5 South Korea	849
6 Canada	634	6 Italy	676
7 Russia	600	7 Taiwan	540
8 China	587	8 France	538
9 Poland	474	9 Mexico	445
10 Kazakhstan	470	10 Brazil	345

Lead

Top 10 producers[a] '000 tonnes		*Top 10 consumers[b]* '000 tonnes	
1 Australia	714	1 United States	1,694
2 China	676	2 China	643
3 United States	461	3 Germany	401
4 Peru	290	4 Japan	321
5 Mexico	282	5 South Korea	312
6 Canada	154	6 United Kingdom	298
7 Sweden	86	7 Italy	283
8 Morocco	80	8 France	254
9 Poland	53	9 Mexico	243
10 South Africa	52	10 Spain	232

Zinc

Top 10 producers[a] '000 tonnes		*Top 10 consumers[c]* '000 tonnes	
1 China	1,693	1 China	1,512
2 Australia	1,518	2 United States	1,107
3 Canada	1,065	3 Japan	633
4 Peru	1,057	4 Germany	531
5 United States	797	5 South Korea	394
6 Mexico	414	6 Italy	355
7 Kazakhstan	345	7 France	336
8 Ireland	302	8 India	278
9 India	211	9 Taiwan	276
10 Spain	165	10 Belgium	275

Tin

Top 5 producers[a] '000 tonnes		*Top 5 consumers[b]* '000 tonnes	
1 China	93.0	1 China	62.0
2 Indonesia	56.3	2 United States	49.7
3 Peru	38.2	3 Germany	21.9
4 Brazil	13.8	4 Japan	21.5
5 Bolivia	12.4	5 South Korea	13.3

Nickel

Top 10 producers[a] '000 tonnes		*Top 10 consumers*[b] '000 tonnes	
1 Russia	267.3	1 Japan	199.1
2 Australia	206.0	2 United States	122.0
3 Canada	194.1	3 Germany	102.7
4 New Calendonia	117.6	4 Taiwan	91.8
5 Indonesia	84.8	5 China	85.0
6 Cuba	76.5	6 Italy	61.5
7 China	51.5	7 South Korea	59.1
8 Colombia	38.0	8 United Kingdom	55.8
9 South Africa	36.4	9 France	49.4
10 Brazil	32.6	10 Spain	48.3

Aluminium

Top 10 producers[d] '000 tonnes		*Top 10 consumers*[e] '000 tonnes	
1 China	3,371	1 United States	5,122
2 Russia	3,302	2 China	3,492
3 United States	2,637	3 Japan	2,014
4 Canada	2,583	4 Germany	1,552
5 Australia	1,784	5 South Korea	850
6 Brazil	1,132	6 Russia	786
7 Norway	1,068	7 France	761
8 South Africa	654	8 Canada	760
9 Germany	652	9 Italy	756
10 India	624	10 India	589

Precious metals

Gold [a] *Top 10 producers* tonnes		*Silver* [a] *Top 10 producers* tonnes	
1 South Africa	393.5	1 Mexico	3,030
2 United States	335.0	2 Peru	2,670
3 Australia	280.1	3 Australia	1,970
4 China	181.8	4 China	1,908
5 Indonesia	166.1	5 United States	1,606
6 Canada	160.2	6 Chile	1,349
7 Russia	155.0	7 Canada	1,320
8 Peru	134.0	8 Poland	1,088
9 Uzbekistan	82.0	9 Kazakhstan	816
10 Ghana	72.5	10 Bolivia	411

Platinum *Top 3 producers* tonnes		*Palladium* *Top 3 producers* tonnes	
1 South Africa	127.5	1 Russia	135.0
2 Russia	40.5	2 South Africa	62.5
3 North America	10.9	3 North America	26.4

a Mine production. b Refined consumption. c Slab consumption.
d Primary refined production. e Primary refined consumption.

Rubber (natural and synthetic)

Top 10 producers		*Top 10 consumers*	
'000 tonnes		*'000 tonnes*	
1 Thailand	2,430	1 United States	2,814
2 United States	2,064	2 China	2,790
3 Indonesia	1,642	3 Japan	1,814
4 China	1,516	4 Germany	857
5 Japan	1,466	5 India	803
6 Russia	919	6 France	746
7 Germany	828	7 South Korea	705
8 India	701	8 Russia	611
9 France	671	9 Brazil	538
10 South Korea	663	10 Spain	438

Raw wool

Top 10 producers[a]		*Top 10 consumers[b]*	
'000 tonnes		*'000 tonnes*	
1 Australia	607	1 China	436
2 China	295	2 Italy	146
3 New Zealand	246	3 Russia	73
4 Russia	129	4 India	63
5 Iran	74	5 Turkey	46
6 Turkey	70	6 South Korea	42
7 Argentina	65	7 Iran	40
8 Uruguay	52	8 United Kingdom	37
9 United Kingdom	51	9 Japan	34
10 South Africa	48	10 Germany	30

Cotton

Top 10 producers		*Top 10 consumers*	
'000 tonnes		*'000 tonnes*	
1 China	5,320	1 China	5,500
2 United States	4,420	2 India	2,900
3 India	2,686	3 Pakistan	1,760
4 Pakistan	1,802	4 United States	1,681
5 Uzbekistan	1,055	5 Turkey	1,300
6 Turkey	922	6 Brazil	860
7 Brazil	766	7 Indonesia	510
8 Australia	723	8 Mexico	430
9 Greece	455	9 Thailand	385
10 Syria	346	10 Russia	340

Major oil seeds[c]

Top 5 producers		*Top 5 consumers*	
'000 tonnes		*'000 tonnes*	
1 United States	89,347	1 United States	60,736
2 China	48,140	2 China	59,847
3 Brazil	44,340	3 EU15	33,456
4 Argentina	34,312	4 Brazil	27,883
5 India	21,590	5 Argentina	25,232

Oil[d]

Top 15 producers
'000 barrels per day

1	Saudi Arabia[e]	8,768
2	United States	7,177
3	Russia	7,056
4	Iran[e]	3,688
5	Mexico	3,560
6	Venezuela[e]	3,418
7	Norway	3,414
8	China	3,308
9	Canada	2,763
10	United Kingdom	2,503
11	United Arab Emirates[e]	2,422
12	Iraq[e]	2,414
13	Nigeria[e]	2,148
14	Kuwait[e]	2,142
15	Algeria[e]	1,563

Top 15 consumers
'000 barrels per day

1	United States	19,633
2	Japan	5,427
3	China	5,041
4	Germany	2,804
5	Russia	2,456
6	South Korea	2,235
7	India	2,072
8	France	2,032
9	Italy	1,946
10	Canada	1,941
11	Brazil	1,865
12	Mexico	1,813
13	United Kingdom	1,649
14	Spain	1,508
15	Saudi Arabia[e]	1,347

Natural gas

Top 10 producers
Billion cubic metres

1	United States	555.4
2	Russia	542.4
3	Canada	172.0
4	United Kingdom	105.8
5	Algeria	78.2
6	Indonesia	62.9
7	Netherlands	61.4
8	Iran	60.6
9	Norway	57.5
10	Saudi Arabia	53.7

Top 10 consumers
Billion cubic metres

1	United States	616.2
2	Russia	372.7
3	United Kingdom	95.4
4	Germany	82.9
5	Japan	79.0
6	Canada	72.6
7	Ukraine	65.8
8	Iran	65.0
9	Italy	64.5
10	Saudi Arabia	53.7

Coal

Top 10 producers
Million tonnes oil equivalent

1	United States	590.7
2	China	548.5
3	Australia	168.1
4	India	161.1
5	South Africa	126.7
6	Russia	120.8
7	Poland	72.5
8	Indonesia	56.9
9	Germany	54.2
10	Ukraine	43.6

Top 10 consumers
Million tonnes oil equivalent

1	United States	555.7
2	China	520.6
3	India	173.5
4	Russia	114.6
5	Japan	103.0
6	Germany	84.4
7	South Africa	80.6
8	Poland	57.5
9	Australia	47.6
10	South Korea	45.7

a Greasy basis.
b Clean basis.
c Soybeans, sunflower seed, cottonseed, groundnuts and rapeseed.
d Includes crude oil, shale oil, oil sands and natural gas liquids.
e Opec members.

Energy

Largest producers
Million tonnnes oil equivalent, 2000

1	United States	1,675.8	16	South Africa	144.5
2	China	1,107.6	17	United Arab Emirates	143.6
3	Russia	966.5	18	Brazil	142.1
4	Saudi Arabia	487.9	19	Germany	134.3
5	India	421.6	20	Iraq	134.1
6	Canada	374.9	21	France	130.7
7	United Kingdom	272.3	22	Kuwait	111.5
8	Iran	242.1	23	Japan	105.5
9	Australia	232.6	24	Ukraine	82.3
10	Mexico	229.7	25	Argentina	81.2
11	Indonesia	229.5	26	Poland	79.0
12	Venezuela	225.5	27	Kazakhstan	78.1
13	Norway	225.0	28	Malaysia	76.8
14	Nigeria	197.7	29	Colombia	74.6
15	Algeria	149.6	30	Libya	73.9

Largest consumers
Million tonnnes oil equivalent, 2000

1	United States	2,300.0	16	Spain	124.9
2	China	1,142.4	17	Iran	112.7
3	Russia	614.0	18	Australia	110.2
4	Japan	524.7	19	South Africa	107.6
5	India	501.9	20	Saudi Arabia	105.3
6	Germany	339.6	21	Nigeria	90.2
7	France	257.1	22	Poland	90.0
8	Canada	251.0	23	Turkey	77.1
9	United Kingdom	232.6	24	Netherlands	75.8
10	South Korea	193.6	25	Thailand	73.6
11	Brazil	183.2	26	Pakistan	64.0
12	Italy	171.6	27	Argentina	61.5
13	Mexico	153.5	28	Venezuela	59.3
14	Indonesia	145.6	29	Belgium	59.2
15	Ukraine	139.6	30	Uzbekistan	50.2

Energy efficiency[a]

Most efficient		Least efficient		
GDP per unit of energy use, 2000		*GDP per unit of energy use, 2000*		
1	Namibia	12.0	1	Tanzania	1.1
2	Costa Rica	11.7	2	Nigeria	1.2
3	Hong Kong	10.9		Uzbekistan	1.2
4	Bangladesh	10.8		Zambia	1.2
5	Colombia	10.3	5	Trinidad & Tobago	1.3
6	Morocco	9.5	6	Turkmenistan	1.4
	Peru	9.5		Ukraine	1.4
8	Uruguay	9.4	8	Bahrain	1.6
9	Italy	8.2		Russia	1.6
10	El Salvador	8.1	10	Kuwait	1.8

a PPP$, per kg of oil equivalent.

Highest net energy importers
% of commercial energy use, 2000

1	Hong Kong	100	13	Ireland	85
	Singapore	100	14	Italy	84
3	Cyprus	98	15	South Korea	83
	Luxembourg	98	16	Dominican Republic	82
	Moldova	98	17	Japan	80
6	Israel	97	18	Belgium	78
	Lebanon	97	19	Georgia	74
8	Jordan	94		Spain	74
	Morocco	94	21	Namibia	72
10	Jamaica	88	22	Panama	71
11	Portugal	87	23	Armenia	69
12	Belarus	86	24	Uruguay	67

Lowest net energy importers
% of commercial energy use, 2000

1	Congo-Brazzaville	-1,538	14	Venezuela	-280
2	Gabon	-975	15	Qatar	-270
3	Brunei	-866	16	Turkmenistan	-231
4	Norway	-778	17	Ecuador	-175
5	Yemen	-525	18	Colombia	-159
6	Oman	-516	19	Nigeria	-119
7	Angola	-470	20	Iran	-115
8	Kuwait	-434	21	Australia	-111
9	Algeria	-415	22	Trinidad & Tobago	-106
10	United Arab Emirates	-386	23	Cameroon	-100
11	Iraq	-384		Kazakhstan	-100
12	Saudi Arabia	-363	25	Syria	-79
13	Libya	-350	26	Paraguay	-75

Largest consumption per head
Kg of oil equivalent, 2000

1	Qatar	26,773	17	Saudi Arabia	5,081
2	Iceland	12,246	18	New Zealand	4,864
3	Kuwait	10,529	19	Netherlands	4,762
4	United Arab Emirates	10,175	20	France	4,366
5	Bahrain	9,858	21	Russia	4,218
6	Luxembourg	8,409	22	Japan	4,136
7	Canada	8,156	23	Germany	4,131
8	United States	8,148	24	South Korea	4,119
9	Trinidad & Tobago	6,660	25	Oman	4,046
10	Finland	6,409	26	United Kingdom	3,962
11	Singapore	6,120	27	Czech Republic	3,931
12	Brunei	5,870	28	Ireland	3,854
13	Belgium	5,776	29	Switzerland	3,704
14	Australia	5,744	30	Denmark	3,643
15	Norway	5,704	31	Austria	3,524
16	Sweden	5,354	32	Estonia	3,303

Note: Consumption data for small countries, especially oil producers, can be unreliable, often leading to unrealistically high consumption per head rates.

Workers of the world

Highest % of population in labour force

2001 or latest

1	China	56.5		21	New Zealand	49.9
2	Switzerland	56.1		22	Ethiopia	49.7
3	Thailand	54.4		23	Ecuador	49.6
4	Iceland	54.2		24	Brazil	49.5
5	Denmark	53.8		25	United States	49.0
6	Japan	53.1		26	Slovakia	48.8
7	Norway	52.5			Slovenia	48.8
8	Canada	52.4		28	Germany	48.6
9	Portugal	51.8		29	Austria	48.5
10	Singapore	51.7		30	Estonia	48.3
11	Macau	51.4		31	Peru	48.0
12	Hong Kong	51.3		32	Cyprus	47.9
	Netherlands	51.3		33	Russia	47.7
14	Romania	51.1		34	Bahamas	47.6
15	Australia	50.8		35	Bangladesh	47.3
16	Finland	50.6			Colombia	47.3
17	Lithuania	50.5		37	South Korea	47.1
18	Czech Republic	50.4		38	Ukraine	47.0
19	Sweden	50.2		39	Uruguay	46.9
	United Kingdom	50.2		40	Kazakhstan	46.8

Most male workforce

Highest % men in workforce

1	Algeria	87.8
2	West Bank and Gaza	86.7
3	Pakistan	84.4
4	Bahrain	82.6
5	Syria	79.7
6	Egypt	79.0
7	Guatemala	77.4
8	Turkey	73.4
9	Malta	70.8
10	Nicaragua	69.2
11	Dominican Republic	68.2
12	Chile	66.7
13	Sri Lanka	66.2
14	Mexico	65.9
15	Malaysia	65.3
16	Costa Rica	64.6
17	Honduras	64.3
	Panama	64.3
19	Suriname	63.1
20	Bangladesh	62.2
21	Indonesia	61.8
	Trinidad & Tobago	61.8
23	Italy	61.3
24	Spain	60.8
25	Philippines	60.7

Most female workforce

Highest % women in workforce

1	Belarus	52.9
2	Cambodia	51.6
3	Malawi	50.2
4	Moldova	50.1
5	Bahamas	49.4
6	Estonia	48.9
7	Lithuania	48.7
8	Ukraine	48.6
9	Latvia	48.4
10	Georgia	48.2
	Zimbabwe	48.2
12	Mongolia	48.0
14	Azerbaijan	47.8
	Sweden	47.8
15	Russia	47.7
16	Finland	47.5
17	Bulgaria	47.4
18	Iceland	46.7
19	Norway	46.6
	United States	46.6
21	Macau	46.4
22	Romania	46.2
23	Canada	46.0
	Poland	46.0
25	Israel	45.8
	Slovenia	45.8

Lowest % of population in labour force
2001 or latest

1	West Bank and Gaza	20.8	26	Italy	41.7
2	Algeria	27.0	27	Sri Lanka	42.0
3	Pakistan	29.0	28	Greece	42.1
4	Togo	29.6	29	Costa Rica	42.3
5	Egypt	29.6	30	Argentina	42.4
6	Puerto Rico	30.4	31	Bulgaria	42.8
7	Congo-Brazzaville	32.3	32	Belgium	43.0
8	Syria	32.6	33	Macedonia	43.1
9	Turkey	32.9		Trinidad & Tobago	43.1
10	Suriname	34.6	35	Philippines	43.3
11	Guatemala	35.0	36	Dominican Republic	43.7
12	Botswana	35.1		Luxembourg	43.7
13	Nicaragua	36.5	38	Jamaica	43.9
14	Mongolia	36.7	39	Croatia	44.0
15	Panama	37.6	40	France	44.3
16	Chile	38.4	41	Moldova	44.5
17	Honduras	38.5		Spain	44.5
18	Malta	39.5	43	Indonesia	44.6
19	El Salvador	39.7	44	Cambodia	44.8
20	Mexico	40.0	45	Poland	45.0
21	Israel	40.4	46	Belarus	45.4
22	Georgia	40.6		Malawi	45.4
23	Hungary	41.3	48	Bahrain	46.0
	Malaysia	41.3	49	Bolivia	46.2
25	Zimbabwe	41.5			

Highest rate of unemployment
% of labour force[a]

1	Macedonia	55.5	21	Panama	14.5
2	Réunion	39.7	22	Venezuela	14.1
3	Lesotho	39.3		West Bank and Gaza	14.1
4	Armenia	29.9	24	Ecuador	13.9
5	Guadeloupe	27.4		Lithuania	13.9
6	Algeria	25.0	26	Latvia	13.8
7	South Africa	23.8	27	Jordan	13.2
8	Colombia	21.3		Netherlands Antilles	13.2
9	Morocco	19.0	29	Spain	13.1
	Slovakia	19.0	30	Estonia	12.6
11	Poland	18.3	31	Trinidad & Tobago	11.8
12	Bulgaria	17.5		Ukraine	11.8
13	Argentina	17.2	33	India	11.6
	Suriname	17.2	34	Greece	11.0
15	Georgia	17.0	35	Italy	10.3
16	Jamaica	16.4		Philippines	10.3
17	Tunisia	15.4	37	Russia	10.2
18	Croatia	15.3	38	El Salvador	10.0
19	Uruguay	15.2	39	Puerto Rico	9.6
20	Dominican Republic	15.0	40	Israel	9.3

a ILO definition.

The business world

Global competitiveness

Overall	Government	Trade blocks
1 United States	Finland	Finland
2 Finland	Singapore	Luxembourg
3 Singapore	Australia	Chile
4 Denmark	Hong Kong	Austria
5 Hong Kong	Luxembourg	Germany
6 Switzerland	United States	France
7 Luxembourg	Malaysia	Denmark
8 Sweden	Canada	Ireland
9 Australia	Denmark	Portugal
10 Netherlands	Switzerland	Belgium
11 Canada	Iceland	Spain
12 Iceland	Thailand	Sweden
13 Austria	New Zealand	Netherlands
14 Ireland	Estonia	Greece
15 Norway	Ireland	Singapore
16 Belgium	Chile	Czech Republic
17 Malaysia	Austria	Malaysia
18 New Zealand	Taiwan	Mexico
19 Germany	Spain	Canada
20 Taiwan	Sweden	Hong Kong
21 United Kingdom	United Kingdom	United States
22 France	Norway	United Kingdom
23 Chile	China	Hungary
24 Estonia	Netherlands	Iceland
25 Spain	Colombia	Slovakia
26 Thailand	Germany	Estonia
27 Japan	France	Thailand
28 China	South Africa	Jordan
29 South Korea	Portugal	Italy
30 Czech Republic	Jordan	China
31 Colombia	Mexico	Colombia
32 Italy	Japan	Turkey
33 South Africa	South Korea	Switzerland
34 Israel	India	New Zealand
35 Hungary	Philippines	Slovenia
36 India	Czech Republic	Philippines
37 Brazil	Brazil	Australia
38 Philippines	Belgium	Taiwan
39 Portugal	Italy	Japan
40 Greece	Hungary	Israel
41 Romania	Romania	South Africa
42 Mexico	Slovakia	Brazil
43 Slovakia	Russia	South Korea
44 Turkey	Israel	Poland

Notes: Rankings reflect assessments for the ability of a country to achieve sustained high rates of GDP growth per head. Column 1 is based on 259 criteria covering: the openness of an economy, the role of the government, the development of financial markets, the quality of infrastructure, technology, business management and judicial and political institutions and labour-market flexibility. Column 2 looks at the extent to which government policies are conducive to competitiveness. Column 3 is based on the extent to which a country is integrated into regional trade blocks.

The business environment

		2003–07 score	1998–2002 score	1998–2002 ranking
1	Netherlands	8.76	8.62	2
2	Canada	8.73	8.58	4
3	Finland	8.63	8.36	8
4	United Kingdom	8.54	8.61	3
5	United States	8.52	8.62	1
6	Singapore	8.49	8.41	7
7	Denmark	8.48	8.12	11
8	Hong Kong	8.47	8.52	5
	Switzerland	8.47	8.44	6
10	Ireland	8.41	8.26	9
11	Sweden	8.28	8.12	10
12	France	8.24	7.81	16
13	Belgium	8.21	7.93	13
14	New Zealand	8.19	8.08	12
15	Australia	8.17	7.88	15
	Germany	8.17	7.89	14
17	Taiwan	8.08	7.34	21
18	Spain	8.06	7.42	19
19	Austria	8.05	7.66	17
20	Chile	8.03	7.38	20
	Norway	8.03	7.61	18
22	Portugal	7.59	6.88	22
23	Israel	7.57	6.72	26
24	Italy	7.47	6.85	23
25	South Korea	7.45	6.43	31
26	Czech Republic	7.40	6.55	27
27	Hungary	7.24	6.72	25
28	Japan	7.19	6.53	29
29	Poland	7.14	6.37	32
30	Greece	7.08	6.24	33
31	Malaysia	6.93	6.83	24
	Thailand	6.93	6.49	30
33	Mexico	6.79	6.53	28
34	Slovakia	6.54	5.78	34
35	Philippines	6.51	5.69	35
36	South Africa	6.37	5.50	38
37	China	6.28	5.35	42
38	Brazil	6.27	5.53	37
	India	6.27	5.31	44
40	Bulgaria	6.24	5.42	41
41	Saudi Arabia	6.19	5.44	40
42	Peru	6.13	5.45	39
43	Sri Lanka	6.10	4.92	49
44	Colombia	6.05	5.32	43
45	Argentina	6.04	5.66	36
46	Russia	5.97	4.54	53

Note: Scores reflect the opportunities for, and hindrances to, the conduct of business, measured by countries' rankings in ten categories including market potential, tax and labour-market policies, infrastructure, skills and the political environment. Scores reflect average and forecast average over given date range.

Business creativity and research

Innovation index[a]

1	United States	6.62	23	Spain	3.37
2	Taiwan	5.89	24	Slovenia	3.33
3	Finland	5.47	25	Italy	3.22
4	Sweden	5.25	26	Latvia	3.09
5	Japan	5.18	27	Estonia	3.05
6	Israel	4.71		Greece	3.05
7	Switzerland	4.51	29	Poland	2.90
8	Canada	4.43	30	Argentina	2.84
9	Australia	4.41	31	Portugal	2.83
10	Germany	4.38	32	Hong Kong	2.78
11	South Korea	4.33	33	Lithuania	2.77
12	Norway	4.13	34	Hungary	2.73
13	Denmark	4.12		Russia	2.73
14	United Kingdom	4.10	36	Costa Rica	2.68
15	Belgium	4.09	37	Chile	2.67
16	Austria	3.88	38	Bulgaria	2.63
17	Netherlands	3.86		Ukraine	2.63
18	France	3.84	40	Thailand	2.57
19	New Zealand	3.76	41	Panama	2.54
	Singapore	3.76	42	Czech Republic	2.53
21	Iceland	3.54	43	Uruguay	2.51
22	Ireland	3.47	44	Slovakia	2.45

Information and communications technology index[b]

1	Sweden	6.29	23	Estonia	5.18
2	Iceland	6.27	24	Portugal	5.12
3	Finland	6.19	25	France	5.09
4	United States	6.09	26	Slovenia	5.08
5	Singapore	6.02	27	Italy	4.94
6	Hong Kong	5.97	28	Czech Republic	4.83
7	Denmark	5.94	29	Hungary	4.77
8	Norway	5.93	30	Spain	4.75
9	Switzerland	5.87	31	Greece	4.59
10	Taiwan	5.86	32	Malaysia	4.43
11	Canada	5.83	33	Chile	4.37
12	Netherlands	5.77	34	Slovakia	4.28
13	United Kingdom	5.71	35	Latvia	4.24
14	Australia	5.70	36	Poland	4.03
15	Israel	5.61	37	Croatia	3.99
16	Germany	5.51	38	Uruguay	3.98
17	Japan	5.50	39	Mauritius	3.95
18	Austria	5.48	40	Lithuania	3.94
19	South Korea	5.40	41	Brazil	3.86
20	Belgium	5.38	42	South Africa	3.72
21	New Zealand	5.37	43	Trinidad & Tobago	3.64
22	Ireland	5.33	44	Bulgaria	3.58

a The innovation index is a measure of human resources skills, market incentive structures and interaction between business and scientific sectors.
b The information and communications technology (ICT) index is a measure of ICT usage and includes per capita measures of telephone lines, internet usage, personal computers and mobile phone users.

Total expenditure on R&D
% of GDP, 2001

1	Sweden	3.6		Slovenia	1.3
2	Finland	3.4	24	Ireland	1.2
3	Iceland	3.1	25	China	1.1
4	Japan	3.0		Italy	1.1
5	South Korea	2.9		New Zealand	1.1
6	Israel	2.8	28	Spain	1.0
	United States	2.8	29	Brazil	0.9
8	Switzerland	2.6		Hungary	0.9
9	Germany	2.5		Romania	0.9
10	France	2.2	32	India	0.8
	Taiwan	2.2	33	Greece	0.7
12	Denmark	2.1		Poland	0.7
	Singapore	2.1		Portugal	0.7
14	Belgium	2.0		Slovakia	0.7
	Netherlands	2.0		South Africa	0.7
16	Austria	1.9	38	Chile	0.6
	Canada	1.9		Hong Kong	0.6
18	United Kingdom	1.8		Turkey	0.6
19	Norway	1.7	41	Argentina	0.5
20	Australia	1.6		Malaysia	0.5
21	Russia	1.4		Venezuela	0.5
22	Czech Republic	1.3			

Patents

No. of patents granted to residents			*No. of patents in force*		
Total, 2000			*Per 100,000 inhabitants, 2000*		
1	Japan	123,978	1	Luxembourg	6,722
2	United States	83,090	2	Switzerland	1,214
3	South Korea	34,052	3	Sweden	1,097
4	Taiwan	20,094	4	Belgium	835
5	Germany	18,328	5	Japan	820
6	Russia	16,340	6	Netherlands	756
7	France	11,290	7	Taiwan	645
8	United Kingdom	4,491	8	Canada	639
9	Italy	3,983	9	France	631
10	China	3,742	10	Ireland	619
11	Netherlands	2,917	11	Denmark	555
12	Sweden	2,336	12	Singapore	549
13	Spain	1,752	13	United Kingdom	523
14	Switzerland	1,371	14	Australia	486
15	Australia	1,313	15	United States	471
16	Austria	1,248	16	Germany	459
17	Canada	1,138	17	South Korea	457
18	Poland	1,045	18	Finland	394
19	Belgium	844	19	Spain	360
20	Israel	433	20	Norway	354

Business costs and corruption

Business operating costs[a]
2001, 100 = highest

1	Japan	100.0	17	Singapore	22.4
2	United States	66.3	18	Venezuela	21.3
3	Germany	66.0	19	Russia	21.0
4	United Kingdom	64.0	20	Mexico	19.6
5	Belgium	58.7	21	Brazil	15.7
6	Sweden	54.5	22	South Africa	15.0
7	France	54.4	23	Czech Republic	13.4
8	Netherlands	54.0	24	Poland	13.1
9	Canada	45.6	25	Malaysia	11.1
10	Italy	45.5	26	Chile	10.4
11	Spain	39.5	27	China	8.7
12	Australia	38.3	28	India	7.7
13	Argentina	36.8	29	Thailand	7.3
14	Hong Kong	27.3	30	Indonesia	1.7
15	South Korea	27.1	31	Hungary	1.0
16	Taiwan	26.6			

Employment costs
Pay, social security and other benefits, $'000

1	Japan	50.6	11	United Kingdom	31.9
2	France	43.3	12	Austria	30.2
3	United States	42.5	13	Italy	29.4
4	Belgium	42.2	14	Ireland	28.4
5	Sweden	38.9	15	Spain	23.6
6	Germany	35.7	16	Portugal	12.6
7	Luxembourg	35.5	17	Greece	12.3
8	Denmark	34.6	18	India	1.8
9	Netherlands	32.6	19	China	1.6
10	Finland	32.3			

Business software piracy
2001, % of software that is pirated

1	Vietnam	94	20	Paraguay	72
2	China	92	21	Nigeria	71
3	Indonesia	88	22	India	70
4	Russia	87		Malaysia	70
	Ukraine	87	24	Honduras	68
6	Pakistan	83		Zimbabwe	68
7	Lebanon	79	26	Croatia	67
8	Nicaragua	78		Jordan	67
	Qatar	78	28	Mauritius	65
10	Bahrain	77	29	Costa Rica	64
	Bolivia	77		Dominican Republic	64
	Kenya	77		Greece	64
	Oman	77	32	Philippines	63
	Thailand	77		Uruguay	63
15	Kuwait	76	34	Argentina	62
16	Bulgaria	75		Ecuador	62
	Romania	75	36	Cyprus	61
18	El Salvador	73		Morocco	61
	Guatemala	73		Panama	61

Corruption perceptions index[b]

2002, 10 = least corrupt

1	Finland	9.7		Jamaica	4.0
2	Denmark	9.5		Peru	4.0
	New Zealand	9.5		Poland	4.0
4	Iceland	9.4	50	Ghana	3.9
5	Singapore	9.3	51	Croatia	3.8
	Sweden	9.3	52	Czech Republic	3.7
7	Canada	9.0		Latvia	3.7
	Luxembourg	9.0		Morocco	3.7
	Netherlands	9.0		Slovakia	3.7
10	United Kingdom	8.7		Sri Lanka	3.7
11	Australia	8.6	57	Colombia	3.6
12	Norway	8.5		Mexico	3.6
13	Switzerland	8.5	59	China	3.5
14	Hong Kong	8.2		Dominican Republic	3.5
15	Austria	7.8		Ethiopia	3.5
16	United States	7.7	62	Egypt	3.4
17	Chile	7.5		El Salvador	3.4
18	Germany	7.3	64	Thailand	3.2
	Israel	7.3		Turkey	3.2
20	Belgium	7.1	66	Senegal	3.1
	Japan	7.1	67	Panama	3.0
	Spain	7.1	68	Malawi	2.9
23	Ireland	6.9		Uzbekistan	2.9
24	Botswana	6.4	70	Argentina	2.8
25	France	6.3	71	Côte d'Ivoire	2.7
	Portugal	6.3		Honduras	2.7
27	Slovenia	6.0		India	2.7
28	Namibia	5.7		Russia	2.7
29	Estonia	5.6		Tanzania	2.7
	Taiwan	5.6		Zimbabwe	2.7
31	Italy	5.2	77	Pakistan	2.6
32	Uruguay	5.1		Philippines	2.6
33	Hungary	4.9		Romania	2.6
	Malaysia	4.9		Zambia	2.6
	Trinidad & Tobago	4.9	81	Albania	2.5
36	Belarus	4.8		Guatemala	2.5
	Lithuania	4.8		Nicaragua	2.5
	South Africa	4.8		Venezuala	2.5
	Tunisia	4.8	85	Georgia	2.4
40	Costa Rica	4.5		Ukraine	2.4
	Jordan	4.5		Vietnam	2.4
	Mauritius	4.5	88	Kazakhstan	2.3
	South Korea	4.5	89	Bolivia	2.2
44	Greece	4.2		Cameroon	2.2
45	Brazil	4.0		Ecuador	2.2
	Bulgaria	4.0		Haiti	2.2

a These costs include labour, business travel, taxes, rents, telecommunications and transport.
b This index ranks countries based on how much corruption is perceived to exist among politicians and public officials.

Businesses and banks

Largest businesses
By sales, $bn

1	Wal-Mart Stores	United States	219.8
2	Exxon Mobil	United States	191.6
3	General Motors	United States	177.3
4	BP	United Kingdom	174.2
5	Ford Motor	United States	162.4
6	DaimlerChrysler	United States	136.9
7	Royal Dutch/Shell Group	United Kingdom/Netherlands	135.2
8	General Electric	United States	126.0
9	Toyota Motor	Japan	120.8
10	Citigroup	United States	112.0
11	Mitsubishi	Japan	105.8
12	Mitsui	Japan	101.2
13	ChevronTexaco	United States	99.7
14	Total Fina Elf	France	94.3
15	Nippon Telegraph & Telephone[a]	Japan	93.4
16	Itochu	Japan	91.2
17	Allianz	Germany	86.0
18	Intl. Business Machines	United States	85.9
19	ING Group	Netherlands	83.0
20	Volkswagen	Germany	79.3
21	Siemens	Germany	77.4
22	Sumitomo	Japan	77.1
23	Altria Group	United States	73.0
24	Marubeni	Japan	71.8
25	Verizon Communications	United States	67.2
26	Deutsche Bank	Germany	66.8
27	E.ON	Germany	66.5
28	U.S. Postal Service[a]	United States	65.8
29	AXA	France	65.6
30	Credit Suisse	Switzerland	64.2
31	Hitachi	Japan	64.0
32	Nippon Life Insurance	Japan	63.8
33	American Intl. Group	United States	62.4
34	Carrefour	France	62.2
35	American Electric Power	United States	61.3
36	Sony	Japan	60.6
37	Royal Ahold	Netherlands	59.6
38	Duke Energy	United States	59.5
39	AT&T	United States	59.1
40	Honda Motor	Japan	58.9
41	Boeing	United States	58.2
42	El Paso	United States	57.5
43	BNP Paribas	France	55.0
	Matsushita Electric Industrial	Japan	55.0

a Government owned.

Notes: Industrial and service corporations. Figures refer to the year ended December 31, 2001, except for Japanese companies, where figures refer to year ended March 31, 2002. They include sales of consolidated subsidiaries but exclude excise taxes, thus differing, in some instances, from figures published by the companies themselves. Enron featured at number 6 in the original list for 2001.

Largest banks

By capital, $m

1	Citigroup	United States	58,448
2	Bank of America Corp	United States	41,972
3	Mizuho Financial Group	Japan	40,498
4	J.P. Morgan Chase	United States	37,713
5	HSBC Holdings	United Kingdom	35,074
6	Sumitomo Mitsui Banking Corporation	Japan	29,952
7	Crédit Agricole Groupe	France	28,876
8	Mitsubishi Tokyo Financial Group	Japan	25,673
9	UFJ Holding	Japan	23,815
10	Industrial and Commercial Bank of China	China	23,107
11	Bank of China	China	22,085
12	Deutsche Bank	Germany	21,859
13	Royal Bank of Scotland	United Kingdom	21,830
14	Bank One Corp	United States	21,749
15	BNP Paribas	France	21,748
16	HypoVereinsbank	Germany	19,154
17	Wachovia Corporation	United States	18,999
18	Wells Fargo & Co.	United States	18,247
19	HBOS	United Kingdom	18,086
20	Barclays Bank	United Kingdom	18,046
21	UBS	Switzerland	17,482
22	ABN-Amro Bank	Netherlands	16,942
23	Agricultural Bank of China	China	15,971
24	Santander Central Hispano	Spain	15,209
25	ING Bank	Netherlands	15,070
26	Rabobank Nederland	Netherlands	14,961
27	FleetBoston Financial Corp	United States	14,864
28	China Construction Bank	China	14,517
29	MetLife	United States	14,342
30	Société Générale	France	13,516
31	Lloyds TSB Group	United Kingdom	13,297
32	Norinchukin Bank	Japan	13,239
33	Banco Bilbao Vizcaya Argentaria	Spain	13,107
34	IntesaBci	Italy	13,041
35	Washington Mutual	United States	12,679
36	Credit Suisse Group	Switzerland	12,613
37	US Bancorp	United States	12,488
38	Fortis Bank	Belgium	11,432
39	Crédit Mutuel	France	10,877
40	Commerzbank	Germany	10,740
41	Abbey National	United Kingdom	10,612
42	Resona Group	Japan	10,230
43	Dresdner Bank	Germany	10,172
44	Groupe Caisse d'Epargne	France	10,013
45	Scotiabank	Canada	9,639
46	National Australia Bank	Australia	9,467

Notes: Capital is essentially equity and reserves.
Figures for Japanese banks refer to the year ended March 31, 2002. Figures for all other countries refer to the year ended December 31, 2001.

Stockmarkets

Largest market capitalisation

$m, end 2001

1	United States	13,810,429	27	Greece	86,538
2	Japan	2,251,814	28	Russia	76,198
3	United Kingdom	2,217,324	29	Ireland	75,298
4	France	1,174,428	30	Saudi Arabia	73,199
5	Germany	1,071,749	31	Israel	70,271
6	Canada	700,751	32	Norway	69,054
7	Italy	527,396	33	Chile	56,310
8	China	523,952	34	Turkey	47,150
9	Switzerland	521,190	35	Portugal	46,338
10	Hong Kong	506,118	36	Iran	43,854
11	Spain	468,203	37	Philippines	41,523
12	Netherlands	458,221	38	Thailand	36,340
13	Australia	374,629	39	Poland	26,017
14	Taiwan	292,621	40	Austria	24,511
15	Sweden	232,561	41	Egypt	24,335
16	South Korea	220,046	42	Luxembourg	23,783
17	Argentina	192,499	43	Indonesia	23,006
18	Finland	190,456	44	New Zealand	17,779
19	Brazil	186,238	45	Colombia	13,217
20	Belgium	165,843	46	Peru	11,134
21	South Africa	139,750	47	Hungary	10,367
22	Mexico	126,258	48	Czech Republic	9,331
23	Malaysia	120,007	49	Morocco	9,087
24	Singapore	117,338	50	Zimbabwe	7,972
25	India	110,396	51	United Arab Emirates	7,881
26	Denmark	94,958	52	Bahrain	6,600

Highest growth in market capitalisation, $ terms

% increase, 1996–2001

1	Bulgaria	7,114	20	Iran	158
2	Romania	3,626	22	Jamaica	149
3	Bolivia	1,264	23	Barbados	137
4	Fiji	544	24	Zimbabwe	119
5	Belgium	388	25	Ireland	117
6	Latvia	362	26	Russia	105
7	China	361	27	Italy	104
8	Argentina	331	28	Panama	103
9	Slovenia	328	29	France	99
10	Botswana	289		Qatar[a]	99
11	Nepal	286	31	Hungary	97
12	Greece	258	32	Israel	96
	Trinidad & Tobago	258	33	Spain	93
14	El Salvador	237	34	Portugal	88
15	Poland	210	35	Egypt	72
16	Finland	202	36	Tanzania[b]	69
17	Iceland	194	37	United States	63
18	Malta	186	38	Germany	60
19	Cyprus	161		Saudi Arabia	60
20	Costa Rica	160	40	South Korea	59

Highest growth in value traded, $ terms
% increase, 1996-2001

1	Kazakhstan[a]	15,900	23	Malta	236
2	Romania	4,167	24	Spain	234
3	Zambia	1,667	25	Saudi Arabia	228
4	Iceland	1,374	26	United Kingdom	224
5	Latvia	1,275	27	Jordan	214
6	Finland	699	28	Netherlands	204
7	Russia	674	29	West Bank and Gaza[a]	200
8	Cyprus	639	30	Hungary	194
9	Nigeria	589	31	India	159
10	Nepal[c]	540	32	South Africa	156
11	Zimbabwe	500	33	Ukraine[b]	143
12	Bulgaria[b]	483	34	Canada	142
13	Italy	439	35	Bermuda[a]	130
14	Swaziland	400	36	Morocco	125
15	Greece	351	37	Sweden	120
16	Lithuania	347	38	Turkey	112
17	United States	308	39	Botswana	110
18	South Korea	297	40	Pakistan	106
19	France	289	41	Denmark	104
20	Portugal	282	42	Slovenia	98
21	Israel	270	43	Jamaica	92
22	Qatar[d]	251	44	Iran	89

Highest growth in number of listed companies
% increase, 1996-2001

1	Romania	30,135		Panama	53
2	Bulgaria	2,560		Taiwan	53
3	Kazakhstan[a]	933		Tunisia	53
4	Spain	308	27	Greece	51
5	Cyprus	272	28	Zambia	50
6	Russia	223	29	Germany	45
7	Canada	217	30	Iran	44
8	Bolivia	190	31	Trinidad & Tobago	35
9	Poland	177		Turkey	35
10	Fiji[e]	125	33	Botswana	33
11	Nigeria	116		Lebanon[a]	33
12	China	115	35	Malaysia	30
13	Finland	114	36	Kuwait[c]	28
14	Malta	100	37	Hungary	27
	Tanzania[b]	100	38	West Bank and Gaza[a]	26
16	Iceland	91	39	Indonesia	25
17	Latvia	85		Uzbekistan[c]	25
	South Korea	85	41	Bangladesh	24
19	Slovenia	81		Sweden	24
20	Singapore	73	42	Côte d'Ivoire	23
21	Egypt	71		Switzerland	23
22	Jordan	64	45	Nepal[c]	22
22	Hong Kong	53		Qatar[d]	22

a 1997–2001   b 1998–2001   c 1996–2000   d 1997–2000   e 1996–99

Transport: *roads and cars*

Longest road networks
Km, 2001 or latest

1	United States	6,304,193	21	Sweden	212,961
2	India	3,319,644	22	Bangladesh	207,486
3	Brazil	1,724,929	23	Philippines	201,994
4	China	1,698,012	24	Austria	200,000
5	Japan	1,166,340	25	Romania	198,603
6	Canada	901,903	26	Nigeria	194,394
7	France	894,000	27	Ukraine	169,630
8	Australia	811,603	28	Hungary	167,839
9	Spain	663,795	29	Iran	167,157
10	Russia	537,289	30	Congo	157,000
11	Italy	479,688	31	Saudi Arabia	152,044
12	United Kingdom	371,913	32	Belgium	149,028
13	Poland	364,697	33	Czech Republic	127,728
14	South Africa	362,099	34	Greece	117,000
15	Turkey	354,373	35	Netherlands	116,500
16	Indonesia	342,700	36	Colombia	112,988
17	Mexico	329,532	37	Algeria	104,000
18	Pakistan	257,683	38	Sri Lanka	96,695
19	Germany	230,735	39	Venezuela	96,155
20	Argentina	215,471	40	Vietnam	93,300

Densest road networks
Km of road per km² land area, 2001 or latest

1	Macau	19.6	21	Sri Lanka	1.5
2	Malta	7.1		United Kingdom	1.5
3	Bahrain	5.2	23	Bangladesh	1.4
4	Belgium	4.9	24	Ireland	1.3
5	Singapore	4.8		Spain	1.3
6	Barbados	3.7	26	Cyprus	1.2
7	Japan	3.1		Estonia	1.2
8	Netherlands	2.8		Lithuania	1.2
9	Puerto Rico	2.6		Poland	1.2
10	Austria	2.4	30	Latvia	1.1
11	Luxembourg	2.0	31	India	1.0
12	Hungary	1.8		Mauritius	1.0
13	Denmark	1.7		Slovenia	1.0
	Hong Kong	1.7		Taiwan	1.0
	Jamaica	1.7	35	Greece	0.9
	Switzerland	1.7		Slovakia	0.9
17	Czech Republic	1.6		South Korea	0.9
	France	1.6	38	Israel	0.8
	Italy	1.6		Portugal	0.8
	Trinidad & Tobago	1.6		Romania	0.8

Most crowded road networks
Number of vehicles per km of road network, 2001 or latest

1	Hong Kong	286.7	26	Switzerland	54.0
2	United Arab Emirates	231.6	27	Russia	47.3
3	Germany	194.5	28	Mexico	47.0
4	Lebanon	190.6	29	Slovenia	45.8
5	Singapore	168.9	30	Guatemala	44.8
6	Macau	163.5	31	Puerto Rico	44.5
7	Kuwait	155.7	32	Croatia	44.1
8	Qatar	154.5	33	Barbados	43.2
9	Taiwan	148.6	34	Jordan	40.4
10	South Korea	138.4		Tunisia	40.4
11	Thailand	108.6	36	France	37.8
12	Israel	105.9	37	Greece	36.6
13	Malta	103.0	38	El Salvador	36.1
14	Malaysia	74.8	39	Belgium	35.4
15	Italy	73.3	40	Macedonia	34.9
16	Brunei	73.2	41	Serbia	34.8
17	Uruguay	63.1	42	United States	34.1
18	Portugal	62.5	43	Cyprus	33.7
19	Japan	62.3	44	Slovakia	33.4
	United Kingdom	62.3	45	Poland	32.5
21	Mauritius	61.2	46	Denmark	31.1
22	Bahrain	61.1	47	Cambodia	30.9
23	Bulgaria	59.6	48	Finland	30.6
24	Netherlands	57.9	49	Argentina	30.4
25	Luxembourg	54.7	50	Dominican Republic	29.8

Most used road networks
'000 vehicle-km per year per km of road network, 2001 or latest

1	Indonesia	8,134	16	Luxembourg	740
2	Hong Kong	5,888	17	Greece	678
3	Taiwan	2,753	18	Japan	665
4	Germany	2,555	19	Chile	631
5	Israel	2,240		Denmark	631
6	Portugal	1,397	21	Sweden	602
7	Bahrain	1,367	22	Finland	591
8	Malta	1,246	23	France	581
9	United Kingdom	1,243	24	Cambodia	563
10	Belgium	1,062	25	Croatia	536
11	Netherlands	944	26	China	495
12	Pakistan	910	27	Macedonia	489
13	Ethiopia	835	28	Slovenia	467
14	South Korea	773	29	El Salvador	423
15	Tunisia	770	30	United States	421

Highest car ownership
Number of cars per 1,000 people, 2001 or latest

1	Lebanon	732		Kuwait	359
2	New Zealand	578	27	Ireland	349
3	Brunei	576	28	Estonia	339
	Luxembourg	576	29	Czech Republic	335
5	Iceland	561	30	Portugal	321
6	Italy	542	31	Lithuania	317
7	Germany	516	32	Poland	259
8	Austria	495	33	Greece	254
9	Malta	494	34	Bahrain	248
10	Switzerland	493	35	Croatia	247
11	Australia	488	36	Hungary	237
12	United States	481	37	Slovakia	236
13	France	477	38	Latvia	235
14	Belgium	462	39	Bulgaria	234
15	Canada	458	40	Israel	233
16	Sweden	450	41	Puerto Rico	230
17	Slovenia	426	42	Qatar	219
18	Japan	413	43	Taiwan	212
19	Norway	411	44	South Korea	171
20	Spain	408	45	Bahamas	161
21	Finland	403	46	Libya	154
22	Cyprus	400		Uruguay	154
23	Netherlands	384	48	Serbia & Montenegro	150
	United Kingdom	384	49	Belarus	145
25	Denmark	359		Malaysia	145

Lowest car ownership
Number of cars per 1,000 people, 2001 or latest

1	Somalia	0.1	17	Liberia	2.6
	Tajikistan	0.1	18	Burundi	2.8
3	Armenia	0.3	19	Mali	2.9
	Central African Rep	0.3	20	Chad	3.2
	Mozambique	0.3	21	Laos	3.4
6	Bangladesh	0.5	22	Burkina Faso	3.6
7	Myanmar	0.6	23	Niger	3.8
8	Tanzania	0.8	24	Sierra Leone	3.9
9	Ethiopia	0.9	25	Madagascar	4.1
10	Guatemala	1.0	26	Haiti	4.4
11	Afghanistan	1.4	27	Ghana	4.7
	Rwanda	1.4	28	Pakistan	5.0
13	Eritrea	1.5	29	India	5.2
14	Uganda	1.8	30	Guinea-Bissau	5.7
15	Guinea	2.0		Lesotho	5.7
16	Malawi	2.3	32	China	6.7

Most accidents

Number of people injured per 100m vehicle-km, 2001 or latest

1	Malawi	2,730	27	Saudi Arabia	89
2	Rwanda	1,764	28	Philippines	86
3	South Korea	510	29	Germany	81
4	Costa Rica	406		Macedonia	81
5	Kenya	363	31	United States	74
6	India	333	32	Spain	73
7	Honduras	317	33	Ghana	72
8	Egypt	222	34	Mexico	66
9	Sri Lanka	205	35	Yemen	59
10	Portugal	194	36	Iceland	58
11	Morocco	183	37	Bahrain	57
12	Turkey	179	38	Hungary	56
13	Hong Kong	176		Senegal	56
14	Japan	149	40	Iran	53
15	Kirgizstan	134		Oman	53
16	Colombia	126		Switzerland	53
17	Latvia	125	43	Malta	42
18	Italy	122	44	Thailand	40
19	Canada	121	45	Slovakia	39
20	Czech Republic	113	46	Ireland	38
21	Belgium	108	47	Estonia	37
22	Slovenia	106	48	Norway	34
23	Israel	100	49	New Zealand	33
	South Africa	100	50	Mauritius	32
25	United Kingdom	94		Sweden	32
26	Mongolia	90		Zimbabwe	32

Most deaths

Number of people killed per 100m vehicle-km, 2001 or latest

1	Malawi	1,117		Saudi Arabia	11
2	India	65		Yemen	11
3	Egypt	44	19	Mexico	10
4	Kenya	41	20	Albania	8
5	Latvia	25	21	South Africa	7
6	Kirgizstan	24		Suriname	7
7	Sri Lanka	23	23	Portugal	6
8	Mongolia	22		Romania	6
9	Colombia	17		Turkey	6
	Morocco	17	26	Czech Republic	5
	South Korea	17		Iran	5
12	Honduras	16	28	Ecuador	4
13	Philippines	14		Macedonia	4
14	Thailand	13		Oman	4
15	Ghana	12		Senegal	4
16	Costa Rica	11			

Transport: *planes and trains*

Most air travel
Million passenger-km[a] per year

1	United States	1,106,347		16	Italy	43,315
2	Japan	198,794		17	Malaysia	41,112
3	United Kingdom	173,822		18	Thailand	40,582
4	China	112,058		19	Switzerland	30,826
5	Germany	111,343		20	Mexico	26,897
6	France	94,994		21	Saudi Arabia	26,238
7	Australia	78,419		22	South Africa	25,507
8	Singapore	70,232		23	India	25,052
9	Canada	69,392		24	Belgium	24,706
10	Hong Kong	65,150		25	United Arab Emirates	23,126
11	South Korea	63,859		26	New Zealand	22,013
12	Netherlands	57,849		27	Argentina	18,008
13	Brazil	52,740		28	Indonesia	16,983
14	Spain	51,316		29	Austria	16,684
15	Russia	48,027		30	Ireland	14,853

Busiest airports

Total passengers, m

				International passengers, m		
1	Atlanta, Hartsfield	76.9		1	London, Heathrow	53.8
2	Chicago, O'Hare	66.5		2	Paris, Charles de Gaulle	42.9
3	London, Heathrow	63.3		3	Frankfurt, Main	39.4
4	Tokyo, Haneda	61.1		4	Amsterdam, Schipol	39.2
5	Los Angeles, Intl.	56.2		5	Hong Kong, Intl.	32.0
6	Dallas, Ft. Worth	52.8		6	London, Gatwick	28.1
7	Frankfurt, Main	48.5		7	Singapore, Changi	25.6
8	Paris, Charles de Gaulle	48.3		8	Tokyo, Narita	22.2
9	Amsterdam, Schipol	40.7		9	Bangkok, Intl.	21.4
10	Denver, Intl.	35.7		10	Zurich	19.7
11	Phoenix, Skyharbor Intl.	35.5		11	Brussels, Zaventem	19.6
12	Las Vegas, McCarran Intl.	35.0		12	Madrid	17.1

- -

Average daily aircraft movements, take-offs and landings

1	Chicago, O'Hare	2,530		11	Detroit, Metro	1,345
2	Atlanta, Hartsfield	2,438		12	Cincinnati, Intl.	1,333
3	Dallas, Ft. Worth	2,096		13	London, Heathrow	1,278
4	Los Angeles, Intl.	1,768		14	Philadelphia, Intl.	1,543
5	Phoenix, Skyharbor Intl.	1,495		15	Frankfurt, Main	1,256
6	Paris, Charles de Gaulle	1,398		16	Houston, George Bush Intercont.	1,252
7	Minneapolis, St Paul	1,388		17	Charlotte/Douglas, Intl.	1,248
8	Los Angeles, Van Nuys	1,366		18	Miami, Intl.	1,220
9	Las Vegas, McCarran Intl.	1,361		19	Pittsburgh, Intl	1,198
10	Denver, Intl.	1,353		20	Amsterdam, Schipol	1,164

a Air passenger–km data refer to the distance travelled by each aircraft of national origin.

Longest railway networks
'000 km

1	United States	230.2	21	Australia	9.5
2	Russia	85.8	22	Czech Republic	9.4
3	India	63.0	23	Turkey	8.7
4	Canada	62.7	24	Hungary	8.0
5	China	59.1	25	Iran	7.9
6	Germany	36.0	26	Pakistan	7.8
7	Argentina	34.2	27	Finland	5.9
8	France	29.5		Sudan	5.9
9	Mexico	26.5	29	Austria	5.8
10	South Africa	22.7	30	Belarus	5.5
11	Ukraine	22.2	31	Egypt	5.1
12	Brazil	22.1	32	Philippines	4.9
13	Japan	20.2	33	Cuba	4.8
14	Poland	20.1	34	North Korea	4.5
15	Italy	16.4	35	Bulgaria	4.3
	United Kingdom	16.4	36	Indonesia	4.2
17	Spain	13.9		Norway	4.2
18	Kazakhstan	13.6	38	Serbia & Montenegro	4.1
19	Romania	11.4	39	New Zealand	3.9
20	Sweden	10.9	40	Slovakia	3.7

Most rail passengers
Km per person per year

1	Switzerland	1,923	11	Luxembourg	865
2	Japan	1,896		Russia	865
3	Belarus	1,542	13	Italy	827
4	Kazakhstan	1,368	14	Belgium	788
5	France	1,209	15	Hungary	739
6	Ukraine	1,062	16	Egypt	720
7	Denmark	1,047	17	Czech Republic	705
8	Austria	1,031	18	United Kingdom	658
9	Netherlands	905	19	Finland	631
10	Germany	902	20	South Korea	619

Most rail freight
Million tonnes-km per year

1	United States	2,151,866	11	Poland	47,656
2	China	1,424,980	12	Australia	38,525
3	Russia	1,249,166	13	Belarus	29,727
4	Canada	313,370	14	Japan	21,800
5	India	312,371	15	Italy	21,785
6	Ukraine	177,465	16	United Kingdom	20,561
7	Kazakhstan	135,653	17	Sweden	17,989
8	South Africa	106,654	18	Austria	16,566
9	Germany	74,555	19	Czech Republic	16,557
10	France	50,396	20	Romania	15,899

Transport: *shipping*

Largest merchant fleets
Number of vessels not less than 100 GRT and built before end of 2002[a]
By country of :

		registration	ownership				registration	ownership
1	Japan	7,458	2,912		46	Bangladesh	325	32
2	Panama	6,247	6		47	Portugal	324	73
3	United States	6,080	1,454		48	Iceland	318	70
4	Russia	4,943	2,548		49	Nigeria	303	43
5	China	3,326	2,320		50	Azerbaijan	285	150
6	Indonesia	2,628	610		51	Finland	283	134
7	South Korea	2,532	855		52	Saudi Arabia	280	121
8	Norway	2,299	1,691		53	Venezuela	274	59
9	Singapore	1,768	714		54	Georgia	261	5
10	Philippines	1,686	337		55	Croatia	256	103
11	Spain	1,568	329		56	Romania	237	104
12	Greece	1,548	3,101		57	North Korea	225	99
13	Liberia	1,535	0		58	Ireland	220	53
14	United Kingdom	1,525	792		59	Ghana	213	19
15	Italy	1,486	638		60	Kuwait	201	32
16	Malta	1,350	14			Neth. Antilles	201	0
17	Bahamas	1,348	28		62	South Africa	196	27
18	Cyprus	1,325	68		63	Senegal	190	1
19	Netherlands	1,316	784			Syria	190	67
20	Honduras	1,155	3		65	Belgium	188	153
21	Turkey	1,147	573		66	Lithuania	184	74
22	Denmark	1,043	690		67	Ecuador	182	31
23	India	1,010	385		68	Estonia	181	82
24	Malaysia	915	306		69	New Zealand	173	42
25	Canada	902	327		70	Bulgaria	165	100
26	Germany	857	2,301		71	Latvia	158	101
27	Ukraine	828	384		72	Mauritania	142	0
28	Hong Kong	766	570		73	Algeria	141	68
29	Cambodia	727	0		74	Libya	140	16
30	Vietnam	721	159		75	Mozambique	131	1
31	Peru	719	24		76	Namibia	126	3
32	France	707	277		77	Angola	124	10
33	Mexico	658	98			Myanmar	124	34
34	Taiwan	649	528		79	Bahrain	115	11
35	Thailand	629	254		80	Bermuda	113	0
36	Australia	624	87		81	Papua New Guinea	111	15
37	Sweden	571	324		82	Colombia	109	19
38	Chile	525	90		83	Madagascar	103	8
39	Morocco	483	38		84	Bolivia	96	0
40	Argentina	481	94		85	Cuba	91	57
41	Brazil	476	162		86	Uruguay	90	16
42	Poland	383	125		87	Lebanon	89	44
43	Iran	380	153		88	Iraq	88	0
44	Egypt	361	125		89	Tunisia	75	13
45	United Arab Emir	356	195		90	Albania	74	3

a Gross Tonnage (GRT) = total volume within the hull and above deck. 1 GRT=100 cu ft.

Tourism

Most tourist arrivals
Number of arrivals, '000

1	France	76,503	21	Turkey	9,628
2	Spain	49,532	22	Singapore	7,077
3	United States	45,495	23	Macau	6,840
4	Italy	38,994	24	Ireland	6,606
5	China	33,165	25	Croatia	6,502
6	United Kingdom	23,338	26	Belgium	6,479
7	Russia	20,207	27	Saudi Arabia	6,306
8	Mexico	19,814	28	South Africa	5,952
9	Canada	19,630	29	Egypt	5,702
10	Austria	18,180	30	South Korea	5,402
11	Germany	17,863	31	Brazil	5,246
12	Hungary	15,337	32	Tunisia	5,153
13	Poland	14,991	33	Indonesia	5,126
14	Hong Kong	13,725	34	Australia	5,122
15	Greece	13,703	35	Czech Republic	5,006
16	Portugal	12,197	36	Japan	4,838
17	Malaysia	11,085	37	Ukraine	4,483
18	Switzerland	10,871	38	Norway	4,291
19	Netherlands	10,084	39	Morocco	4,187
20	Thailand	9,923	40	United Arab Emirates	3,922

Biggest tourist spenders
$m

1	United States	58,008	11	Netherlands	9,193
2	Germany	47,494	12	Belgium	8,719
3	United Kingdom	34,301	13	Russia	7,645
4	Japan	28,764	14	Switzerland	6,771
5	Spain	21,502	15	Sweden	6,249
6	France	17,584	16	Poland	6,040
7	Italy	15,177	17	Taiwan	5,473
8	Canada	12,733	18	Mexico	4,825
9	Austria	11,050	19	South Korea	4,712
10	China	9,799	20	Denmark	4,417

Largest tourist receipts
$m

1	United States	68,448	11	Poland	8,051
2	France	29,283	12	Greece	7,511
3	Spain	27,392	13	Switzerland	7,077
4	Italy	24,439	14	Australia	6,708
5	United Kingdom	19,252	15	Hong Kong	6,464
6	Germany	14,358	16	Russia	6,297
7	China	14,314	17	South Korea	6,294
8	Austria	11,010	18	Netherlands	6,217
9	Canada	9,146	19	Singapore	6,162
10	Mexico	8,204	20	Turkey	5,523

Education

Highest primary enrolment
Number enrolled as % of relevant age group, 2000 or latest available

1	Brazil	166		Suriname	119
2	Malawi	158	17	Liberia	118
3	Haiti	154		Tunisia	118
4	Gabon	151	19	Libya	117
5	Uganda	141	20	Bolivia	116
6	Peru	128	21	Laos	115
7	Nepal	126	22	Algeria	114
8	Dominican Republic	125		Ecuador	114
	Swaziland	125		Israel	114
10	Togo	124	25	Colombia	113
11	Portugal	123		Mexico	113
12	Rwanda	122		Namibia	113
13	Argentina	119		Netherlands Antilles	113
	Ireland	119		Paraguay	113
	South Africa	119		Philippines	113

Lowest primary enrolment
Number enrolled as % of relevant age group, 2000 or latest available

1	Bhutan	21	15	Serbia & Montenegro	69
2	Niger	32	16	Chad	70
3	Burkina Faso	43	17	Ethiopia	71
4	Congo	47	18	Oman	73
5	Mali	55		Senegal	73
	Sudan	55	20	Gambia, The	75
7	Central African Rep	56	21	Côte d'Ivoire	77
8	Eritrea	61	22	Ghana	78
9	Burundi	62		Uzbekistan	78
10	Guinea	63		Yemen	78
	Tanzania	63	25	Zambia	79
12	Angola	64	26	Singapore	80
13	Sierra Leone	65	27	Ukraine	81
14	Saudi Arabia	68			

Highest tertiary enrolment[a]
Number enrolled as % of relevant age group, 2000 or latest available

1	Finland	84	11	United Kingdom	58
2	South Korea	72	12	Barbados	57
3	United States	72		Belgium	57
4	Norway	68	14	Austria	56
5	New Zealand	66		Denmark	56
	Sweden	66	16	Greece	55
7	Russia	65	17	Estonia	53
8	Australia	63		France	53
9	Canada	60		Slovenia	53
10	Spain	58	20	Netherlands	52

Notes: The gross enrolment ratios shown are the actual number enrolled as a percentage of the number of children in the official primary age group. They may exceed 100 when children outside the primary age group are receiving primary education either because they have not moved on to secondary education or because they have started primary education early.

Least literate
% adult literacy rate, 2000 or latest available

1	Niger	16.0		16	Yemen	46.4
2	Burkina Faso	23.9		17	Central African Rep	46.7
3	Mali	25.6		18	Burundi	48.0
4	Gambia, The	36.6		19	Côte d'Ivoire	48.6
5	Benin	37.4		20	Morocco	48.8
	Senegal	37.4		21	Haiti	49.8
7	Guinea-Bissau	38.4		22	Liberia	53.5
8	Ethiopia	39.1		23	Egypt	55.3
9	Iraq	39.3		24	Eritrea	55.7
10	Bangladesh	40.0		25	Togo	57.1
11	Mauritania	40.2		26	India	57.2
12	Nepal	41.7		27	Sudan	57.7
13	Chad	42.6		28	Malawi	60.1
14	Pakistan	43.2		29	Congo-Brazzaville	61.4
15	Mozambique	44.0		30	Papua New Guinea	63.9

Highest education spending
% of GDP, 2000 or latest available

1	Zimbabwe	10.4		15	Kenya	6.4
2	Lesotho	10.1			Lithuania	6.4
3	Yemen	10.0		17	Jamaica	6.3
4	Saudi Arabia	9.5			Malaysia	6.3
5	Botswana	8.6		19	Finland	6.1
6	Cuba	8.5			New Zealand	6.1
7	Denmark	8.2		21	Belarus	6.0
8	Namibia	8.1		22	Belgium	5.9
9	Sweden	7.8			Latvia	5.9
10	Estonia	7.5			Panama	5.9
11	Israel	7.3		25	Austria	5.8
12	Barbados	7.1			France	5.8
13	Norway	6.9			Portugal	5.8
14	Tunisia	6.8				

Lowest education spending
% of GDP, 2000 or latest available

1	Myanmar	0.5		13	China	2.1
2	Sierra Leone	1.0			Guinea-Bissau	2.1
3	Haiti	1.1			Tajikistan	2.1
4	Swaziland	1.5			Tanzania	2.1
5	Ecuador	1.6		17	Egypt	2.3
6	Guatemala	1.7			Laos	2.3
7	Pakistan	1.8			Uganda	2.3
8	Cambodia	1.9			Zambia	2.3
	Central African Rep	1.9		21	Mongolia	2.4
	Guinea	1.9			Mozambique	2.4
11	Chad	2.0		23	Bangladesh	2.5
	United Arab Emirates	2.0			Dominican Republic	2.5

a Tertiary education includes all levels of post-secondary education including courses
leading to awards not equivalent to a university degree, courses leading to a first
university degree and postgraduate courses.

Life expectancy

Highest life expectancy
Years, 2000–05

1	Andorra[a]	83.5		New Zealand	78.3
2	Japan	81.6	27	United Kingdom	78.2
3	Sweden	80.1	28	Costa Rica	78.1
4	Hong Kong	79.9		Singapore	78.1
5	Iceland	79.8	30	Finland	78.0
6	Canada	79.3		Virgin Islands	78.0
	Spain	79.3	32	Bermuda[a]	77.3
8	Australia	79.2	33	Barbados	77.2
	Israel	79.2	34	United States	77.1
10	Martinique	79.1	35	Ireland	77.0
	Switzerland	79.1	36	Cuba	76.7
12	France	79.0		Taiwan[a]	76.7
13	Macau	78.9	38	Denmark	76.6
	Norway	78.9		Kuwait	76.6
15	Belgium	78.8	40	Brunei	76.3
16	Italy	78.7		Netherlands Antilles	76.3
17	Aruba[b]	78.5		Slovenia	76.3
	Austria	78.5	43	Portugal	76.2
19	Luxembourg	78.4	44	Chile	76.1
	Malta	78.4	45	Jamaica	75.7
21	Cyprus	78.3	46	Puerto Rico	75.6
	Germany	78.3	47	South Korea	75.5
	Greece	78.3	48	Czech Republic	75.4
	Guadeloupe	78.3	49	Uruguay	75.3
	Netherlands	78.3	50	Réunion	75.2

Highest male life expectancy
Years, 2000–05

1	Andorra[a]	80.6	9	Australia	76.4
2	Japan	77.9	10	Uruguay	76.1
3	Iceland	77.6	11	Cyprus	76.0
	Sweden	77.6		Norway	76.0
5	Hong Kong	77.3	13	Malta	75.9
6	Israel	77.1		Singapore	75.9
7	Canada	76.7		Spain	75.9
8	Macau	76.5		Switzerland	75.9

Highest female life expectancy
Years, 2000–05

1	Andorra	86.6	10	Aruba[b]	82.0
2	Japan	85.1		Australia	82.0
3	France	82.8		Virgin Islands	82.0
	Hong Kong	82.8	13	Belgium	81.9
	Spain	82.8		Canada	81.9
6	Sweden	82.6		Iceland	81.9
7	Martinique	82.3		Italy	81.9
	Switzerland	82.3		Norway	81.9
9	Macau	82.1	18	Guadeloupe	81.7

a 2002 estimate.   b 2001

Lowest life expectancy

Years, 2000–05

1	Zambia	32.4		Uganda	46.2
2	Zimbabwe	33.1	27	South Africa	47.7
3	Sierra Leone	34.2	28	Somalia	47.9
4	Swaziland	34.4	29	Congo-Brazzaville	48.2
5	Lesotho	35.1	30	Mali	48.6
6	Malawi	37.5	31	Guinea	49.1
7	Mozambique	38.1	32	Haiti	49.5
8	Rwanda	39.3	33	Togo	49.7
9	Central African Rep	39.5	34	Benin	50.6
10	Botswana	39.7	35	Nigeria	51.5
11	Angola	40.1	36	Mauritania	52.5
12	Burundi	40.9	37	Eritrea	52.7
13	Côte d'Ivoire	41.0	38	Senegal	52.9
14	Liberia	41.4	39	Madagascar	53.6
15	Congo	41.8	40	Gambia, The	54.1
16	Afghanistan	43.1	41	Laos	54.5
17	Tanzania	43.3	42	Cambodia	54.7
18	Namibia	44.3	43	Sudan	55.6
19	Kenya	44.6	44	Gabon	56.6
20	Chad	44.7	45	Myanmar	57.3
21	Guinea-Bissau	45.3	46	Papua New Guinea	57.6
22	Ethiopia	45.5	47	Ghana	57.9
23	Burkina Faso	45.7	48	Nepal	59.9
24	Cameroon	46.2	49	Yemen	60.0
	Niger	46.2	50	Iraq	60.7

Lowest male life expectancy

Years, 2000–05

1	Lesotho	32.3	11	Botswana	38.9
2	Zambia	32.7	12	Burundi	40.4
3	Sierra Leone	33.1	13	Liberia	40.7
4	Swaziland	33.3	14	Congo	40.8
5	Zimbabwe	33.7		Côte d'Ivoire	40.8
6	Mozambique	36.6	16	Tanzania	42.5
7	Malawi	37.3	17	Namibia	42.9
8	Central African Rep	38.5	18	Afghanistan	43.0
9	Angola	38.8	19	Kenya	43.5
	Rwanda	38.8	20	Chad	43.7

Lowest female life expectancy

Years, 2000–05

1	Zambia	32.1	10	Central African Rep	40.6
2	Zimbabwe	32.6	11	Côte d'Ivoire	41.2
3	Swaziland	35.4	12	Burundi	41.4
4	Sierra Leone	35.5	13	Angola	41.5
5	Lesotho	37.7	14	Liberia	42.2
	Malawi	37.7	15	Congo	42.8
7	Mozambique	39.6	16	Afghanistan	43.3
8	Rwanda	39.7	17	Tanzania	44.1
9	Botswana	40.5			

Death rates and infant mortality

Highest death rates
Number of deaths per 1,000 population, 2000–05

1	Sierra Leone	29.3	49	Eritrea	11.9
2	Zambia	28.0	50	Croatia	11.8
3	Zimbabwe	27.0	51	Sudan	11.7
4	Lesotho	25.7	52	Lithuania	11.6
5	Swaziland	25.4	53	Gabon	11.5
6	Malawi	24.1	54	Denmark	11.3
7	Angola	23.6	55	Myanmar	11.2
8	Mozambique	23.5	56	North Korea	11.0
9	Central African Rep	22.1	57	Italy	10.9
10	Rwanda	21.8	58	Czech Republic	10.8
11	Afghanistan	21.5		Portugal	10.8
	Liberia	21.5	60	Moldova	10.7
13	Botswana	21.4	61	Germany	10.6
	Congo	21.4		Serbia & Montenegro	10.6
15	Burundi	20.6		Sweden	10.6
16	Côte d'Ivoire	20.0	64	Greece	10.5
17	Guinea-Bissau	19.6	65	United Kingdom	10.4
18	Chad	19.5	66	Belgium	10.0
19	Niger	19.1		Cambodia	10.0
20	Tanzania	18.1		Ghana	10.0
21	Namibia	17.9		Poland	10.0
22	Ethiopia	17.7	70	Austria	9.9
	Somalia	17.7		Georgia	9.9
24	Burkina Faso	17.4		Norway	9.9
25	Cameroon	16.9	73	Finland	9.8
	South Africa	16.9		Slovakia	9.8
27	Kenya	16.7		Slovenia	9.8
	Uganda	16.7		Switzerland	9.8
29	Mali	16.2	77	Nepal	9.7
30	Guinea	16.1	78	Pakistan	9.6
31	Congo-Brazzaville	15.4	79	Kazakhstan	9.5
32	Bulgaria	15.1	80	Papua New Guinea	9.4
33	Togo	14.7	81	France	9.3
34	Haiti	14.6	82	Yemen	9.2
	Russia	14.6	83	Spain	9.1
36	Benin	14.3	84	Uruguay	9.1
37	Mauritania	14.2	85	Netherlands	8.9
	Ukraine	14.2	86	Iraq	8.8
39	Nigeria	13.7	87	Bhutan	8.6
40	Estonia	13.6	88	India	8.5
	Latvia	13.6	89	Macedonia	8.4
42	Hungary	13.5	90	Bangladesh	8.3
43	Belarus	13.2		Ireland	8.3
	Madagascar	13.2		Puerto Rico	8.3
45	Gambia, The	12.7		United States	8.3
46	Laos	12.6	94	Bahamas	8.2
47	Romania	12.5		Japan	8.2
48	Senegal	12.2		Luxembourg	8.2

Note: Both death and, in particular, infant mortality rates can be underestimated in certain countries where not all deaths are officially recorded.   a 2002 estimate.

Highest infant mortality
Number of deaths per 1,000 live births, 2000–05

1	Sierra Leone	177.2	21	Mauritania	96.7
2	Afghanistan	161.7	22	Burkina Faso	93.2
3	Liberia	147.4	23	Benin	92.7
4	Angola	140.3	24	Lesotho	92.1
5	Niger	125.7	25	Madagascar	91.5
6	Mozambique	122.0	26	Cameroon	88.1
7	Guinea-Bissau	120.0	27	Laos	88.0
8	Congo	119.6	28	Pakistan	86.5
9	Mali	118.7	29	Uganda	86.1
10	Somalia	117.7	30	Congo-Brazzaville	84.0
11	Malawi	115.4	31	Myanmar	83.5
12	Chad	115.3	32	Iraq	83.3
13	Rwanda	111.5	33	Togo	81.5
14	Burundi	107.4	34	Gambia, The	80.5
15	Zambia	104.8	35	Nigeria	78.8
16	Guinea	101.7	36	Swaziland	78.3
17	Côte d'Ivoire	101.3	37	Sudan	77.0
18	Central African Rep	100.4	38	Cambodia	73.2
	Ethiopia	100.4	39	Eritrea	73.0
20	Tanzania	99.8	40	Nepal	70.9

Lowest death rates
No. deaths per 1,000 pop., 2000–05

1	Kuwait	1.9
2	United Arab Emirates	2.4
3	Brunei	2.8
4	Bahrain	3.1
5	Oman	3.3
6	Qatar	3.7
	Saudi Arabia	3.7
8	Costa Rica	3.9
	Syria	3.9
10	Libya	4.2
11	Jordan	4.3
	West Bank and Gaza	4.3
13	Malaysia	4.6
	Venezuela	4.6
15	Macau	4.7
16	Guam	4.9
17	Mexico	5.0
	Panama	5.0
19	Nicaragua	5.1
	Paraguay	5.1
	Philippines	5.1
22	Singapore	5.2
23	Iran	5.3
24	Albania	5.4
	Colombia	5.4
	Lebanon	5.4

Lowest infant mortality
No. deaths per 1,000 live births, 2000–05

1	Singapore	2.9
2	Japan	3.2
3	Iceland	3.4
	Sweden	3.4
5	Finland	4.0
6	Andorra[a]	4.1
	Hong Kong	4.1
8	Belgium	4.2
9	Germany	4.5
	Netherlands	4.5
	Norway	4.5
12	Austria	4.7
13	Switzerland	4.8
14	Denmark	5.0
	France	5.0
	South Korea	5.0
17	Spain	5.1
18	Canada	5.3
19	Italy	5.4
	Luxembourg	5.4
	United Kingdom	5.4
22	Australia	5.5
	Slovenia	5.5
24	Czech Republic	5.6
25	Ireland	5.8
	New Zealand	5.8

Death and disease

Heart attack
Deaths per 100,000 pop.[a]

1	Finland	138.2
2	Sweden	137.2
3	Norway	125.5
4	Ireland	118.6
5	Hungary	115.9
6	United Kingdom	112.3
7	Czech Republic	110.5
8	Malta	110.0
9	Croatia	102.9
10	Macedonia	95.5
11	Austria	95.1
12	Germany	93.8
13	Mauritius	90.9
14	Romania	89.4
15	New Zealand	89.2
16	Greece	86.6
17	Netherlands	85.1
18	Bulgaria	83.8
19	Australia	80.2
20	Belgium	79.8
21	Denmark	76.6

Infectious/parasitic dis.
Deaths per 100,000 pop.[a]

1	South Africa	92.4
2	Turkmenistan	47.2
3	Brazil	45.3
4	Kazakhstan	38.1
5	Kirgizstan	34.9
6	Argentina	34.8
7	El Salvador	32.8
8	Panama	32.5
9	Tajikistan	31.5
10	Dominican Republic	31.2
11	Ecuador	26.8
12	Ukraine	25.8
13	Russia[b]	25.1
14	Venezuela	24.7
15	Peru	24.3
16	Portugal	22.8
17	Uzbekistan	22.6
18	United States	22.0
19	Paraguay	20.9
20	Moldova	20.2
21	Azerbaijan	19.6

Intentional injury[c]
Deaths per 100,000 pop.[a]

1	Colombia	65.1
2	El Salvador	61.9
3	Russia	53.7
4	Lithuania	45.8
5	Estonia	42.9
6	Belarus	41.4
7	Latvia	38.6
8	Ukraine	36.9
9	Kazakhstan	36.7
10	Puerto Rico	28.6
11	Brazil	27.7
12	Albania	26.7
	Moldova	26.7
14	Trinidad & Tobago	26.1
15	Slovenia	26.0
16	Hungary	25.9
17	Cuba	23.5
18	Finland	23.3
19	Venezuela	23.2
20	Kirgizstan	22.6
21	Croatia	21.4
22	Ecuador	20.8
23	Mexico	19.8

Tuberculosis
Incidence per 100,000 pop., 2000

1	Botswana	757
2	Swaziland	600
3	Zimbabwe	584
4	Lesotho	578
5	Cambodia	572
6	Zambia	529
7	South Africa	526
8	Namibia	521
9	Kenya	484
10	Malawi	447
11	Central African Rep	445
12	Mozambique	433
13	Burundi	406
14	Rwanda	405
15	Ethiopia	397
16	Côte d'Ivoire	389
17	Somalia	360
18	Tanzania	359
19	Uganda	351
20	Haiti	350
21	Cameroon	341
22	Congo-Brazzaville	338
23	Philippines	330

a Statistics are available for only a limited number of countries and many less developed countries are excluded. Latest available.
b Excluding Chechnya. c Homicide, suicide, war and other acts of violence.

Measles immunisation
Lowest % of children under 12 months

1	Central African Rep	29
2	North Korea	34
3	Congo-Brazzaville	35
4	Chad	36
5	Mali	37
	Sierra Leone	37
7	Somalia	38
8	Nigeria	40
9	Afghanistan	46
	Burkina Faso	46
	Congo	46
12	Guinea-Bissau	48
	Senegal	48
14	Venezuela	49
15	Laos	50
16	Niger	51
17	Ethiopia	52
	Guinea	52
19	Haiti	53
20	Pakistan	54

DPT[d] immunisation
Lowest % of children under 12 months

1	Central African Rep	23
2	Nigeria	26
3	Chad	27
4	Congo-Brazzaville	31
	Niger	31
6	Somalia	33
7	North Korea	37
8	Gabon	38
9	Congo	40
	Laos	40
11	Angola	41
	Burkina Faso	41
13	Cameroon	43
	Guinea	43
	Haiti	43
16	Afghanistan	44
	Sierra Leone	44
18	Sudan	46
19	Guinea-Bissau	47
20	Mali	51

AIDS
Cases per 100,000 population[e]

1	Namibia	1449.8	21	Kenya	260.4
2	Congo-Brazzaville	1311.1	22	Trinidad & Tobago	260.3
3	Bahamas	1166.0	23	Togo	256.3
4	Bermuda	706.7	24	Uganda	232.8
5	Lesotho	697.1	25	Jamaica	213.2
6	Botswana	636.1	26	Guadeloupe	202.3
7	Zimbabwe	579.7	27	Central African Rep	184.6
8	Eritrea	535.5	28	Honduras	180.8
9	Malawi	469.9	29	Chad	165.2
10	Swaziland	435.2	30	Congo	162.0
11	Zambia	424.0	31	Spain	158.5
12	Gabon	417.2	32	Ethiopia	155.6
13	Barbados	399.7	33	Burkina Faso	143.5
14	Burundi	390.2	34	Suriname	137.5
15	Tanzania	362.2	35	Mozambique	134.5
16	Côte d'Ivoire	343.3	36	Panama	125.3
17	Thailand	295.8	37	Brazil	125.0
18	Rwanda	286.0	38	Cameroon	124.9
19	United States	282.0	39	Netherlands Antilles	117.5
20	Ghana	264.5	40	Martinique	109.0

d Diptheria, whooping cough (pertussis) and tetanus.
e AIDS data refer to the total number of cases reported to the World Health Organisation up to November 22 2002. The number of cases diagnosed and reported depends on the quality of medical practice and administration and is likely to be under-recorded in a number of countries.

Health

Highest health spending

As % of GDP[a]

1	United States	13.0
2	Nicaragua	12.5
3	Lebanon	12.2
4	Saudi Arabia	11.0
5	Switzerland	10.8
6	Germany	10.7
7	Croatia	9.6
8	United Arab Emirates	9.5
9	Israel	9.4
10	Brunei	9.1
	Latvia	9.1
	Uruguay	9.1
13	Canada	8.9
14	Netherlands	8.8
15	Iceland	8.7
16	Honduras	8.6
17	Australia	8.5
	Austria	8.5
	France	8.5
20	Italy	8.3
21	Zimbabwe	8.1
22	Jordan	8.0
	New Zealand	8.0
24	Sweden	7.9
25	Kenya	7.8
26	Portugal	7.7
27	Belgium	7.6
	Slovenia	7.6
29	Greece	7.5
	South Africa	7.5

Lowest health spending

As % of GDP[a]

1	Taiwan	0.4
2	Colombia	1.0
	Ecuador	1.0
4	Peru	1.2
5	Indonesia	1.4
	Venezuela	1.4
7	Azerbaijan	1.6
8	Myanmar	1.8
9	Madagascar	2.1
10	Brazil	2.2
11	Chile	2.5
	Laos	2.5
	Syria	2.5
14	Niger	2.6
	Togo	2.6
16	Georgia	2.8
17	Chad	2.9
18	Central African Rep	3.0
	Malaysia	3.0
	Tanzania	3.0
21	Gabon	3.1
22	Mexico	3.2
	Papua New Guinea	3.2
24	Albania	3.3
	Benin	3.3
	Nigeria	3.3
	Singapore	3.3
	Sudan	3.3
	Ukraine	3.3
30	Mauritius	3.4

Highest population per doctor

Latest available year

1	Philippines	25,709	16	Malaysia	1,181
2	Indonesia	7,557	17	Tunisia	1,160
3	Saudi Arabia	6,261	18	Colombia	1,054
4	Nigeria	5,188	19	Algeria	1,034
5	Thailand	3,633	20	Peru	999
6	Morocco	2,537	21	Iceland	890
7	India	2,169	22	Venezuela	868
8	Chile	1,950	23	Mexico	783
9	Vietnam	1,922	24	Turkey	765
10	Bolivia	1,901	25	Ecuador	704
11	United Arab Emirates	1,880	26	Singapore	692
12	Kuwait	1,817	27	Hong Kong	690
13	Egypt	1,735	28	Cyprus	665
14	Pakistan	1,507	29	Taiwan	642
15	South Africa	1,382	30	Croatia	629

a Latest available year.

Most hospital beds
Beds per 1,000 pop.

1	Japan	17.0		Turkmenistan	7.2
2	Norway	14.0	31	Belgium	6.8
3	Russia	13.1		Bulgaria	6.8
4	Moldova	12.9		Germany	6.8
5	Estonia	12.0	34	Switzerland	6.6
6	Belarus	11.8	35	Israel	6.3
7	Netherlands	11.5		Kazakhstan	6.3
8	Martinique	10.7	37	New Zealand	6.1
9	Georgia	10.5	38	Thailand	6.0
10	Kirgizstan	10.4	39	Croatia	5.9
11	Mongolia	9.7		South Korea	5.9
12	Tajikistan	9.6	41	Italy	5.5
13	Ukraine	9.2	42	Macedonia	5.4
14	Austria	9.1	43	Slovenia	5.3
15	Latvia	8.7		Taiwan	5.3
	Lithuania	8.7	45	Poland	5.1
17	Uzbekistan	8.5	46	Hong Kong	5.0
18	Czech Republic	8.4	47	Greece	4.9
19	Hungary	8.2	48	Cuba	4.6
20	Armenia	8.1	49	Denmark	4.3
	Azerbaijan	8.1	50	Uruguay	4.2
	France	8.1	51	Australia	4.1
	Guadeloupe	8.1	52	Namibia	4.0
24	Barbados	7.9		Portugal	4.0
25	Romania	7.7	54	Albania	3.9
26	Finland	7.6		Argentina	3.9
27	Suriname	7.5		United Kingdom	3.9
28	Bermuda	7.3	57	Réunion	3.7
29	Slovakia	7.2			

Lowest population per doctor
Latest available year

1	Argentina	52	16	Austria	304
2	Italy	169		France	304
3	Hungary	209		Kazakhstan	304
4	Slovakia	213	19	Portugal	305
5	Ukraine	217	20	Sweden	306
6	Greece	218	21	Estonia	320
7	Spain	219	22	Finland	322
8	Russia	226	23	Czech Republic	337
9	Belarus	243	24	Denmark	338
10	Belgium	255	25	United States	356
11	Lithuania	264	26	Australia	378
12	Israel	273	27	Latvia	387
13	Germany	275	28	Turkmenistan	397
14	Azerbaijan	290	29	Brazil	402
15	Bulgaria	296	30	Netherlands	407

Marriage and divorce

Highest marriage rates[a]
Number of marriages per 1,000 population

1	Bermuda	16.7	31	China	6.5
2	Barbados	13.1	32	Costa Rica	6.4
3	Cyprus	12.3		Greece	6.4
4	Jamaica	10.4		Portugal	6.4
5	Ethiopia	10.2		Tunisia	6.4
6	Fiji	10.1	36	Ecuador	6.3
7	Guam	9.7		Japan	6.3
8	Bangladesh	9.5	38	Malta	6.2
9	Bahamas	9.3		Russia	6.2
	Sri Lanka	9.3		Ukraine	6.2
11	Mauritius	9.2	41	Bosnia	6.1
12	Syria	8.5		Romania	6.1
13	Iran	8.4	43	Moldova	6.0
14	Egypt	8.2	44	Australia	5.9
	Jordan	8.2	45	Algeria	5.8
	United States	8.2		Kazakhstan	5.8
17	South Korea	7.7		Thailand	5.8
	Taiwan	7.7		Trinidad & Tobago	5.8
	Turkey	7.7	49	Nicaragua	5.7
20	Mexico	7.6	50	El Salvador	5.6
21	Albania	7.4		Iceland	5.6
22	Belarus	7.3		Netherlands	5.6
	Philippines	7.3		Norway	5.6
24	Uzbekistan	7.1	54	Bahrain	5.5
25	Aruba	7.0		New Zealand	5.5
	Brunei	7.0		Poland	5.5
	Macedonia	7.0		Singapore	5.5
	Puerto Rico	7.0	58	Kirgizstan	5.4
29	Denmark	6.7		Turkmenistan	5.4
30	Israel	6.6	60	Mongolia	5.3

Lowest marriage rates[a]
Number of marriages per 1,000 population

1	United Arab Emirates	2.5		Libya	3.9
2	Macau	2.8		Slovenia	3.9
3	Armenia	2.9	16	Dominican Republic	4.0
	Georgia	2.9		Estonia	4.0
5	Peru	3.2	18	Argentina	4.2
	Saudi Arabia	3.2	19	Belgium	4.3
7	Andorra	3.4		Bulgaria	4.3
	Qatar	3.4	21	Hong Kong	4.5
9	South Africa	3.5		Sweden	4.5
	Tajikistan	3.5	23	Brazil	4.6
11	Panama	3.7		Chile	4.6
12	Venezuela	3.8		Lithuania	4.6
13	Latvia	3.9	26	Netherlands Antilles	4.7

a Latest available year.
Note: Marriage rates refer to registered marriages only and, therefore, reflect the customs surrounding registry and efficiency of administration. The data are based on latest available figures and hence will be affected by the population age structure at the time.

Highest divorce rates[a]
Number of divorces per 1,000 population

1	Belarus	4.3		Romania	2.0
	Guam	4.3		Suriname	2.0
	United States	4.3	35	Hong Kong	1.8
4	Puerto Rico	3.9		Iceland	1.8
5	Bermuda	3.7		Japan	1.8
6	Cuba	3.5		Kirgizstan	1.8
7	Ukraine	3.4		Luxembourg	1.8
8	Lithuania	3.3		Singapore	1.8
9	New Zealand	3.2		Taiwan	1.8
10	Czech Republic	3.1	42	Egypt	1.6
	Estonia	3.1		Portugal	1.6
12	Moldova	3.0		Slovakia	1.6
	Russia	3.0	45	Kuwait	1.5
14	Aruba	2.8		South Korea	1.5
15	Australia	2.7		Tajikistan	1.5
	Switzerland	2.7		Uzbekistan	1.5
17	Denmark	2.6	49	Bahamas	1.4
	Finland	2.6		Barbados	1.4
	Netherlands Antilles	2.6		Cyprus	1.4
	United Kingdom	2.6		Georgia	1.4
21	Hungary	2.5	53	Guadeloupe	1.3
	Latvia	2.5		Jordan	1.3
23	Belgium	2.4		Réunion	1.3
24	Germany	2.3		Turkmenistan	1.3
	Norway	2.3	57	Bahrain	1.2
26	Austria	2.2		Bulgaria	1.2
	Canada	2.2		Dominican Republic	1.2
	Kazakhstan	2.2	60	Costa Rica	1.1
	Uruguay	2.2		Poland	1.1
30	France	2.0		Tunisia	1.1
	Israel	2.0		United Arab Emirates	1.1
	Netherlands	2.0			

Lowest divorce rates[a]
Number of divorces per 1,000 population

1	Guatemala	0.2	15	Azerbaijan	0.7
	Honduras	0.2		Brazil	0.7
	Nicaragua	0.2		Ecuador	0.7
	Sri Lanka	0.2		Iran	0.7
5	Jamaica	0.3		Martinique	0.7
6	Armenia	0.4		Mauritius	0.7
	Bosnia	0.4		Panama	0.7
	El Salvador	0.4		Qatar	0.7
	Macedonia	0.4		Syria	0.7
	Mongolia	0.4	24	Albania	0.8
11	Chile	0.5		Brunei	0.8
	Mexico	0.5		Iraq	0.8
13	Libya	0.6		Italy	0.8
	Turkey	0.6		Spain	0.8

Households and prices

Biggest households[a]
Population per dwelling

1	Saudi Arabia	7.8		Uzbekistan	5.6
2	Gabon	7.0		Yemen	5.6
3	Pakistan	6.5	29	Central African Rep	5.5
4	Algeria	6.4		Guinea	5.5
	Bosnia	6.4		Laos	5.5
	United Arab Emirates	6.4		Sri Lanka	5.5
7	Swaziland	6.2	33	Bangladesh	5.4
8	Congo-Brazzaville	6.1		Chad	5.4
	North Korea	6.1		Gambia, The	5.4
	Rwanda	6.1		India	5.4
	Sudan	6.1		Iran	5.4
12	Burundi	6.0		Iraq	5.4
	Guam	6.0	39	Fiji	5.3
	Jordan	6.0		Madagascar	5.3
	Sierra Leone	6.0		Morocco	5.3
16	Kuwait	5.9		Tanzania	5.3
	Malawi	5.9		Uganda	5.3
	Niger	5.9	44	Guinea-Bissau	5.2
	Papua New Guinea	5.9		Mauritius	5.2
	Philippines	5.9	46	Afghanistan	5.1
	Réunion	5.9		Haiti	5.1
	Togo	5.9		Kirgizstan	5.1
23	Ghana	5.8		Liberia	5.1
24	Senegal	5.7		Mongolia	5.1
25	Lesotho	5.6		Turkmenistan	5.1
	Mozambique	5.6			

Highest cost of living[b]
December 2002, USA=100

1	Japan	139	17	Sweden	89
2	Norway	123	18	Germany	87
3	Gabon	115	19	Mexico	86
	Hong Kong	115	20	Ireland	85
5	United Kingdom	108		Israel	85
6	Switzerland	105	22	Belgium	84
7	Denmark	104		Russia	84
8	France	103	24	Côte d'Ivoire	83
9	Singapore	99	25	Jordan	82
10	Iceland	97	26	Italy	79
	South Korea	97		Luxembourg	79
12	Austria	95	28	Australia	78
13	China	94		Bahrain	78
14	Finland	93		Nigeria	78
	Netherlands	93		Spain	78
16	Taiwan	92			

a Latest available year.
b The cost of living index shown is compiled by The Economist Intelligence Unit for use
  by companies in determining expatriate compensation: it is a comparison of the cost
  of maintaining a typical international lifestyle in the country rather than a
  comparison of the purchasing power of a citizen of the country. The index is based on
  typical urban prices an international executive and family will face abroad. The prices

Smallest households[a]
Population per dwelling

1	Sweden	2.0		New Zealand	2.7
2	Denmark	2.1		Portugal	2.7
3	Finland	2.2		Slovakia	2.7
	Germany	2.2	31	Greece	2.8
	Norway	2.2		Poland	2.8
	Switzerland	2.2		Russia	2.8
7	Iceland	2.3	34	Cyprus	2.9
	Netherlands	2.3		Luxembourg	2.9
	United Kingdom	2.3		Romania	2.9
10	Austria	2.4		Slovenia	2.9
	Belgium	2.4	38	Ireland	3.1
	Hungary	2.4		Mali	3.1
13	Australia	2.5	40	Malta	3.2
	Canada	2.5		Myanmar	3.2
	Estonia	2.5		Spain	3.2
	France	2.5	43	Hong Kong	3.3
	Latvia	2.5		Macau	3.3
	Ukraine	2.5		South Korea	3.3
	United States	2.5		Taiwan	3.3
20	Croatia	2.6	47	Brazil	3.4
	Italy	2.6	48	Albania	3.5
	Lithuania	2.6		Argentina	3.5
	Uruguay	2.6		China	3.5
24	Belarus	2.7		Israel	3.5
	Bulgaria	2.7		Kazakhstan	3.5
	Czech Republic	2.7		Singapore	3.5
	Japan	2.7			

Lowest cost of living[b]
December 2002, USA=100

1	Zimbabwe	30	16	Colombia	54
2	Tehran	31		Sri Lanka	54
3	Paraguay	40		Tunisia	54
4	Argentina	41		Uzbekistan	54
	India	41	20	Chile	55
6	Philippines	42		Costa Rica	55
7	Libya	44	22	Cambodia	56
8	Pakistan	45		Venezuela	56
	South Africa	45	24	Bangladesh	57
10	Brazil	46	25	Hungary	58
	Uruguay	46		Syria	58
12	Romania	49	27	Thailand	59
13	Serbia & Montenegro	51	28	Kenya	61
	Zambia	51		Peru	61
15	Algeria	53		Turkey	61

are for products of international comparable quality found in a supermarket or department store. Prices found in local markets and bazaars are not used unless the available merchandise is of the specified quality and the shopping area itself is safe for executive and family members. New York City prices are used as the base, so United States = 100.

Consumer goods ownership

TV

Colour TVs per 100 households

1	United States	99.5	26	Denmark	92.2
2	Saudi Arabia	99.4	27	Jordan	91.9
	Taiwan	99.4	28	Australia	91.7
4	Hong Kong	99.2	29	Venezuela	91.5
	Ireland	99.2	30	Greece	91.2
6	Finland	99.1	31	Slovenia	90.6
	Japan	99.1	32	Hungary	90.5
8	Belgium	99.0	33	Malaysia	90.3
9	Canada	98.7	34	Andorra	89.5
10	United Kingdom	98.6	35	Mexico	89.4
11	Singapore	98.5	36	Tunisia	88.9
12	Netherlands	98.4	37	Kuwait	88.7
13	Spain	98.3	38	Croatia	87.6
14	Portugal	97.6	39	Czech Republic	86.9
15	Austria	97.4	40	Brazil	86.3
	Switzerland	97.4	41	Slovakia	86.0
17	New Zealand	97.3	42	Colombia	85.6
	Sweden	97.3	43	Estonia	83.8
19	Germany	97.1	44	Poland	82.6
20	France	95.9	45	Thailand	81.7
	United Arab Emirates	95.9	46	Russia	78.4
22	Israel	95.8	47	Belarus	75.8
23	Italy	94.8	48	Ukraine	73.6
24	Norway	93.0	49	Lithuania	70.8
	South Korea	93.0	50	Algeria	70.0

Telephone

Telephone lines per 100 people

1	Bermuda	87.2	23	Israel	47.6
2	Luxembourg	78.3		South Korea	47.6
3	Sweden	73.9	25	Singapore	47.2
4	Denmark	72.3	26	Italy	47.1
5	Norway	72.0		New Zealand	47.1
6	Switzerland	71.8	28	Austria	46.8
7	United States	66.5	29	Barbados	46.3
8	Iceland	66.4	30	Guadeloupe	44.9
9	Cyprus	64.3	31	Spain	43.1
10	Germany	63.5	32	Martinique	43.0
11	Netherlands	62.1	33	Portugal	42.4
12	Japan	59.7	34	Slovenia	40.1
13	Hong Kong	58.1	35	Bahamas	40.0
14	United Kingdom	57.8	36	United Arab Emirates	39.7
15	France	57.4	37	Macau	39.4
16	Taiwan	57.3	38	Czech Republic	37.4
17	Finland	54.8		Hungary	37.4
18	Malta	53.0	40	Croatia	36.5
19	Greece	52.9	41	Bulgaria	35.9
20	Australia	52.0	42	Estonia	35.2
21	Belgium	49.3	43	Aruba	35.0
22	Ireland	48.5	44	Puerto Rico	33.6

CD players

CD players per 100 households

1	Netherlands	88.2	13	Japan	64.7
2	Denmark	86.9	14	Philippines	64.1
3	Norway	85.7	15	Finland	62.0
4	New Zealand	85.3	16	Switzerland	59.5
5	United Kingdom	83.1	17	Singapore	56.8
6	Germany	81.9	18	United States	55.6
7	Sweden	81.1	19	Hong Kong	54.8
8	Australia	79.8	20	Ireland	40.3
9	Canada	76.0	21	Spain	37.6
10	Austria	70.0	22	Portugal	35.9
11	Taiwan	67.9	23	Saudi Arabia	30.5
12	Belgium	65.7			

Computer

Computers per 100 people

1	United States	62.3	18	Japan	34.9
2	Sweden	56.1	19	Belgium	34.5
3	Australia	51.7	20	France	33.7
4	Luxembourg	51.5	21	Germany	33.6
5	Norway	50.8	22	Austria	28.0
	Singapore	50.8	23	Slovenia	27.6
7	Switzerland	50.0	24	Cyprus	25.1
8	Bermuda	49.5		South Korea	25.1
9	Denmark	43.2	26	Israel	24.6
10	Netherlands	42.9	27	Malta	23.0
11	Finland	42.4	28	Taiwan	22.3
12	Iceland	41.8	29	Guadeloupe	21.7
13	Ireland	39.1	30	Italy	19.5
14	Canada	39.0	31	Macau	17.9
15	New Zealand	38.6	32	Estonia	17.5
16	Hong Kong	38.5	33	Spain	16.8
17	United Kingdom	36.6	34	Qatar	16.4

Mobile telephone

Subscribers per 100 people

1	Luxembourg	96.7	16	Netherlands	73.9
2	Taiwan	96.6	17	Denmark	73.7
3	Hong Kong	84.4	18	Ireland	72.9
4	Italy	83.9	19	Switzerland	72.4
5	Norway	82.5	20	United Arab Emirates	72.0
6	Iceland	82.0	21	Martinique	71.5
7	Israel	80.8	22	Singapore	69.2
8	Austria	80.7	23	Germany	68.3
9	United Kingdom	78.3	24	Czech Republic	65.9
10	Finland	77.8	25	Spain	65.5
11	Portugal	77.4	26	Guadeloupe	63.6
12	Sweden	77.1	27	New Zealand	62.1
13	Slovenia	75.9	28	South Korea	60.8
14	Greece	75.1	29	France	60.5
15	Belgium	74.7	30	Australia	57.8

Books and newspapers

Book sales

	$m			*Per head, $*	
1	United States	28,021	1	Japan	158
2	Japan	20,150	2	Norway	117
3	Germany	8,969	3	Germany	109
4	United Kingdom	4,300	4	Singapore	100
5	Mexico	3,217	5	United States	98
6	China	2,904	6	Finland	88
7	France	2,497	7	Belgium	86
8	Italy	2,355	8	Switzerland	84
9	Spain	2,158	9	United Kingdom	72
10	Canada	1,610	10	Sweden	70
11	Australia	1,046	11	Denmark	62
12	Belgium	890	12	New Zealand	59
13	Colombia	761	13	Australia	54
14	Venezuela	750		Spain	54
15	India	728	15	Ireland	53
16	South Korea	693	16	Canada	52
17	Argentina	660	17	France	42
18	Taiwan	634	18	Italy	41
19	Sweden	619	19	Austria	39
20	Switzerland	604	20	Mexico	32
21	Norway	528		Portugal	32
22	Finland	457	22	Venezuela	30
23	Singapore	412	23	Taiwan	28
24	Poland	395	24	Israel	26
25	Netherlands	374	25	Netherlands	24
26	Chile	339	26	Chile	22
27	Vietnam	333	27	Greece	21
28	Denmark	326	28	Czech Republic	19
29	Portugal	324	29	Argentina	18
30	Austria	312		Colombia	18
			31	South Korea	15

Daily newspapers

Copies per '000 population, latest year

1	Japan	563	16	Bulgaria	183
2	Norway	562	17	Slovenia	171
3	Sweden	471	18	Ukraine	169
4	Finland	444	19	Hungary	168
5	Switzerland	366		Czech Republic	168
6	Austria	307	21	Australia	161
7	United Kingdom	301	22	Ireland	155
8	Germany	291	23	Belgium	150
9	Netherlands	275	24	Latvia	143
	Denmark	275	25	France	139
11	Singapore	256	26	Spain	108
12	Hong Kong	204	27	Malaysia	106
13	New Zealand	201	28	Croatia	105
14	United States	194	29	China	98
15	Estonia	184	30	Slovakia	93

Music and the internet

Music sales[a]

$m, 2002			$ per head, 2002	
1	United States	12,920.1	1	Norway	56
2	Canada	5,879.0	2	United Kingdom	48
3	Japan	4,593.3	3	United States	45
4	United Kingdom	2,859.4	4	Japan	36
5	France	1,989.7	5	Switzerland	35
6	Germany	1,988.0	6	France	33
7	Italy	554.7	7	Denmark	32
8	Spain	542.3		Ireland	32
9	Australia	499.9		Sweden	32
10	Mexico	445.5	10	Austria	30
11	Netherlands	397.6	11	Australia	26
12	Brazil	354.0	12	Netherlands	25
13	Sweden	281.9	13	Germany	24
14	Russia	257.2	14	New Zealand	23
15	Norway	254.0	15	Belgium	22
16	Switzerland	253.2	16	Finland	21
17	Austria	245.2	17	Canada	19
18	Belgium	225.3	18	Portugal	14
19	South Korea	216.1		Spain	14
20	India	172.3	20	Hong Kong	13
21	Denmark	167.2	21	Singapore	11
22	Taiwan	143.9	22	Italy	10

Internet hosts

By country, January 2003			Per 1,000 pop., January 2003	
1	United States[b]	107,233,631	1	United States[b]	375.1
2	Japan	9,260,117	2	Iceland	227.6
3	Italy	3,864,315	3	Finland	219.4
4	Canada	2,993,982	4	Denmark	217.7
5	Germany	2,891,407	5	Netherlands	151.9
6	United Kingdom	2,583,753	6	Sweden	137.4
7	Australia	2,564,339	7	Australia	132.9
8	Netherlands	2,415,286	8	Norway	131.0
9	Brazil	2,237,527	9	New Zealand	113.9
10	Taiwan	2,170,233	10	Austria	103.5
11	France	2,157,628	11	Belgium	102.2
12	Spain	1,694,601	12	Switzerland	100.5
13	Sweden	1,209,266	13	Taiwan	97.3
14	Denmark	1,154,053	14	Canada	96.6
15	Finland	1,140,838	15	Singapore	82.5
16	Mexico	1,107,795	16	Estonia	78.3
17	Belgium	1,052,706	17	Japan	72.7
18	Poland	843,475	18	Italy	67.2
19	Austria	838,026	19	Hong Kong	56.9
20	Switzerland	723,243	20	United Kingdom	43.4
21	Norway	589,621	21	Luxembourg	43.2
22	Argentina	495,920	22	Spain	42.5
23	Russia	477,380	23	Israel	37.1

a Vinyl, tape and compact disc sales.
b Includes all hosts ending ".com", ".net" and ".org", which exaggerates the numbers.

Nobel prize winners: *1901–2002*

Peace

1	United States	17
2	United Kingdom	11
3	France	9
4	Sweden	5
5	Belgium	4
	Germany	4
7	Norway	3
	South Africa	3
9	Argentina	2
	Austria	2
	Israel	2
	Russia	2
	Switzerland	2

Economics[a]

1	United States	26
2	United Kingdom	8
3	Norway	2
	Sweden	2
5	France	1
	Germany	1
	Netherlands	1
	Russia	1

Literature

1	France	14
2	United States	12
3	United Kingdom	9
4	Germany	7
5	Sweden	6
6	Italy	5
7	Spain	5
8	Norway	3
9	Poland	3
10	Russia	3

Physiology or medicine

1	United States	47
2	United Kingdom	20
3	Germany	14
4	Sweden	7
5	France	6
	Switzerland	6
7	Austria	5
	Denmark	5
9	Belgium	3
	Italy	3

Physics

1	United States	44
2	United Kingdom	19
3	Germany	17
4	France	8
5	Netherlands	6
6	Russia	5
7	Japan	4
	Sweden	4
	Switzerland	4
10	Austria	3
	Italy	3

Chemistry

1	United States	38
2	United Kingdom	22
3	Germany	14
4	France	6
	Switzerland	6
6	Sweden	5
7	Canada	4
	Japan	4
9	Argentina	1
	Austria	1
	Belgium	1
	Czech Republic	1
	Denmark	1
	Finland	1
	Italy	1
	Netherlands	1
	Norway	1
	Russia	1

a Since 1969.
Prizes by country of residence at time awarded. When prizes have been shared in the same field, one credit given to each country. Only top rankings in each field are included.

Olympic medal winners

Summer games, 1896–2000

		Gold	Silver	Bronze
1	United States	872	659	581
2	Soviet Union[a]	517	423	382
3	Germany	374	392	417
4	France	189	195	216
5	United Kingdom	188	243	232
6	Italy	179	144	155
7	Hungary	150	134	158
8	Sweden	138	157	176
9	Australia	103	110	139
10	Finland	101	81	114
11	Japan	98	97	103
12	China	80	79	64
13	Romania	74	83	108
14	Netherlands	61	66	85
15	Cuba	57	47	41
16	Poland	56	72	113
17	Canada	52	80	99
18	Bulgaria	48	82	65
19	Switzerland	47	74	62
20	Denmark	41	63	58

Winter games, 1924–2002

		Gold	Silver	Bronze
1	Germany	108	105	87
2	Norway	94	94	75
3	Soviet Union[a]	87	63	67
4	United States	69	72	52
5	Finland	42	51	49
6	Austria	41	57	63
7	Sweden	39	30	29
8	Switzerland	32	33	38
9	Italy	31	31	27
10	Canada	31	28	37
11	Russia	27	20	13
12	Netherlands	22	28	19
13	France	22	22	28
14	South Korea	11	5	4
15	Japan	8	10	13
16	United Kingdom	8	4	15
17	Croatia	3	1	0
18	China	2	12	8
19	Czech Republic	2	1	2
20	Australia	2	0	1

a Includes unified team in 1992.

Drinking and smoking

Beer drinkers
Litres consumed per head

1	Czech Republic	158.1
2	Ireland	150.8
3	Germany	123.1
4	Austria	106.9
5	Luxembourg	100.9
6	Denmark	98.6
7	Belgium	98.0
8	United Kingdom	97.1
9	Australia	93.0
10	Slovakia	86.4
11	United States	83.2
12	Netherlands	80.5
13	Finland	80.2
14	New Zealand	80.0
	Venezuela	80.0
16	Spain	75.0
17	Canada	68.8
18	Hungary	64.0
19	Portugal	61.3
20	Poland	60.5
21	Cyprus	60.3
22	Switzerland	57.1
23	South Africa	55.8

Wine drinkers
Litres consumed per head

1	Luxembourg	64.4
2	France	56.9
3	Italy	50.0
	Portugal	50.0
5	Switzerland	43.1
6	Spain	36.2
7	Argentina	34.0
	Greece	34.0
9	Uruguay	31.9
10	Denmark	31.2
11	Austria	31.0
	Hungary	31.0
13	Romania	30.0
14	Germany	23.9
15	Bulgaria	21.4
16	Finland	20.1
17	Australia	20.0
18	Malta	19.3
19	Netherlands	18.9
20	Belgium	18.7
21	United Kingdom	17.5
22	Cyprus	16.8
23	New Zealand	16.7

Alcoholic drinks
Litres of pure alcohol consumed per head

1	Luxemburg	12.4
2	Czech Republic	10.9
3	Ireland	10.8
4	Portugal	10.6
	Romania	10.6
6	France	10.5
	Spain	10.5
8	Germany	10.4
9	Hungary	9.8
10	Denmark	9.5
11	Austria	9.2
12	Switzerland	9.1
13	Russia	8.6
14	United Kingdom	8.5
15	Belgium	8.2
	Cyprus	8.2
	Slovakia	8.2
18	Netherlands	8.1
19	Greece	7.9
20	Italy	7.6
	New Zealand	7.6
22	Latvia	7.5
23	Australia	7.4
	Finland	7.4

Smokers
Av. ann. consumption of
cigarettes per head per day, 2002

1	Greece	8.6
2	Bulgaria	7.7
3	Japan	6.8
4	Bosnia	6.4
5	Slovenia	6.2
6	Spain	6.1
7	Cyprus	6.0
8	Latvia	5.8
	Russia	5.8
10	Hungary	5.7
11	Albania	5.6
12	Poland	5.4
	Switzerland	5.4
14	Macedonia	5.3
	South Korea	5.3
16	Czech Republic	5.1
	Ukraine	5.1
18	Austria	5.0
	Taiwan	5.0
20	Ireland	4.9
	Portugal	4.9
22	Germany	4.8
	Italy	4.8

Crime and punishment

Serious assault[a]

No. per 100,000 pop., latest avail. yr.

1	Australia	736.8
2	Sweden	667.4
3	Swaziland	632.7
4	South Africa	597.8
5	Belgium	553.0
6	Namibia	533.6
7	Ghana	472.8
8	New Zealand	425.2
9	Botswana	369.3
10	Jamaica	352.3
11	United States	318.6
12	Argentina	316.2
13	Netherlands	242.8
14	Lebanon	214.7
15	France	211.3
16	Barbados	200.8
17	Bermuda	188.1
18	Côte d'Ivoire	174.6
19	Lesotho	156.9
20	El Salvador	155.4

Theft[a]

No. per 100,000 pop., latest avail. yr.

1	Sweden	7,484.0
2	New Zealand	6,978.3
3	Australia	6,653.2
4	United Kingdom	5,656.9
5	Netherlands	5,302.5
6	Norway	4,676.7
7	Belgium	4,258.4
8	France	4,224.6
9	Germany	3,819.8
10	United States	3,804.6
11	South Africa	3,565.8
12	Finland	3,441.3
13	Denmark	3,404.1
14	Switzerland	3,346.5
15	Estonia	3,296.7
16	Luxembourg	3,275.3
17	Bermuda	3,254.8
18	Israel	3,221.0
19	Austria	3,114.7
20	Canada	2,758.2

Prisoners

Total prison pop., latest available year

1	United States	2,021,223
2	China	1,428,126
3	Russia	919,330
4	India	281,380
5	Brazil	233,859
6	Thailand	217,697
7	Ukraine	198,885
8	South Africa	176,893
9	Iran	163,526
10	Mexico	154,765
11	Rwanda[b]	112,000
12	Kazakhstan[b]	84,000
13	Poland	82,173
14	United Kingdom	80,144
15	Egypt[b]	80,000
16	Pakistan	78,938
17	Germany	78,707
18	Philippines	70,383
19	Bangladesh[b]	70,000
20	Uzbekistan[b]	65,000
21	Indonesia	62,886

Per 100,000 pop., latest available year

1	United States	707
2	Russia	638
3	Belarus	554
4	Kazakhstan[b]	522
5	Turkmenistan	489
6	Bermuda	447
7	Suriname	437
8	Bahamas	416
9	Ukraine	406
10	South Africa	404
11	Virgin Islands	402
12	Kirgizstan	390
13	Botswana	381
14	Guam	371
15	Puerto Rico	368
16	Swaziland	362
17	Latvia	361
18	Singapore	359
19	Trinidad & Tobago	351
20	Thailand	342
21	Estonia	337

a Crime statistics are based on offences recorded by the police. The number will therefore depend partly on the efficiency of police administration systems, the definition of offences, and the proportion of crimes reported, and therefore may not be strictly comparable.

b Estimate.

Stars...

Space missions
Firsts and selected events

1957 Man-made satellite
Dog in space, Laika

1961 Human in space, Yuri Gagarin
Entire day in space, Gherman Titov

1963 Woman in space, Valentina Tereshkova

1964 Space crew, one pilot and two passengers

1965 Space walk, Alexei Leonov
Computer guidance system
Eight days in space achieved (needed to travel to moon and back)

1966 Docking between space craft and target vehicle
Autopilot re-entry and landing

1968 Live television broadcast from space
Moon orbit

1969 Astronaut transfer from one craft to another in space
Moon landing

1971 Space station, Salyut
Drive on the moon

1973 Space laboratory, Skylab

1978 Non-Amercian, non-Soviet, Vladimir Remek (Czechoslovakia)

1982 Space shuttle, Columbia (first craft to carry four crew members)

1983 Five crew mission

1984 Space walk, untethered
Capture, repair and redeployment of satellite in space
Seven crew mission

1986 Space shuttle explosion, Challenger
Mir space station activated

1990 Hubble telescope deployed

2001 Dennis Tito, first paying space tourist

2003 Space shuttle explosion, Columbia. Shuttle programme suspended.

Astronauts
Longest time in space, hours

United States		Yuri Ramanenko	10,344
John Blaha	3,864	Alexandr Volkov	9,384
Norman Thagard	3,360	Leonid Kizim	9,024
Andrew Thomas	3,268	**Other nations**	
David Wolf	3,216	Jean-Loup Chrétien	784
Edward Gibson	2,017	Ulf Merbold	441
Russia		Pedro Duque	381
Musa Manarov	12,984	Claude Andre-Deshays	379
Sergi Krikalev	11,064		

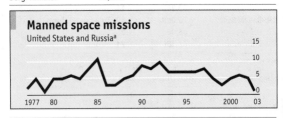

Manned space missions
United States and Russia[a]

1977 80   85   90   95   2000   03

...and Wars

Defence spending

As % of GDP

1	Eritrea	20.9		Iran	5.8
2	Angola	17.0		Rwanda	5.8
3	Oman	14.4	23	Liberia	5.6
4	Saudi Arabia	14.1	24	Brunei	5.5
5	Afghanistan	12.2		Burundi	5.5
6	Kuwait	12.1	26	Suriname	5.3
7	North Korea	11.6	27	Singapore	5.1
8	Syria	10.9		Sri Lanka	5.1
9	Ethiopia	9.8	29	Turkey	5.0
10	Israel	9.5	30	Bahrain	4.8
11	Iraq	9.3		Greece	4.8
12	Congo-Brazzaville	8.9	32	Egypt	4.7
13	Jordan	8.5	33	United Arab Emirates	4.6
14	Yemen	8.1	34	Chile	4.4
15	Vietnam	7.2		Pakistan	4.4
16	Qatar	7.1		Somalia	4.4
17	Armenia	6.5	37	Russia	4.3
18	Algeria	6.3		Sudan	4.3
	Serbia & Montenegro	6.3	39	Cuba	4.1
20	Cambodia	5.8		Libya	4.1

Armed forces

'000

		Regulars	Reserves				Regulars	Reserves
1	China	2,310	550	21	France	274	419
2	United States	1,368	1,201	22	Japan	240	47
3	India	1,263	535	23	Italy	230	65
4	North Korea	1,082	4,700	24	Ethiopia	217	253
5	Russia	977	2,400	25	United Kingdom	211	247
6	South Korea	683	4,500	26	Poland	206	406
7	Pakistan	620	513	27	Saudi Arabia	201	
8	Turkey	515	379	28	Morocco	199	150
9	Iran	513	350	29	Mexico	193	300
10	Vietnam	484	3,000	30	Israel	164	425
11	Egypt	443	254	31	Greece	159	291
12	Iraq	424	650	32	Colombia	158	61
13	Taiwan	370	1,658	33	Spain	144	329
14	Myanmar	344		34	Cambodia	140	
15	Syria	321	354	35	Bangladesh	137	
16	Germany	308	364	36	Angola	131	
17	Thailand	306	200	37	Peru	128	100
18	Ukraine	304	1,000	38	Algeria	124	150
19	Indonesia	297	400	39	Sri Lanka	121	
20	Brazil	288	1,115	40	Philippines	107	131

a Previously Soviet Union; United States only from 1984; up to May 2003.

Environment

Ecological footprints

Highest, hectares per person[a]

1	United Arab Emirates	11.87
2	United States	9.62
3	Kuwait	9.38
4	Australia	8.57
5	New Zealand	8.08
	Norway	8.08
7	Finland	8.01
8	Canada	7.81
9	Denmark	7.18
10	Sweden	6.54
11	Belgium	6.38
12	Ireland	5.84
13	Saudi Arabia	5.52
14	Estonia	5.51
15	France	5.50
16	United Kingdom	5.46
17	Netherlands	5.43
18	Greece	5.12
19	Israel	5.02
20	Austria	4.79

Lowest, hectares per person[a]

1	Libya	3.53
2	Slovakia	3.61
	Ukraine	3.61
4	Italy	3.72
5	Kazakhstan	3.75
6	South Africa	3.81
7	Belarus	3.85
8	Lithuania	3.88
9	Poland	3.90
	Malaysia	3.90
11	Chile	3.95
12	Slovenia	3.99
13	Trinidad & Tobago	4.05
14	Switzerland	4.30
15	Portugal	4.45
16	Spain	4.52
17	Russia	4.57
18	Japan	4.68
19	Germany	4.76
20	Czech Republic	4.78

Environmental sustainability index[b]

Highest

1	Finland	73.9
2	Norway	73.0
3	Sweden	72.6
4	Canada	70.6
5	Switzerland	66.5
6	Uruguay	66.0
7	Austria	64.2
8	Iceland	63.9
9	Costa Rica	63.2
10	Latvia	63.0
11	Hungary	62.7
12	Croatia	62.5
13	Botswana	61.8
14	Slovakia	61.6
15	Argentina	61.5
16	Australia	60.3
17	Estonia	60.0
	Panama	60.0
19	New Zealand	59.9
20	Brazil	59.6

Lowest

1	Kuwait	23.9
2	United Arab Emirates	25.7
3	North Korea	32.3
4	Iraq	33.2
5	Saudi Arabia	34.2
6	Haiti	34.8
7	Ukraine	35.0
8	South Korea	35.9
9	Sierra Leone	36.5
10	Nigeria	36.7
11	Somalia	37.1
12	Turkmenistan	37.3
13	Liberia	37.7
14	China	38.5
15	Guinea-Bissau	38.8
	Madagascar	38.8
17	Mauritania	38.9
18	Belgium	39.1
19	Libya	39.3
20	Niger	39.4

a Productive land and water areas required to produce the resources consumed and assimilate the wastes generated, per person.
b Based on 20 key indicators, including: environmental systems and stresses; human vulnerability to environmental risks; institutional capacities on environmental issues; shared resources

Water poverty index[a]

Top		Bottom	
1 Finland	78.0	1 Haiti	35.1
2 Canada	77.7	2 Niger	35.2
3 Iceland	77.1	3 Ethiopia	35.4
4 Norway	77.0	4 Eritrea	37.4
5 Austria	74.6	5 Malawi	38.0
6 Ireland	73.4	6 Chad	38.5
7 Sweden	72.4	7 Benin	39.3
8 Switzerland	72.1	8 Rwanda	39.4
9 United Kingdom	71.5	9 Burundi	40.2
10 Slovakia	71.2	10 Mali	40.6
11 Turkmenistan	70.0	11 Angola	41.3
12 New Zealand	69.1	12 Burkina Faso	41.5
Slovenia	69.1	13 Sierra Leone	41.9
14 Chile	68.9	14 Lesotho	43.2
15 Netherlands	68.5	15 Yemen	43.8

Renewable freshwater resources

Cubic metres per person, highest		Cubic metres per person, lowest	
1 Congo-Brazzaville	275,679	1 Kuwait	0
2 Papua New Guinea	156,140	2 United Arab Emirates	69
3 Gabon	133,333	3 Libya	113
4 Canada	94,314	4 Saudi Arabia	116
5 Norway	87,508	5 Jordan	143
6 New Zealand	85,361	6 Yemen	234
7 Liberia	74,121	7 Israel	273
8 Peru	67,852	8 Oman	415
9 Laos	63,175	9 Algeria	471
10 Chile	58,115	10 Tunisia	481
11 Panama	51,647	11 Burundi	529
12 Colombia	49,930	12 Rwanda	611
13 Costa Rica	47,901	13 Kenya	1,004
14 Brazil	43,022	14 Morocco	1,010
15 Uruguay	39,856	15 Egypt	1,071
16 Cambodia	39,613	16 Lebanon	1,109
17 Central African Rep	37,934	17 Zimbabwe	1,117
18 Nicaragua	37,409	18 Denmark	1,124
19 Bolivia	37,305	19 South Africa	1,168
20 Ecuador	34,164	20 Burkina Faso	1,286

Annual freshwater withdrawals

% for agricultural use		% for industrial use	
1 Afghanistan	99	1 Serbia & Montenegro	86
Madagascar	99	2 Finland	85
Nepal	99	3 Slovenia	80
4 Mali	97	4 United Kingdom	77
Pakistan	97	5 Poland	76
Somalia	97	6 Bulgaria	75
7 Sri Lanka	96	7 Ireland	74
Swaziland	96	8 Switzerland	73

a Based on five measures: resources; access; capacity; use; and environmental impact.

Forests

Highest % of land area, 2000

1	Gabon	84.7
2	Bahamas	84.1
3	Brunei	83.9
4	Finland	72.0
5	North Korea	68.2
6	Papua New Guinea	67.6
7	Sweden	65.9
8	Congo-Brazzaville	64.6
9	Brazil	64.3
10	Bhutan	64.2
11	Japan	64.0
12	South Korea	63.3
13	Guinea-Bissau	60.5
14	Congo	59.6
15	Paraguay	58.8

Lowest % of land area, 2000

1	Oman	0.0
2	Egypt	0.1
	Qatar	0.1
4	Libya	.0.2
5	Iceland	0.3
	Kuwait	0.3
	Mauritania	0.3
8	Lesotho	0.5
9	Saudi Arabia	0.7
10	Algeria	0.9
	Yemen	0.9
12	Jordan	1.0
	Niger	1.0
14	Iraq	1.8
15	Afghanistan	2.1

Annual rate of reforestation

%, 1990–2000

1	Qatar	9.6
2	Oman	5.3
3	Uruguay	5.0
4	Israel	4.9
5	Cyprus	3.7
6	Kuwait	3.5
7	Egypt	3.3
8	Belarus	3.2
9	Ireland	3.0
10	United Arab Emirates	2.8
11	Kirgizstan	2.6
12	Iceland	2.2
	Kazakhstan	2.2
14	Guadeloupe	2.1
15	Portugal	1.7

'000 hectares, 1990–2000

1	China	1,806
2	United States	388
3	Belarus	256
4	Russia	135
5	Spain	86
6	France	62
7	Portugal	57
8	Vietnam	52
9	Uruguay	50
10	New Zealand	39
11	India	38
12	Norway	31
	Ukraine	31

Annual rate of deforestation

%, 1990–2000

1	Burundi	-9.0
2	Haiti	-5.7
3	El Salvador	-4.6
4	Rwanda	-3.9
5	Niger	-3.7
6	Togo	-3.4
7	Côte d'Ivoire	-3.1
8	Nicaragua	-3.0
9	Sierra Leone	-2.9
10	Mauritania	-2.7
11	Nigeria	-2.6
12	Malawi	-2.4
	Zambia	-2.4
14	Benin	-2.3

'000 hectares, 1990–2000

1	Brazil	-2,309
2	Indonesia	-1,312
3	Sudan	-959
4	Zambia	-851
5	Mexico	-631
6	Congo	-532
7	Myanmar	-517
8	Nigeria	-398
9	Zimbabwe	-320
10	Australia	-282
11	Peru	-269
12	Côte d'Ivoire	-265
13	Venezuela	-218

CO_2 emissions
Tonnes per person

1	Qatar	91.5	14	Ireland	10.8
2	United Arab Emirates	31.3	15	Czech Republic	10.6
3	Bahrain	29.4	16	Belgium	10.2
4	Kuwait	24.9	17	Israel	10.0
5	United States	19.7	18	Russia	9.8
6	Trinidad & Tobago	19.4	19	Germany	9.7
7	Australia	18.2	20	North Korea	9.4
8	Canada	14.4	21	Denmark	9.3
9	Brunei	14.2	22	United Kingdom	9.2
10	Singapore	13.7	23	Japan	9.1
11	Estonia	11.7	24	Norway	8.7
	Saudi Arabia	11.7	25	Netherlands	8.5
13	Finland	11.3		Oman	8.5

CO_2 emissions per unit of GDP
Kg/PPP$

1	Trinidad & Tobago	2.4	10	Kazakhstan	1.5
2	Uzbekistan	2.2	11	Estonia	1.4
3	Turkmenistan	2.1		Kuwait	1.4
	Ukraine	2.1		Yemen	1.4
5	Bahrain	2.0	14	Jamaica	1.2
6	Mongolia	1.9	15	Syria	1.1
7	Azerbaijan	1.8	16	Lebanon	1.0
8	Russia	1.6		Macedonia	1.0
	United Arab Emirates	1.6		Venezuela	1.0

Sulphur dioxide emissions
'000 tons per populated sq km

1	Belgium	21.39	12	Netherlands	4.19
2	South Korea	19.43	13	Egypt	4.09
3	Jamaica	17.05	14	Poland	3.90
4	Czech Republic	7.98	15	Israel	3.31
5	North Korea	7.64	16	Libya	3.22
6	Kuwait	7.12	17	Denmark	2.86
7	United Kingdom	5.37	18	Australia	2.84
8	Germany	5.10	19	Canada	2.79
9	Slovakia	4.85		Italy	2.79
10	Bulgaria	4.61	21	Jordan	2.71
11	Chile	4.38	22	China	2.68

Land area under protected status

Highest, %		Lowest, %	
1 Venezuela	60.72	1 Kuwait	1.04
2 Saudi Arabia	34.17	2 Liberia	1.16
3 Zambia	30.09	3 Turkey	1.20
4 Austria	29.23	4 Ukraine	1.34
5 Tanzania	27.74	5 Papua New Guinea	1.49
6 Germany	25.24	6 Moldova	1.50
7 Denmark	23.96	7 Uzbekistan	1.83
8 New Zealand	23.84	8 Madagascar	2.07
9 Slovakia	21.64	9 Sierra Leone	2.12
10 Bhutan	21.40	10 Philippines	2.17
11 Uganda	20.78	11 Algeria	2.44
12 United States	20.13	12 Russia	2.46
13 Guatemala	19.90	13 North Korea	2.58
14 Costa Rica	19.21	14 Gabon	2.70
15 Panama	19.08	Kazakhstan	2.70
16 Chile	18.74	16 Belgium	2.81
17 Switzerland	18.04	17 Vietnam	2.93
18 United Kingdom	17.73	18 Jordan	3.10

Mammals under threat

% of species threatened

1 New Zealand	80.00	10 South Korea	26.53
2 Iceland	54.55	11 Papua New Guinea	26.13
3 Cuba	35.48	12 Dominican Republic	25.00
4 Madagascar	35.46	13 Australia	24.23
5 Philippines	31.65	14 United Kingdom	24.00
6 Indonesia	30.63	15 Chile	23.08
7 Spain	29.27	16 Sri Lanka	22.73
8 India	27.22	17 Jamaica	20.83
9 Portugal	26.98	18 Romania	20.24

Environmental quality of life

Highest cities, New York = 100		Lowest cities, New York = 100	
1 Calgary, Canada	166.0	1 Mexico city, Mexico	29.5
2 Honolulu, US	161.5	2 Baku, Azerbaijan	31.5
3 Helsinki, Finland	158.0	3 Dacca, Bangladesh	35.0
Katsuyama, Japan	158.0	4 Bombay, India	41.5
5 Minneapolis, US	154.0	5 Almaty, Kazakhstan	44.5
Ottawa, Canada	154.0	6 New Delhi, India	50.0
7 Victoria, Seychelles	152.5	7 Antananarivo, Madag.	52.0
Wellington, New Zea.	152.5	8 Novosibirsk, Russia	52.5
9 Auckland, New Zea.	150.0	9 Belgrade, Yugoslavia	53.0
10 Kobe, Japan	149.5	10 Bangkok, Thailand	58.0
Omuta, Japan	149.5	Rayong, Thailand	58.0
Oslo, Norway	149.5	12 Quito, Ecuador	60.0
Perth, Australia	149.5	13 Port au Prince, Haiti	61.0
Stockholm, Sweden	149.5	14 Bangalore, India	62.0
Tsukuba, Japan	149.5	15 Ndjamena, Chad	62.5
Zurich, Switzerland	149.5	16 Bamako, Mali	64.0

Country
profiles

ALGERIA

Area	2,381,741 sq km	Capital	Algiers
Arable as % of total land	3	Currency	Algerian dinar (AD)

People

Population	30.8m	Life expectancy: men	68.1 yrs
Pop. per sq km	13	women	78.3 yrs
Av. ann. growth		Adult literacy	67.8%
in pop. 2000–05	1.67%	Fertility rate (per woman)	2.8
Pop. under 15	35.1%	Urban population	57.7%
Pop. over 60	6.0%		per 1,000 pop.
No. of men per 100 women	102	Crude birth rate	23.5
Human Development Index	69.7	Crude death rate	5.5

The economy

GDP	AD4,222bn	GDP per head	$1,770
GDP	$54.7bn	GDP per head in purchasing	
Av. ann. growth in real		power parity (USA=100)	17.2
GDP 1991–2001	1.7%	Economic freedom index	3.25

Origins of GDP[a]		Components of GDP[a]	
	% of total		% of total
Agriculture	10.5	Private consumption	31.8
Industry, of which:	51.5	Public consumption	16.3
manufacturing	8.9	Investment	18.0
Services	38.0	Exports	45.7
		Imports	-14.0

Structure of employment[b]

	% of total		% of labour force
Agriculture	25	Unemployed 2001	25.0
Industry	26	Av. ann. rate 1995–2001	26.7
Services	49		

Energy

	m TOE		
Total output	149.6	Net energy imports as %	
Total consumption	29.1	of energy use	-415
Consumption per head,			
kg oil equivalent	956		

Inflation and finance

Consumer price		av. ann. increase 1996–2001	
inflation 2002	1.4%	Narrow money (M1)	16.0%
Av. ann. inflation 1996–2002	3.0%	Broad money	17.8%
Money market rate, 2002	4.20%		

Exchange rates

	end 2002		December 2002
AD per $	79.90	Effective rates	1995 = 100
AD per SDR	108.40	– nominal	77.26
AD per euro	76.19	– real	95.01

Trade

Principal exports[a]	$bn fob	Principal imports[a]	$bn cif
Other energy & products	9.4	Capital goods	2.8
Natural gas	6.8	Food	2.4
Crude oil	4.8		
Total including others	**21.7**	**Total incl. others**	**9.3**

Main export destinations	% of total	Main origins of imports	% of total
Italy	22.8	France	37.3
France	14.6	United States	11.3
Spain	13.9	Italy	10.0
United States	13.9	Germany	7.6

Balance of payments, reserves and debt, $bn

Visible exports fob	19.1	Overall balance[c]	1.2
Visible imports fob	-9.8	Change in reserves	6.1
Trade balance	9.3	Level of reserves	
Invisibles inflows	1.8	end Dec.	19.6
Invisibles outflows	-5.0	No. months of import cover	16.0
Net transfers	0.7	Foreign debt	22.5
Current account balance	6.8	– as % of GDP	46
– as % of GDP	12.4	– as % of total exports	114
Capital balance[c]	-2.3	Debt service ratio	22

Health and education

Health spending, % of GDP[d]	3.6	Education spending, % of GDP	6.0
Doctors per 1,000 pop.[d]	1.0	Enrolment, %: primary	112
Hospital beds per 1,000 pop.[d]	2.1	secondary	71
Improved-water source access,		tertiary	15
% of pop.[a]	92		

Society

No. of households	4.7m	Colour TVs per 100 households	70.0
Av. no. per household	6.3	Telephone lines per 100 pop.	6.0
Marriages per 1,000 pop.	5.8	Mobile telephone subscribers	
Divorces per 1,000 pop.	...	per 100 pop.	0.3
Cost of living, Dec. 2002		Computers per 100 pop.	0.7
New York = 100	53	Internet hosts per 1,000 pop.	...

a 2000
b 1996
c 1997
d 1998

ARGENTINA

Area	2,766,889 sq km	Capital	Buenos Aires
Arable as % of total land	9	Currency	Peso (P)

People

Population	37.5m	Life expectancy: men		70.6 yrs
Pop. per sq km	14		women	77.7 yrs
Av. ann. growth		Adult literacy		96.9%
in pop. 2000–05	1.17%	Fertility rate (per woman)		2.4
Pop. under 15	27.7%	Urban population		88.3%
Pop. over 60	13.4%			per 1,000 pop.
No. of men per 100 women	96	Crude birth rate		19.0
Human Development Index	84.4	Crude death rate		7.6

The economy

GDP	P269bn	GDP per head	$7,170
GDP	$269bn	GDP per head in purchasing	
Av. ann. growth in real		power parity (USA=100)	32.0
GDP 1991–2001	3.7%	Economic freedom index	2.95

Origins of GDP		**Components of GDP**	
	% of total		% of total
Agriculture	4.6	Private consumption	68.9
Industry, of which:	25.3	Public consumption	14.2
manufacturing	16.1	Investment	14.2
Services	70.1	Exports	11.5
		Imports	-10.2

Structure of employment[a]

	% of total		% of labour force
Agricultural	1	Unemployed 2001	17.2
Industry	25	Av. ann. rate 1995–2001	15.7
Services	74		

Energy

	m TOE		
Total output	81.2	Net energy imports as %	
Total consumption	61.5	of energy use	-32
Consumption per head			
kg oil equivalent	1,660		

Inflation and finance

Consumer price		*av. ann. increase 1996–2001*	
inflation 2002	25.9%	Narrow money (M1)	-3.6%
Av. ann. inflation 1996–2002	3.6%	Broad money	7.1%
Money market rate, 2002	41.35%		

Exchange rates

	end 2002		December 2002
			1995 = 100
P per $	3.32	Effective rates	
P per SDR	4.51	– nominal	...
P per euro	3.17	– real	...

Trade

Principal exports		Principal imports	
	$bn fob		*$bn cif*
Manufactures	8.3	Capital goods	7.6
Agricultural products	7.4	Intermediate goods	7.3
Fuels	4.8	Consumer goods	4.0
Total incl. others	**26.6**	**Total incl. others**	**20.3**

Main export destinations		Main origins of imports	
	% of total		*% of total*
Brazil	23.3	Brazil	26.2
Chile	10.7	United States	18.4
United States	10.7	China	5.2
China	4.6	Germany	5.2

Balance of payments, reserves and debt, $bn

Visible exports fob	26.6	Overall balance	-21.4
Visible imports fob	-19.2	Change in reserves	-10.6
Trade balance	7.5	Level of reserves	
Invisibles inflows	10.0	end Dec.	14.6
Invisibles outflows	-22.2	No. months of import cover	4.2
Net transfers	0.2	Foreign debt	136.7
Current account balance	-4.6	– as % of GDP	50
– as % of GDP	-1.7	– as % of total exports	375
Capital balance	-13.5	Debt service ratio	67

Health and education

Health spending, % of GDP[b]	8.6	Education spending, % of GDP	4.0
Doctors per 1,000 pop.[c]	2.7	Enrolment, %: primary	120
Hospital beds per 1,000 pop.[c]	3.3	secondary	97
Improved-water source access,		tertiary	48
% of pop.[c]	79		

Society

No. of households	10.3m	Colour TVs per 100 households	89.5
Av. no. per household	3.5	Telephone lines per 100 pop.	21.6
Marriages per 1,000 pop.	4.2	Mobile telephone subscribers	
Divorces per 1,000 pop.	...	per 100 pop.	18.6
Cost of living, Dec. 2002		Computers per 100 pop.	5.3
New York = 100	41	Internet hosts per 1,000 pop.	13.2

a 1998
b 2000
c 1997

AUSTRALIA

Area	7,682,300 sq km	Capital	Canberra
Arable as % of total land	7	Currency	Australian dollar (A$)

People

Population	19.3m	Life expectancy: men		76.4 yrs
Pop. per sq km	2		women	82.0 yrs
Av. ann. growth		Adult literacy		99.0%
in pop. 2000–05	0.96%	Fertility rate (per woman)		1.7
Pop. under 15	20.5%	Urban population		91.2%
Pop. over 60	16.4%			per 1,000 pop.
No. of men per 100 women	99	Crude birth rate		12.7
Human Development Index	93.9	Crude death rate		7.4

The economy

GDP	A$713bn	GDP per head	$19,070
GDP	$369bn	GDP per head in purchasing	
Av. ann. growth in real		power parity (USA=100)	71.8
GDP 1991–2001	3.6%	Economic freedom index	1.85

Origins of GDP

	% of total
Agriculture & mining	7.9
Manufacturing	11.6
Other	80.5

Components of GDP

	% of total
Private consumption	59.9
Public consumption	18.5
Investment	21.3
Exports	22.1
Imports	-22.0

Structure of employment

	% of total		% of labour force
Agriculture	5	Unemployed 2001	6.7
Industry	21	Av. ann. rate 1995–2001	7.7
Services	74		

Energy

	m TOE		
Total output	232.6	Net energy imports as %	
Total consumption	110.2	of energy use	-111
Consumption per head,			
kg oil equivalent	5,744		

Inflation and finance

		av. ann. increase 1996–2001	
Consumer price			
inflation 2002	3.0%	Narrow money (M1)	11.8%
Av. ann. inflation 1996–2002	2.4%	Broad money	8.6%
Money market, 2002	4.55%	Household saving rate	3.5%

Exchange rates

	end 2002		December 2002
			1995 = 100
A$ per $	1.77	Effective rates	
A$ per SDR	2.40	– nominal	91.3
A$ per euro	1.68	– real	97.1

Trade

Principal exports		Principal imports	
	$bn fob		$bn cif
Minerals & metals	25.3	Intermediate & other goods	27.0
Rural goods	15.3	Consumption goods	19.4
Manufacturing goods	14.2	Capital goods	14.1
Other goods	7.9	Other	2.7
Total incl. others	**62.7**	Total incl. others	**63.1**

Main export destinations		Main origins of imports	
	% of total		% of total
Japan	18.8	EU15	22.7
Asean[a]	12.2	United States	18.0
EU15	12.0	Asean[a]	14.7
United States	9.9	Japan	12.9

Balance of payments, reserves and aid, $bn

Visible exports fob	63.7	Capital balance	8.3
Visible imports fob	-61.8	Overall balance	1.1
Trade balance	1.9	Change in reserves	-0.2
Invisibles inflows	24.2	Level of reserves	
Invisibles outflows	-35.0	end Dec.	18.7
Net transfers	0.0	No. months of import cover	2.3
Current account balance	-15.3	Aid given	0.87
– as % of GDP	-2.4	– as % of GDP	0.25

Health and education

Health spending, % of GDP	8.5	Education spending, % of GDP	4.7
Doctors per 1,000 pop.	2.6	Enrolment, %: primary	102
Hospital beds per 1,000 pop.	4.1	secondary	161
Improved-water source access,		tertiary	63
% of pop.	100		

Society

No. of households	7.3m	Colour TVs per 100 households	91.7
Av. no. per household	2.5	Telephone lines per 100 pop.	52.0
Marriages per 1,000 pop.	5.9	Mobile telephone subscribers	
Divorces per 1,000 pop.	2.7	per 100 pop.	57.8
Cost of living, Dec. 2002		Computers per 100 pop.	51.7
New York = 100	78	Internet hosts per 1,000 pop.	132.8

a Brunei, Indonesia, Laos, Malaysia, Myanmar, Philippines, Singapore, Thailand, Vietnam.

AUSTRIA

Area	83,855 sq km	Capital	Vienna
Arable as % of total land	17	Currency	Euro (€)

People

Population	8.1m	Life expectancy:	men	75.4 yrs
Pop. per sq km	96		women	81.5 yrs
Av. ann. growth		Adult literacy		99.0%
in pop. 2000–05	0.05%	Fertility rate (per woman)		1.3
Pop. under 15	16.7%	Urban population		67.4%
Pop. over 60	20.7%			per 1,000 pop.
No. of men per 100 women	96	Crude birth rate		8.3
Human Development Index	92.6	Crude death rate		9.9

The economy

GDP	€211bn	GDP per head	$23,350
GDP	$189bn	GDP per head in purchasing	
Av. ann. growth in real		power parity (USA=100)	77.0
GDP 1991–2001	2.2%	Economic freedom index	2.10

Origins of GDP

	% of total
Agriculture	2.3
Industry, of which:	29.9
manufacturing	...
Services	67.8

Components of GDP

	% of total
Private consumption	57.4
Public consumption	19.1
Investment	22.3
Exports	52.5
Imports	-52.5

Structure of employment

	% of total		% of labour force
Agriculture	6	Unemployed 2001	3.4
Industry	30	Av. ann. rate 1995–2001	3.9
Services	64		

Energy

	m TOE		
Total output	9.7	Net energy imports as %	
Total consumption	28.6	of energy use	66
Consumption per head,			
kg oil equivalent	3,524		

Inflation and finance

Consumer price		*av. ann. increase 1996–2001*	
inflation 2002	1.8%	Euro area:	
Av. ann. inflation 1996–2002	1.6%	Narrow money (M1)	7.6%
Interbank rate, 2001	4.26%	Broad money	5.8%
		Household saving rate	5.5%

Exchange rates

	end 2002		December 2002
			1995 = 100
Euro per $	0.95	Effective rates	
Euro per SDR	1.30	– nominal	94.7
		– real	86.6

Trade

Principal exports		Principal imports	
	$bn fob		*$bn cif*
Machinery & transport equipment	29.4	Machinery & transport equipment	27.6
Consumer goods	8.8	Consumer goods	10.9
Chemicals	6.4	Chemicals	7.2
Food, drink & tobacco	3.4	Raw materials	7.2
Paper	3.1	Food, drink & tobacco	3.9
Total incl. others	**66.6**	Total incl. others	**70.4**

Main export destinations		Main origins of imports	
	% of total		*% of total*
Germany	32.4	Germany	40.5
Italy	8.6	Italy	6.8
United States	5.3	United States	5.4
United Kingdom	4.8	France	4.1

Balance of payments, reserves and aid, $bn

Visible exports fob	66.9	Capital balance	1.3
Visible imports fob	-68.2	Overall balance	-1.9
Trade balance	-1.3	Change in reserves	-2.1
Invisibles inflows	45.2	Level of reserves	
Invisibles outflows	-46.8	end Dec.	15.6
Net transfers	-1.1	No. months of import cover	1.6
Current account balance	-4.1	Aid given	0.53
– as % of GDP	-2.2	– as % of GDP	0.29

Health and education

Health spending, % of GDP	8.5	Education spending, % of GDP	5.8
Doctors per 1,000 pop.	3.3	Enrolment, %: primary	104
Hospital beds per 1,000 pop.	9.1	secondary	99
Improved-water source access,		tertiary	58
% of pop.	100		

Society

No. of households	3.3m	Colour TVs per 100 households	97.4
Av. no. per household	2.4	Telephone lines per 100 pop.	46.8
Marriages per 1,000 pop.	4.8	Mobile telephone subscribers	
Divorces per 1,000 pop.	2.4	per 100 pop.	80.7
Cost of living, Dec. 2002		Computers per 100 pop.	28.0
New York = 100	95	Internet hosts per 1,000 pop.	103.4

BANGLADESH

Area	143,998 sq km	Capital	Dhaka
Arable as % of total land	63	Currency	Taka (Tk)

People

Population	140.4m	Life expectancy: men	61.0 yrs
Pop. per sq km	975	women	61.8 yrs
Av. ann. growth		Adult literacy	35.0%
in pop. 2000–05	2.02%	Fertility rate (per woman)	3.5
Pop. under 15	39.2%	Urban population	25.6%
Pop. over 60	5.0%		per 1,000 pop.
No. of men per 100 women	105	Crude birth rate	29.9
Human Development Index	47.8	Crude death rate	8.3

The economy

GDP	Tk2,535bn	GDP per head	$330
GDP	$46.7bn	GDP per head in purchasing	
Av. ann. growth in real		power parity (USA=100)	4.7
GDP 1991–2001	4.8%	Economic freedom index	3.50

Origins of GDP[a]		Components of GDP[a]	
	% of total		% of total
Agriculture	34	Private consumption	77.5
Industry, of which:	19	Public consumption	4.5
manufacturing	12	Investment	23.1
Services	47	Exports	15.4
		Imports	-21.5

Structure of employment[b]

	% of total		% of labour force
Agriculture	63	Unemployed 2001	2.3
Industry	10	Av. ann. rate 1995–2001	2.4
Services	27		

Energy

	m TOE		
Total output	15.1	Net energy imports as %	
Total consumption	18.7	of energy use	19
Consumption per head,			
kg oil equivalent	142		

Inflation and finance

Consumer price		av. ann. increase 1996–2001	
inflation 2002	2.1%	Narrow money (M1)	11.3%
Av. ann. inflation 1996–2002	4.3%	Broad money	14.1%
Deposit rate, 2002	8.17%		

Exchange rates

	end 2002		December 2002
Tk per $	57.90	Effective rates	1995 = 100
Tk per SDR	78.72	– nominal	...
Tk per euro	55.21	– real	...

Trade

Principal exports[a]		Principal imports[a]	
	$bn fob		*$bn cif*
Clothing	4.9	Machinery & transport	
Fish & fish products	0.4	equipment	2.4
Leather	0.3	Fuels	0.8
Jute goods	0.2	Textiles & yarn	0.8
		Cereal & dairy products	0.4
Total incl. others	**6.0**	Total incl. others	**9.4**

Main export destinations		Main origins of imports	
	% of total		*% of total*
United States	29.6	India	13.1
Germany	10.3	Singapore	9.1
United Kingdom	8.5	China	8.5
France	5.4	Japan	7.9
Italy	4.6	Hong Kong	5.4

Balance of payments, reserves and debt, $bn

Visible exports fob	6.1	Overall balance	-0.1
Visible imports fob	-8.1	Change in reserves	-0.2
Trade balance	-2.0	Level of reserves	
Invisibles inflows	0.8	end Dec.	1.3
Invisibles outflows	-1.9	No. months of import cover	1.6
Net transfers	2.6	Foreign debt	15.2
Current account balance	-0.5	– as % of GDP	33
– as % of GDP	-1.1	– as % of total exports	178
Capital balance	0.5	Debt service ratio	8

Health and education

Health spending, % of GDP[c]	3.6	Education spending, % of GDP	2.5
Doctors per 1,000 pop.	0.1	Enrolment, %: primary	100
Hospital beds per 1,000 pop.	0.3	secondary	46
Improved-water source access,		tertiary	7
% of pop.	97		

Society

No. of households	24.1m	Colour TVs per 100 households	0.6
Av. no. per household	5.4	Telephone lines per 100 pop.	0.4
Marriages per 1,000 pop.	9.5	Mobile telephone subscribers	
Divorces per 1,000 pop.	...	per 100 pop.	0.4
Cost of living, Dec. 2002		Computers per 100 pop.	0.2
New York = 100	57	Internet hosts per 1,000 pop.	...

a Fiscal year ending June 30 2001.
b Fiscal year ending June 30 1996.
c 1998

BELGIUM

Area	30,520 sq km	Capital	Brussels
Arable as % of total land	25	Currency	Euro (€)

People

Population	10.3m	Life expectancy: men	75.7 yrs
Pop. per sq km	337	women	81.9 yrs
Av. ann. growth		Adult literacy	99.0%
in pop. 2000–05	0.21%	Fertility rate (per woman)	1.7
Pop. under 15	17.4%	Urban population	97.4%
Pop. over 60	22.1%		per 1,000 pop.
No. of men per 100 women	96	Crude birth rate	9.7
Human Development Index	93.9	Crude death rate	10.0

The economy

GDP	€257bn	GDP per head	$22,370
GDP	$230bn	GDP per head in purchasing	
Av. ann. growth in real		power parity (USA=100)	76.3
GDP 1991–2001	2.1%	Economic freedom index	2.10

Origins of GDP

Components of GDP

	% of total		% of total
Agriculture	1.3	Private consumption	53.8
Industry, of which:	24.4	Public consumption	21.3
manufacturing	...	Investment	21.6
Services	74.3	Exports	88.1
		Imports	-84.7

Structure of employment

	% of total		% of labour force
Agriculture	2	Unemployed 2001	6.8
Industry	27	Av. ann. rate 1995–2001	8.5
Services	71		

Energy

	m TOE		
Total output	13.2	Net energy imports as %	
Total consumption	59.2	of energy use	78
Consumption per head,			
kg oil equivalent	5,776		

Inflation and finance

Consumer price		*av. ann. increase 1996–2001*	
inflation 2002	1.6%	Euro area:	
Av. ann. inflation 1996–2002	1.7%	Narrow money (M1)	7.6%
Treasury bill rate, 2002	3.17%	Broad money	5.8%
		Household saving rate	13.0%

Exchange rates

	end 2002		December 2002
Euro per $	0.95	Effective rates	1995 = 100
Euro per SDR	1.30	– nominal	92.2
		– real	86.3

Trade

Principal exports		Principal imports	
	$bn fob		*$bn cif*
Machinery & transport equip.	59.4	Machinery & transport	56.5
Manufactured materials	41.3	Manufactures	34.0
Chemicals	40.2	Chemicals	31.9
Food & animals	15.3	Mineral fuels	15.4
Total incl. others	**190.2**	Total incl. others	**178.5**

Main export destinations		Main origins of imports	
	% of total		*% of total*
Germany	18.1	Netherlands	17.5
France	17.3	Germany	16.8
Netherlands	12.1	France	13.8
United Kingdom	9.6	United Kingdom	8.0
EU15	75.3	EU15	68.7

Balance of payments[a], reserves and aid, $bn

Visible exports fob	163.5	Capital balance	-8.0
Visible imports fob	-159.8	Overall balance	0.0
Trade balance	3.7	Change in reserves	1.3
Invisibles inflows	129.2	Level of reserves	
Invisibles outflows	-119.2	end Dec.	13.6
Net transfers	-4.2	No. months of import cover	0.6
Current account balance	9.4	Aid given	0.87
– as % of GDP	4.1	– as % of GDP	0.37

Health and education

Health spending, % of GDP	8.7	Education spending, % of GDP	5.9
Doctors per 1,000 pop.	3.9	Enrolment, %: primary	105
Hospital beds per 1,000 pop.	6.8	secondary	...
Improved-water source access,		tertiary	57
% of pop.	...		

Society

No. of households	4.2m	Colour TVs per 100 households	99.0
Av. no. per household	2.4	Telephone lines per 100 pop.	49.3
Marriages per 1,000 pop.	4.3	Mobile telephone subscribers	
Divorces per 1,000 pop.	2.4	per 100 pop.	74.7
Cost of living, Dec. 2002		Computers per 100 pop.	34.5
New York = 100	84	Internet hosts per 1,000 pop.	102.2

a Including Luxembourg.

BRAZIL

Area	8,511,965 sq km	Capital	Brasilia
Arable as % of total land	6	Currency	Real (R)

People

Population	172.6m	Life expectancy: men	64.0 yrs
Pop. per sq km	20	women	72.6 yrs
Av. ann. growth		Adult literacy	85.6%
in pop. 2000–05	1.24%	Fertility rate (per woman)	2.2
Pop. under 15	29.3%	Urban population	81.7%
Pop. over 60	7.8%		per 1,000 pop.
No. of men per 100 women	97	Crude birth rate	19.2
Human Development Index	75.7	Crude death rate	7.1

The economy

GDP	R1,185bn	GDP per head	$2,910
GDP	$503bn	GDP per head in purchasing	
Av. ann. growth in real		power parity (USA=100)	20.6
GDP 1991–2001	2.6%	Economic freedom index	3.00

Origins of GDP		Components of GDP[a]	
	% of total		% of total
Agriculture	8.4	Private consumption	60.6
Industry, of which:	37.6	Public consumption	19.2
manufacturing	...	Investment	21.2
Services	54.0	Exports	13.2
		Imports	-14.2

Structure of employment

	% of total		% of labour force
Agriculture	24	Unemployed 2001	7.7
Industry	19	Av. ann. rate 1995–2001	6.4
Services	57		

Energy

	m TOE		
Total output	142.1	Net energy imports as %	
Total consumption	183.2	of energy use	22
Consumption per head,			
kg oil equivalent	1,077		

Inflation and finance

Consumer price		av. ann. increase 1996–2001	
inflation 2002	8.4%	Narrow money (M1)	14.9%
Av. ann. inflation 1996–2002	6.2%	Broad money	10.3%
Money market rate, 2002	19.11%		

Exchange rates

	end 2002		December 2002
R per $	3.53	Effective rates	1995 = 100
R per SDR	4.80	– nominal	...
R per euro	3.37	– real	...

Trade

Principal exports		Principal imports	
	$bn fob		*$bn fob*
Transport equipment & parts	10.2	Machines & electrical	
Metal goods	5.6	equipment	17.5
Soyabeans etc.	5.2	Chemical products	9.1
Chemical products	1.2	Transport equipment & parts	6.9
		Oil & derivatives	6.3
Total incl. others	**58.2**	Total incl. others	**55.6**

Main export destinations		Main origins of imports	
	% of total		*% of total*
United States	24.2	United States	27.4
Argentina	11.6	Argentina	13.5
Germany	5.4	Germany	8.9
Netherlands	4.4	Japan	5.0

Balance of payments, reserves and debt, $bn

Visible exports fob	58.2	Overall balance	-3.4
Visible imports fob	-55.6	Change in reserves	2.9
Trade balance	2.6	Level of reserves	
Invisibles inflows	12.6	end Dec.	35.9
Invisibles outflows	-40.1	No. months of import cover	4.5
Net transfers	1.6	Foreign debt	226.4
Current account balance	-23.2	– as % of GDP	43
– as % of GDP	-4.6	– as % of total exports	337
Capital balance	20.0	Debt service ratio	81

Health and education

Health spending, % of GDP	6.5	Education spending, % of GDP	4.7
Doctors per 1,000 pop.	2.5	Enrolment, %: primary	162
Hospital beds per 1,000 pop.	2.9	secondary	108
Improved-water source access,		tertiary	17
% of pop.	87		

Society

No. of households	48.6m	Colour TVs per 100 households	86.3
Av. no. per household	3.4	Telephone lines per 100 pop.	21.7
Marriages per 1,000 pop.	4.6	Mobile telephone subscribers	
Divorces per 1,000 pop.	0.7	per 100 pop.	16.7
Cost of living, Dec. 2002		Computers per 100 pop.	6.3
New York = 100	46	Internet hosts per 1,000 pop.	12.9

BULGARIA

Area	110,994 sq km	Capital	Sofia
Arable as % of total land	40	Currency	Lev (BGL)

People

Population	7.9m	Life expectancy: men	67.4 yrs
Pop. per sq km	71	women	74.6 yrs
Av. ann. growth		Adult literacy	98.5%
in pop. 2000–05	-0.85%	Fertility rate (per woman)	1.1
Pop. under 15	15.8%	Urban population	67.4%
Pop. over 60	21.7%		per 1,000 pop.
No. of men per 100 women	94	Crude birth rate	7.9
Human Development Index	77.9	Crude death rate	15.1

The economy

GDP	BGL29.6bn	GDP per head	$1,720
GDP	$13.6bn	GDP per head in purchasing	
Av. ann. growth in real		power parity (USA=100)	19.7
GDP 1991–2001	-1.2%	Economic freedom index	3.35

Origins of GDP

	% of total
Agriculture	13.7
Industry, of which:	28.5
manufacturing	...
Services	57.9

Components of GDP

	% of total
Private consumption	77.4
Public consumption	9.8
Investment	20.4
Exports	55.7
Imports	-63.2

Structure of employment[a]

	% of total		% of labour force
Agriculture	27	Unemployed 2001	17.5
Industry	29	Av. ann. rate 1995–2001	15.5
Services	44		

Energy

	m TOE		
Total output	10.0	Net energy imports as %	
Total consumption	18.8	of energy use	47
Consumption per head,			
kg oil equivalent	2,299		

Inflation and finance

			av. ann change 1996–2001
Consumer price			
inflation 2002	5.8%	Narrow money (M1)	82%
Av. ann. inflation 1996–2002	61.4%	Broad money	57%
Money market rate 2002	2.47%		

Exchange rates

	end 2002		December 2002
BGL per $	1.89	Effective rates	1995 = 100
BGL per SDR	2.56	– nominal	6.87
BGL per euro	1.80	– real	139.89

Trade

Principal exports		Principal imports	
	$bn fob		*$bn fob*
Textiles & clothing	1.4	Machinery & transport	
Metals	0.9	equipment	2.1
Fuels	0.8	Fuels	1.9
Machinery & transport		Textiles & clothing	1.2
equipment	0.6	Chemicals	0.9
Total incl. others	**5.1**	Total incl. others	**7.3**

Main export destinations		Main origins of imports	
	% of total		*% of total*
Italy	15.0	Russia	20.0
Germany	9.5	Germany	15.3
Greece	8.8	Italy	9.6
Turkey	8.1	France	6.0

Balance of payments, reserves and debt, $bn

Visible exports fob	5.1	Overall balance	0.2
Visible imports fob	-6.7	Change in reserves	0.1
Trade balance	-1.6	Level of reserves	
Invisibles inflows	2.8	end Dec.	3.6
Invisibles outflows	-2.6	No. months of import cover	4.7
Net transfers	0.5	Foreign debt	9.6
Current account balance	-0.9	– as % of GDP	75
– as % of GDP	-6.2	– as % of total exports	136
Capital balance	1.1	Debt service ratio	19

Health and education

Health spending, % of GDP	4.5	Education spending, % of GDP	3.4
Doctors per 1,000 pop.	3.4	Enrolment, %: primary	103
Hospital beds per 1,000 pop.	6.8	secondary	94
Improved-water source access,		tertiary	41
% of pop.	100		

Society

No. of households	3.0m	Colour TVs per 100 households	62.5
Av. no. per household	2.7	Telephone lines per 100 pop.	35.9
Marriages per 1,000 pop.	4.3	Mobile telephone subscribers	
Divorces per 1,000 pop.	1.2	per 100 pop.	19.1
Cost of living, Dec. 2002		Computers per 100 pop.	4.4
New York = 100	...	Internet hosts per 1,000 pop.	2.1

a 1999

CAMEROON

Area	475,442 sq km	Capital	Yaoundé
Arable as % of total land	13	Currency	CFA franc (CFAfr)

People

Population	15.2m	Life expectancy: men	45.1 yrs
Pop. per sq km	32	women	47.4 yrs
Av. ann. growth		Adult literacy	76.9%
in pop. 2000–05	1.83%	Fertility rate (per woman)	4.6
Pop. under 15	43.2%	Urban population	49.7%
Pop. over 60	4.5%		per 1,000 pop.
No. of men per 100 women	99	Crude birth rate	36.3
Human Development Index	51.2	Crude death rate	16.9

The economy

GDP	CFAfr6,320bn	GDP per head	$560
GDP	$8.5bn	GDP per head in purchasing	
Av. ann. growth in real		power parity (USA=100)	4.6
GDP 1991–2001	1.7%	Economic freedom index	3.35

Origins of GDP[a]

	% of total
Agriculture	28.8
Industry, of which:	31.0
manufacturing	...
Services	40.2

Components of GDP[a]

	% of total
Private consumption	68.7
Public consumption	8.3
Investment	21.6
Exports	26.2
Imports	-24.8

Structure of employment[b]

	% of total		% of labour force
Agriculture	70	Unemployed 2001	...
Industry	9	Av. ann. rate 1995–2001	...
Services	21		

Energy

	m TOE		
Total output	12.7	Net energy imports as %	
Total consumption	6.4	of energy use	-100
Consumption per head,			
kg oil equivalent	427		

Inflation and finance

Consumer price		*av. ann. change 1996–2001*	
inflation 2001	4.6%	Narrow money (M1)	17.8%
Av. ann. inflation 1996–2001	2.4%	Broad money	14.7%
Deposit rate, 2002	5.00%		

Exchange rates

	end 2002		December 2002
CFAfr per $	625.50	Effective rates	1995 = 100
CFAfr per SDR	850.37	– nominal	103.8
CFAfr per euro	596.45	– real	106.4

Trade

Principal exports[a]		Principal imports[a]	
	$bn fob		*$bn fob*
Mineral fuels	0.9	Manufactures	0.7
Timber & cork	0.5	Mineral fuels	0.6
Cocoa	0.1	Primary products	0.6
Total incl. others	**2.0**	Total incl. others	**1.5**

Main export destinations		Main origins of imports	
	% of total		*% of total*
Italy	21.7	France	28.8
Spain	12.2	Nigeria	11.9
France	10.6	Italy	2.7

Balance of payments[c], reserves and debt, $bn

Visible exports fob	2.0	Overall balance[a]	-0.3
Visible imports fob	-1.5	Change in reserves	0.1
Trade balance	0.5	Level of reserves	
Invisibles inflows	0.6	end Dec.	0.3
Invisibles outflows	-1.2	No. months of import cover	2.0
Net transfers	0.1	Foreign debt	8.3
Current account balance	0.0	– as % of GDP	99
– as % of GDP	0.2	– as % of total exports	324
Capital balance[a]	-0.1	Debt service ratio	6

Health and education

Health spending, % of GDP[c]	4.3	Education spending, % of GDP	3.2
Doctors per 1,000 pop.	0.1	Enrolment, %: primary	108
Hospital beds per 1,000 pop.	1.8	secondary	20
Improved-water source access,		tertiary	5
% of pop.	62		

Society

No. of households	4.1m	Colour TVs per 100 households	3.2
Av. no. per household	3.9	Telephone lines per 100 pop.	0.7
Marriages per 1,000 pop.	...	Mobile telephone subscribers	
Divorces per 1,000 pop.	...	per 100 pop.	2.0
Cost of living, Dec. 2002		Computers per 100 pop.	0.4
New York = 100	71	Internet hosts per 1,000 pop.	...

a Fiscal year ending June 30 2001.
b 1990
c 2000

CANADA

Area[a]	9,970,610 sq km	Capital	Ottawa
Arable as % of total land	5	Currency	Canadian dollar (C$)

People

Population	31.0m	Life expectancy: men	76.7 yrs
Pop. per sq km	3	women	81.9 yrs
Av. ann. growth		Adult literacy	99.0%
in pop. 2000–05	0.77%	Fertility rate (per woman)	1.5
Pop. under 15	19.0%	Urban population	78.9%
Pop. over 60	16.7%		per 1,000 pop.
No. of men per 100 women	98	Crude birth rate	10.9
Human Development Index	94.0	Crude death rate	7.5

The economy

GDP	C$1,076bn	GDP per head	$22,390
GDP	$695bn	GDP per head in purchasing	
Av. ann. growth in real		power parity (USA=100)	77.4
GDP 1991–2001	2.7%	Economic freedom index	2.05

Origins of GDP		**Components of GDP**	
	% of total		% of total
Agriculture	2.3	Private consumption	57.2
Industry, of which:	29.4	Public consumption	18.4
manufacturing & mining	21.2	Investment	19.2
Services	68.1	Exports	43.3
		Imports	-38.2

Structure of employment

	% of total		% of labour force
Agriculture	3	Unemployed 2001	7.2
Industry	23	Av. ann. rate 1995–2001	8.3
Services	74		

Energy

	m TOE		
Total output	374.9	Net energy imports as %	
Total consumption	251.0	of energy use	-49
Consumption per head,			
kg oil equivalent	8,156		

Inflation and finance

Consumer price		av. ann. increase 1996–2001	
inflation 2002	2.2%	Narrow money (M1)	10.3%
Av. ann. inflation 1996–2002	2.0%	Broad money	7.3%
Money market rate, 2002	2.45%	Household saving rate	4.6%

Exchange rates

	end 2002		December 2002
C$ per $	1.58	Effective rates	1995 = 100
C$ per SDR	2.15	– nominal	91.5
C$ per euro	1.51	– real	92.3

Trade

Principal exports	$bn fob	Principal imports	$bn fob
Machinery & industrial equipment	64.4	Machinery & industrial equipment	72.6
Motor vehicles & parts	59.7	Motor vehicles & parts	46.8
Industrial supplies	43.1	Industrial supplies	44.2
Energy products	35.3	Consumer goods	27.7
Forest products	25.4	Agric. products	13.2
Agricultural products	20.0	Energy products	11.5
Total incl. others	**267.7**	Total incl. others	**226.4**

Main export destinations	% of total	Main origins of imports	% of total
United States	84.6	United States	72.7
Japan	2.2	United Kingdom	3.4
United Kingdom	1.6	Japan	3.0
EU15 (excl. UK)	3.8	EU15 (excl. UK)	6.6

Balance of payments, reserves and aid, $bn

Visible exports fob	267.9	Capital balance	-11.3
Visible imports fob	-226.5	Overall balance	2.2
Trade balance	41.4	Change in reserves	2.0
Invisibles inflows	59.2	Level of reserves	
Invisibles outflows	-82.4	end Dec.	34.3
Net transfers	1.3	No. months of import cover	1.3
Current account balance	19.5	Aid given	1.53
– as % of GDP	2.8	– as % of GDP	0.22

Health and education

Health spending, % of GDP	8.9	Education spending, % of GDP	5.5
Doctors per 1,000 pop.	2.0	Enrolment, %: primary	99
Hospital beds per 1,000 pop.	4.6	secondary	103
Improved-water source access, % of pop.	100	tertiary	60

Society

No. of households	12.0m	Colour TVs per 100 households	98.7
Av. no. per household	2.5	Telephone lines per 100 pop.	65.5
Marriages per 1,000 pop.	5.1	Mobile telephone subscribers	
Divorces per 1,000 pop.	2.2	per 100 pop.	32.0
Cost of living, Dec. 2002		Computers per 100 pop.	39.0
New York = 100	72	Internet hosts per 1,000 pop.	96.5

a Including freshwater.

CHILE

Area	756,945 sq km	Capital	Santiago
Arable as % of total land	3	Currency	Chilean peso (Ps)

People

Population	15.4m	Life expectancy: men	73 yrs
Pop. per sq km	20	women	79 yrs
Av. ann. growth		Adult literacy	95.9%
in pop. 2000–05	1.23%	Fertility rate (per woman)	2.4
Pop. under 15	28.4%	Urban population	86.1%
Pop. over 60	10.3%		per 1,000 pop.
No. of men per 100 women	98	Crude birth rate	18.2
Human Development Index	83.1	Crude death rate	5.6

The economy

GDP	42,192bn pesos	GDP per head	$4,310
GDP	$66.5bn	GDP per head in purchasing	
Av. ann. growth in real		power parity (USA=100)	25.8
GDP 1991–2001	6.2%	Economic freedom index	2.00

Origins of GDP		**Components of GDP**	
	% of total		% of total
Agriculture	5.6	Private consumption	62.7
Industry, of which:	32.2	Public consumption	11.0
manufacturing	15.7	Investment	22.1
Services	62.2	Exports	34.3
		Imports	-30.2

Structure of employment

	% of total		% of labour force
Agriculture	13	Unemployed 2001	7.9
Industry	24	Av. ann. rate 1995–2001	6.8
Services	63		

Energy

	m TOE		
Total output	8.3	Net energy imports as %	
Total consumption	24.3	of energy use	66
Consumption per head,			
kg oil equivalent	1,604		

Inflation and finance

Consumer price		*av. ann. increase 1996–2001*	
inflation 2002	2.5%	Narrow money (M1)	8.9%
Av. ann. inflation 1996–2002	4.1%	Broad money	10.2%
Money market rate, 2002	4.08%		

Exchange rates

	end 2002		December 2002
Ps per $	712.38	Effective rates	1995 = 100
Ps per SDR	968.49	– nominal	76.1
Ps per Ecu	679.30	– real	87.2

Trade

Principal exports		Principal imports	
	$bn fob		$bn cif
Copper	6.7	Intermediate goods	10.1
Paper products	1.2	Capital goods	3.4
Fruit	1.1	Consumer goods	2.9
Total incl. others	**18.5**	Total incl. others	**17.8**

Main export destinations		Main origins of imports	
	% of total		% of total
United States	17.9	Argentina	18.1
Japan	12.2	United States	17.0
United Kingdom	5.9	Brazil	8.5
Brazil	5.2	China	5.9

Balance of payments, reserves and debt, $bn

Visible exports fob	18.5	Overall balance	-0.6
Visible imports fob	-16.4	Change in reserves	-0.7
Trade balance	2.1	Level of reserves	
Invisibles inflows	5.1	end Dec.	14.4
Invisibles outflows	-8.8	No. months of import cover	6.8
Net transfers	0.4	Foreign debt	38.4
Current account balance	-1.2	– as % of GDP	55
– as % of GDP	-1.9	– as % of total exports	164
Capital balance	1.8	Debt service ratio	28

Health and education

Health spending, % of GDP[a]	7.2	Education spending, % of GDP	4.2
Doctors per 1,000 pop.	1.7	Enrolment, %: primary	103
Hospital beds per 1,000 pop.	2.8	secondary	75
Improved-water source access,		tertiary	38
% of pop.	97		

Society

No. of households	3.9m	Colour TVs per 100 households	60.0
Av. no. per household	3.8	Telephone lines per 100 pop.	23.9
Marriages per 1,000 pop.	4.6	Mobile telephone subscribers	
Divorces per 1,000 pop.	0.5	per 100 pop.	34.0
Cost of living, Dec. 2002		Computers per 100 pop.	8.4
New York = 100	55	Internet hosts per 1,000 pop.	8.7

a 2000

CHINA

Area	9,560,900 sq km	Capital	Beijing
Arable as % of total land	13	Currency	Yuan

People

Population	1,285.0m	Life expectancy: men	68.9 yrs
Pop. per sq km	134	women	73.3 yrs
Av. ann. growth		Adult literacy	84.7%
in pop. 2000–05	0.73%	Fertility rate (per woman)	1.8
Pop. under 15	24.8%	Urban population	36.7%
Pop. over 60	10.1%		per 1,000 pop.
No. of men per 100 women	106	Crude birth rate	14.3
Human Development Index	72.6	Crude death rate	7.0

The economy

GDP	Yuan9,593bn	GDP per head	$900
GDP	$1,159bn	GDP per head in purchasing	
Av. ann. growth in real		power parity (USA=100)	11.5
GDP 1991–2001	9.8%	Economic freedom index	3.55

Origins of GDP[a]		**Components of GDP**[a]	
	% of total		% of total
Agriculture	16.4	Private consumption	48.0
Industry, of which:	51.1	Public consumption	13.1
manufacturing	39.0	Investment	36.5
Services	32.5	Exports	27.4
		Imports	-24.8

Structure of employment

	% of total		% of labour force
Agriculture	50	Unemployed 2001	3.1
Industry	23	Av. ann. rate 1995–2001	3.0
Services	27		

Energy

	m TOE		
Total output	1,107.6	Net energy imports as %	
Total consumption	1,142.4	of energy use	3
Consumption per head,			
kg oil equivalent	905		

Inflation and finance

		av. ann. increase 1996–2001	
Consumer price			
inflation 2002	-0.8%	Narrow money (M1)	17.5%
Av. ann. inflation 1996–2002	0.1%	Broad money	15.5%
Deposit rate, 2002	2.25%		

Exchange rates

	end 2002		December 2002
Yuan per $	8.28	Effective rates	1995 = 100
Yuan per SDR	11.25	– nominal	117.7
Yuan per euro	7.89	– real	105.0

Trade

Principal exports		Principal imports	
	$bn fob		*$bn cif*
Machinery & transport equipment	94.9	Machinery & transport equipment	107.0
Electric & electronic products	51.3	Electronic circuits	16.6
Garments & accessories	36.7	Crude oil	11.7
Computer & telecoms products	36.2	Plastics	11.7
Textiles	16.8	Steel	9.0
Total incl. others	**266.1**	**Total incl. others**	**243.6**

Main export destinations		Main origins of imports	
	% of total		*% of total*
United States	20.4	Japan	17.6
Hong Kong	17.5	Taiwan	11.2
Japan	16.9	United States	10.8
South Korea	4.7	South Korea	9.6
Germany	3.7	Germany	5.7

Balance of payments, reserves and debt, $bn

Visible exports fob	266.1	Overall balance	47.4
Visible imports fob	-232.1	Change in reserves	48.3
Trade balance	34.0	Level of reserves	
Invisibles inflows	42.7	end Dec.	220.1
Invisibles outflows	-67.9	No. months of import cover	8.8
Net transfers	8.5	Foreign debt	170.1
Current account balance	17.4	– as % of GDP	16
– as % of GDP	1.5	– as % of total exports	61
Capital balance	34.8	Debt service ratio	9

Health and education

Health spending, % of GDP	5.6	Education spending, % of GDP	2.1
Doctors per 1,000 pop.	1.6	Enrolment, %: primary	106
Hospital beds per 1,000 pop.	2.3	secondary	63
Improved-water source access, % of pop.	75	tertiary	7

Society

No. of households	353.3m	Colour TVs per 100 households	45.5
Av. no. per household	3.8	Telephone lines per 100 pop.	13.8
Marriages per 1,000 pop.	6.5	Mobile telephone subscribers	
Divorces per 1,000 pop.	0.9	per 100 pop.	11.2
Cost of living, Dec. 2002		Computers per 100 pop.	1.9
New York = 100	94	Internet hosts per 1,000 pop.	0.1

Note: Data excludes Special Administrative Regions, ie Hong Kong and Macau.
a 2000 estimates.

COLOMBIA

Area	1,141,748 sq km	Capital	Bogota
Arable as % of total land	3	Currency	Colombian peso (peso)

People

Population	42.8m	Life expectancy: men	69.2 yrs
Pop. per sq km	37	women	75.3 yrs
Av. ann. growth		Adult literacy	92.0%
in pop. 2000–05	1.59%	Fertility rate (per woman)	2.6
Pop. under 15	32.8%	Urban population	75.5%
Pop. over 60	6.9%		per 1,000 pop.
No. of men per 100 women	98	Crude birth rate	22.3
Human Development Index	77.2	Crude death rate	5.4

The economy

GDP	189,526bn pesos	GDP per head	$1,930
GDP	$82.4bn	GDP per head in purchasing	
Av. ann. growth in real		power parity (USA=100)	19.8
GDP 1991–2001	2.6%	Economic freedom index	3.00

Origins of GDP		**Components of GDP**	
	% of total		% of total
Agriculture	13.1	Private consumption	64.7
Industry, of which:	26.6	Public consumption	21.9
manufacturing	13.9	Investment	15.3
Services	60.3	Exports	19.0
		Imports	-20.9

Structure of employment[ab]

	% of total		% of labour force
Agriculture	1	Unemployed 2001	21.3
Industry	26	Av. ann. rate 1995–2001	15.7
Services	73		

Energy

	m TOE		
Total output	74.6	Net energy imports as %	
Total consumption	28.8	of energy use	-159
Consumption per head,			
kg oil equivalent	681		

Inflation and finance

		av. ann. increase 1996–2001	
Consumer price			
inflation 2002	6.3%	Narrow money (M1)	15.8%
Av. ann. inflation 1996–2002	12.4%	Broad money	10.7%
Money market rate, 2002	6.06%		

Exchange rates

	end 2002		December 2002
			1995 = 100
Peso per $	2,865	Effective rates	
Peso per SDR	3,895	– nominal	43.0
Peso per euro	2,732	– real	91.8

Trade

Principal exports		Principal imports	
	$bn fob		*$bn cif*
Oil	3.1	Intermediate goods &	
Coal	1.2	raw materials	5.8
Coffee	0.7	Capital goods	4.4
		Consumer goods	2.6
Total incl. others	**12.8**	Total	**12.3**

Main export destinations		Main origins of imports	
	% of total		*% of total*
United States	44.9	United States	30.9
Venezuela	10.5	Venezuela	8.0
Ecuador	3.7	Mexico	5.3
Germany	3.6	Japan	4.8

Balance of payments, reserves and debt, $bn

Visible exports fob	12.8	Overall balance	1.2
Visible imports fob	-12.3	Change in reserves	1.2
Trade balance	0.5	Level of reserves	
Invisibles inflows	2.9	end Dec.	10.2
Invisibles outflows	-7.3	No. months of import cover	6.3
Net transfers	2.1	Foreign debt	36.7
Current account balance	-1.8	– as % of GDP	45
– as % of GDP	-2.2	– as % of total exports	214
Capital balance	2.5	Debt service ratio	37

Health and education

Health spending, % of GDP	9.6	Education spending, % of GDP[c]	4.1
Doctors per 1,000 pop.	1.0	Enrolment, %: primary	112
Hospital beds per 1,000 pop.	1.1	secondary	70
Improved-water source access,		tertiary	23
% of pop.	91		

Society

No. of households	9.2m	Colour TVs per 100 households	85.6
Av. no. per household	3.8	Telephone lines per 100 pop.	17.1
Marriages per 1,000 pop.	...	Mobile telephone subscribers	
Divorces per 1,000 pop.	...	per 100 pop.	7.4
Cost of living, Dec. 2002		Computers per 100 pop.	4.2
New York = 100	54	Internet hosts per 1,000 pop.	2.2

a 2000
b Main cities.
c 1997

CÔTE D'IVOIRE

Area	322,463 sq km	Capital	Abidjan/Yamoussoukro
Arable as % of total land	9	Currency	CFA franc (CFAfr)

People

Population	16.3m	Life expectancy: men	40.8 yrs
Pop. per sq km	50	women	41.2 yrs
Av. ann. growth		Adult literacy	48.2%
in pop. 2000–05	1.67%	Fertility rate (per woman)	4.7
Pop. under 15	42.7%	Urban population	44.0%
Pop. over 60	5.0%		per 1,000 pop.
No. of men per 100 women	104	Crude birth rate	35.3
Human Development Index	42.8	Crude death rate	20.0

The economy

GDP	CFAfr7,631bn	GDP per head	$640
GDP	$10.4bn	GDP per head in purchasing	
Av. ann. growth in real		power parity (USA=100)	4.1
GDP 1991–2001	2.2%	Economic freedom index	3.05

Origins of GDP

	% of total
Agriculture	29.1
Industry, of which:	21.6
manufacturing	...
Services	49.9

Components of GDP

	% of total
Private consumption	65.7
Public consumption	12.8
Investment	11.0
Exports	44.5
Imports	-34.9

Structure of employment[a]

	% of total		% of labour force
Agriculture	60	Unemployed 2001	...
Industry	10	Av. ann. rate 1995–2001	...
Services	30		

Energy

	m TOE		
Total output	6.1	Net energy imports as %	
Total consumption	6.9	of energy use	12
Consumption per head,			
kg oil equivalent	433		

Inflation and finance

Consumer price		av. ann. change 1996–2001	
inflation 2002	3.1%	Narrow money (M1)	6.5%
Av. ann. inflation 1996–2002	3.5%	Broad money	4.4%
Money market rate, 2002	4.95%		

Exchange rates

	end 2002		December 2002
CFAfr per $	625.5	Effective rates	1995 = 100
CFAfr per SDR	850.4	– nominal	77.4
CFAfr per euro	596.5	– real	103.0

Trade

Principal exports		**Principal imports**	
	$bn fob		*$bn cif*
Cocoa beans & products	1.0	Fuel & lubricants	0.8
Petroleum products	0.7	Capital goods	0.7
Coffee & products	0.3	Food products	0.4
Timber	0.2		
Total incl. others	**3.9**	Total incl. others	**2.6**

Main export destinations		**Main origins of imports**	
	% of total		*% of total*
France	13.3	Nigeria	23.0
Netherlands	9.4	France	22.6
United States	8.3	China	5.5
Mali	5.8	Italy	3.8
Germany	5.4	United States	3.4

Balance of payments, reserves and debt, $bn

Visible exports fob	3.9	Overall balance	-0.1
Visible imports fob	-2.4	Change in reserves	0.4
Trade balance	1.5	Level of reserves	
Invisibles inflows	0.6	end Dec.	1.0
Invisibles outflows	-1.9	No. months of import cover	2.8
Net transfers	-0.3	Foreign debt	11.6
Current account balance	-0.1	– as % of GDP	111
– as % of GDP	-0.6	– as % of total exports	240
Capital balance	-0.0	Debt service ratio	13

Health and education

Health spending, % of GDP[b]	2.7	Education spending, % of GDP	4.6
Doctors per 1,000 pop.[b]	0.1	Enrolment, %: primary	81
Hospital beds per 1,000 pop.	0.6	secondary	23
Improved-water source access,		tertiary[c]	7
% of pop.	77		

Society

No. of households	3.4m	Colour TVs per 100 households	38.7
Av. no. per household	4.6	Telephone lines per 100 pop.	1.8
Marriages per 1,000 pop.	...	Mobile telephone subscribers	
Divorces per 1,000 pop.	...	per 100 pop.	4.5
Cost of living, Dec. 2002		Computers per 100 pop.	0.6
New York = 100	83	Internet hosts per 1,000 pop.	...

a 1990
b 2000
c 1999

CZECH REPUBLIC

Area	78,864 sq km	Capital	Prague
Arable as % of total land	40	Currency	Koruna (Kc)

People

Population	10.3m	Life expectancy: men	72.1 yrs
Pop. per sq km	130	women	78.7 yrs
Av. ann. growth		Adult literacy	99.0%
in pop. 2000–05	-0.10	Fertility rate (per woman)	1.2
Pop. under 15	16.4%	Urban population	74.5%
Pop. over 60	18.3%		per 1,000 pop.
No. of men per 100 women	95	Crude birth rate	8.8
Human Development Index	84.9	Crude death rate	10.8

The economy

GDP	Kcs2,158bn	GDP per head	$5,530
GDP	$56.8bn	GDP per head in purchasing	
Av. ann. growth in real		power parity (USA=100)	41.8
GDP 1991–2001	0.4%	Economic freedom index	2.50

Origins of GDP

	% of total
Agriculture	3.8
Industry, of which:	36.8
manufacturing	...
Services	59.4

Components of GDP

	% of total
Private consumption	53.6
Public consumption	19.2
Investment	29.9
Exports	71.3
Imports	-74.1

Structure of employment

	% of total		% of labour force
Agriculture	5	Unemployed 2001	7.9
Industry	40	Av. ann. rate 1995–2001	6.5
Services	55		

Energy

	m TOE		
Total output	29.9	Net energy imports as %	
Total consumption	40.4	of energy use	26
Consumption per head,			
kg oil equivalent	3,931		

Inflation and finance

		av. ann. increase 1996–2001	
Consumer price			
inflation 2002	1.8%	Narrow money (M1)	5.3%
Av. ann. inflation 1996–2002	5.2%	Broad money	6.8%
Money market rate, 2002	2.63%	Household saving rate	8.7%

Exchange rates

	end 2002		December 2002
Kc per $	30.14	Effective rates	1995 = 100
Kc per SDR	40.98	– nominal	114.4
Kc per euro	28.74	– real	130.6

Trade

Principal exports	$bn fob	Principal imports	$bn cif
Machinery & transport equipment	15.8	Machinery & transport equipment	15.5
Semi-manufactures	5.3	Chemicals	4.7
Iron & steel	2.9	Fuels	3.3
Chemicals	2.7	Road vehicles	3.0
		Food	1.6
Total incl. others	**33.4**	**Total incl. others**	**38.3**

Main export destinations	% of total	Main origins of imports	% of total
Germany	35.4	Germany	40.3
Slovakia	7.3	Slovakia	6.4
United Kingdom	5.5	Russia	6.0
Austria	5.3	France	5.9
Poland	5.2	Italy	5.8
EU15	68.9	EU15	61.8

Balance of payments, reserves and debt, $bn

Visible exports fob	33.4	Overall balance	1.8
Visible imports fob	-36.5	Change in reserves	1.3
Trade balance	-3.1	Level of reserves	
Invisibles inflows	9.3	end Dec.	14.5
Invisibles outflows	-9.3	No. months of import cover	3.8
Net transfers	0.5	Foreign debt	21.7
Current account balance	-2.6	– as % of GDP	41
– as % of GDP	-4.6	– as % of total exports	56
Capital balance	4.1	Debt service ratio	12

Health and education

Health spending, % of GDP	7.2	Education spending, % of GDP	4.4
Doctors per 1,000 pop.	3.0	Enrolment, %: primary	104
Hospital beds per 1,000 pop.	8.4	secondary	95
Improved-water source access, % of pop.	...	tertiary	30

Society

No. of households	3.7m	Colour TVs per 100 households	86.9
Av. no. per household	2.7	Telephone lines per 100 pop.	37.4
Marriages per 1,000 pop.	5.2	Mobile telephone subscribers	
Divorces per 1,000 pop.	3.1	per 100 pop.	65.9
Cost of living, Dec. 2002		Computers per 100 pop.	12.1
New York = 100	69	Internet hosts per 1,000 pop.	23.2

DENMARK

Area	43,075 sq km	Capital	Copenhagen
Arable as % of total land	54	Currency	Danish krone (DKr)

People

Population	5.3m	Life expectancy: men	74.2 yrs
Pop. per sq km	123	women	79.1 yrs
Av. ann. growth		Adult literacy	99.0%
in pop. 2000–05	0.24	Fertility rate (per woman)	1.8
Pop. under 15	18.3%	Urban population	85.1%
Pop. over 60	20.0%		per 1,000 pop.
No. of men per 100 women	98	Crude birth rate	11.0
Human Development Index	92.6	Crude death rate	11.3

The economy

GDP	DKr1,344bn	GDP per head	$30,290
GDP	$161.5bn	GDP per head in purchasing	
Av. ann. growth in real		power parity (USA=100)	83.1
GDP 1991–2001	2.2%	Economic freedom index	1.80

Origins of GDP

	% of total
Agriculture	2.8
Industry, of which:	26.2
manufacturing	...
Services	71.0

Components of GDP

	% of total
Private consumption	47.3
Public consumption	25.1
Investment	21.7
Exports	43.8
Imports	-37.9

Structure of employment

	% of total		% of labour force
Agriculture	3	Unemployed 2001	4.8
Industry	20	Av. ann. rate 1995–2001	5.8
Services	77		

Energy

	m TOE		
Total output	27.8	Net energy imports as %	
Total consumption	19.5	of energy use	-43
Consumption per head,			
kg oil equivalent	3,643		

Inflation and finance

		av. ann. increase 1996–2001	
Consumer price			
inflation 2002	2.4%	Narrow money (M1)	5.0%
Av. ann. inflation 1996–2002	2.3%	Broad money	1.4%
Money market rate, 2002	3.56%	Household saving rate	5.3%

Exchange rates

	end 2002		December 2002
DKr per $	7.08	Effective rates	1995 = 100
DKr per SDR	9.63	– nominal	94.7
DKr per euro	6.75	– real	98.5

Trade

Principal exports		Principal imports	
	$bn fob		*$bn cif*
Manufactured goods	38.2	Intermediate goods	19.8
Agric. products	5.6	Consumer goods	12.6
Energy & products	3.4	Capital goods	5.9
Ships	0.2	Transport equipment	2.5
Total incl. others	**50.7**	Total incl. others	**43.4**

Main export destinations		Main origins of imports	
	% of total		*% of total*
Germany	19.6	Germany	21.9
Sweden	11.8	Sweden	12.1
United Kingdom	9.5	United Kingdom	7.5
United States	6.9	Netherlands	7.1
Norway	5.5	France	5.7
Netherlands	4.5	Italy	4.5
EU15	64.7	EU15	69.9

Balance of payments, reserves and aid, $bn

Visible exports fob	50.4	Capital balance	-3.5
Visible imports fob	-43.7	Overall balance	3.3
Trade balance	6.8	Change in reserves	2.0
Invisibles inflows	38.0	Level of reserves	
Invisibles outflows	-38.1	end Dec.	17.7
Net transfers	-2.6	No. months of import cover	2.6
Current account balance	4.1	Aid given	1.63
– as % of GDP	2.6	– as % of GDP	1.03

Health and education

Health spending, % of GDP[a]	8.3	Education spending, % of GDP	8.2
Doctors per 1,000 pop.	3.0	Enrolment, %: primary	102
Hospital beds per 1,000 pop.	4.3	secondary	128
Improved-water source access, % of pop.	100	tertiary	59

Society

No. of households	2.5m	Colour TVs per 100 households	92.2
Av. no. per household	2.1	Telephone lines per 100 pop.	72.3
Marriages per 1,000 pop.	6.7	Mobile telephone subscribers	
Divorces per 1,000 pop.	2.6	per 100 pop.	73.7
Cost of living, Dec. 2002		Computers per 100 pop.	43.2
New York = 100	104	Internet hosts per 1,000 pop.	217.7

a 2000

EGYPT

Area	1,000,250 sq km	Capital	Cairo
Arable as % of total land	3	Currency	Egyptian pound (£E)

People

Population	69.1m	Life expectancy: men		66.7 yrs
Pop. per sq km	69		women	71.0 yrs
Av. ann. growth		Adult literacy		56.1%
in pop. 2000–05	1.99%	Fertility rate (per woman)		3.3
Pop. under 15	36.3%	Urban population		42.7%
Pop. over 60	6.8%			per 1,000 pop.
No. of men per 100 women	100	Crude birth rate		23.3
Human Development Index	64.2	Crude death rate		6.2

The economy

GDP	£E362bn	GDP per head	$1,430
GDP	$98.5bn	GDP per head in purchasing	
Av. ann. growth in real		power parity (USA=100)	10.4
GDP 1991–2001	4.2%	Economic freedom index	3.35

Origins of GDP[a]		Components of GDP[b]	
	% of total		% of total
Agriculture	16.4	Private consumption	75.0
Industry, of which:	27.4	Public consumption	10.1
manufacturing	...	Investment	18.6
Services	56.2	Exports	15.8
		Imports	-19.6

Structure of employment[c]

	% of total		% of labour force
Agriculture	30	Unemployed 2001	8.2
Industry	22	Av. ann. rate 1995–2001	9.1
Services	48		

Energy

	m TOE		
Total output	57.6	Net energy imports as %	
Total consumption	46.4	of energy use	-24
Consumption per head, kg oil equivalent	726		

Inflation and finance

Consumer price		av. ann. increase 1996–2001	
inflation 2002	2.7%	Narrow money (M1)	8.5%
Av. ann. inflation 1996–2002	3.3%	Broad money	10.4%
Treasury bill rate, 2002	5.5%		

Exchange rates

	end 2002		December 2002
		Effective rates	1995 = 100
£E per $	4.50	– nominal	...
£E per SDR	6.12	– real	...
£E per euro	4.29		

Trade

Principal exports[b]		**Principal imports**[b]	
	$bn fob		*$bn fob*
Petroleum & products	1.9	Intermediate goods	3.7
Cotton yarn & textiles	0.4	Investment goods	3.0
Metals	0.4	Consumer goods	2.8
Agricultural products	0.1	Fuels	2.4
Total incl. others	**4.1**	Total incl. others	**12.8**

Main export destinations		**Main origins of imports**	
	% of total		*% of total*
Italy	15.0	United States	18.6
United States	14.4	Italy	6.6
United Kingdom	9.3	Germany	6.5
France	4.7	France	4.9

Balance of payments, reserves and debt, $bn

Visible exports fob	7.0	Overall balance	-1.3
Visible imports fob	-14.0	Change in reserves	-0.2
Trade balance	-6.9	Level of reserves	
Invisibles inflows	10.5	end Dec.	13.6
Invisibles outflows	-7.9	No. months of import cover	7.5
Net transfers	4.0	Foreign debt	29.2
Current account balance	-0.4	– as % of GDP	30
– as % of GDP	-0.4	– as % of total exports	140
Capital balance	0.2	Debt service ratio	9

Health and education

Health spending, % of GDP	3.8	Education spending, % of GDP	2.3
Doctors per 1,000 pop.[d]	1.6	Enrolment, %: primary	100
Hospital beds per 1,000 pop.	2.2	secondary	86
Improved-water source access,		tertiary[d]	39
% of pop.	95		

Society

No. of households	14m	Colour TVs per 100 households	47.3
Av. no. per household	4.4	Telephone lines per 100 pop.	10.3
Marriages per 1,000 pop.	8.2	Mobile telephone subscribers	
Divorces per 1,000 pop.	1.6	per 100 pop.	4.3
Cost of living, Dec. 2002		Computers per 100 pop.	1.6
New York = 100	64	Internet hosts per 1,000 pop.	0.2

a Year ending June 30, 2001.
b Year ending June 30, 2002.
c 1998
d 1999

FINLAND

Area	338,145 sq km	Capital	Helsinki
Arable as % of total land	7	Currency	Euro (€)

People

Population	5.2m	Life expectancy:	men	74.4 yrs
Pop. per sq km	15		women	81.5 yrs
Av. ann. growth		Adult literacy		99.0%
in pop. 2000–05	0.18%	Fertility rate (per woman)		1.7
Pop. under 15	18.1%	Urban population		58.5%
Pop. over 60	19.9%			per 1,000 pop.
No. of men per 100 women	95	Crude birth rate		9.7
Human Development Index	93.0	Crude death rate		9.8

The economy

GDP	€135bn	GDP per head	$23,340
GDP	$120.9bn	GDP per head in purchasing	
Av. ann. growth in real		power parity (USA=100)	70.1
GDP 1991–2001	2.0%	Economic freedom index	1.90

Origins of GDP		**Components of GDP**	
	% of total		% of total
Agriculture	3.5	Private consumption	49.0
Industry, of which:	29.9	Public consumption	19.9
manufacturing & mining	26.1	Investment	18.4
Services	70.4	Exports	47.4
		Imports	-34.7

Structure of employment

	% of total		% of labour force
Agriculture	6	Unemployed 2001	9.1
Industry	27	Av. ann. rate 1995–2001	11.8
Services	67		

Energy

	m TOE		
Total output	15.1	Net energy imports as %	
Total consumption	33.1	of energy use	54
Consumption per head,			
kg oil equivalent	6,409		

Inflation and finance

Consumer price		av. ann. increase 1996–2001	
inflation 2002	1.8%	Euro area:	
Av. ann. inflation 1996–2002	1.9%	Narrow money (M1)	7.6%
Money market rate, 2002	3.32%	Broad money	5.8%
		Household saving rate	2.4%

Exchange rates

	end 2002		December 2002
Euro per $	0.95	Effective rates	1995 = 100
Euro per SDR	1.30	– nominal	91.2
		– real	79.3

Trade

Principal exports		Principal imports	
	$bn fob		*$bn cif*
Metals, machinery &		Raw materials	12.6
transport equipment	12.0	Consumer goods	7.9
Electrical & optical equipment	11.8	Capital goods	7.8
Paper & products	9.2	Other goods	4.5
Chemicals	3.2		
Total incl. others	**42.8**	Total incl. others	**32.1**

Main export destinations		Main origins of imports	
	% of total		*% of total*
Germany	12.4	Germany	14.5
United States	9.7	Sweden	10.2
United Kingdom	9.6	Russia	9.6
Sweden	8.4	United States	6.9
Russia	5.9	United Kingdom	6.4
France	4.6	Japan	4.5

Balance of payments, reserves and aid, $bn

Visible exports fob	43.0	Capital balance	-10.7
Visible imports fob	-30.3	Overall balance	0.4
Trade balance	12.6	Change in reserves	0.0
Invisibles inflows	14.3	Level of reserves	
Invisibles outflows	-17.7	end Dec.	8.4
Net transfers	-0.7	No. months of import cover	2.1
Current account balance	8.6	Aid given	0.39
– as % of GDP	7.1	– as % of GDP	0.32

Health and education

Health spending, % of GDP	6.6	Education spending, % of GDP	6.1
Doctors per 1,000 pop.	3.1	Enrolment, %: primary	102
Hospital beds per 1,000 pop.	7.6	secondary	126
Improved-water source access,		tertiary[a]	83
% of pop.	100		

Society

No. of households	2.3m	Colour TVs per 100 households	99.1
Av. no. per household	2.2	Telephone lines per 100 pop.	54.8
Marriages per 1,000 pop.	5.1	Mobile telephone subscribers	
Divorces per 1,000 pop.	2.6	per 100 pop.	77.8
Cost of living, Dec. 2002		Computers per 100 pop.	42.4
New York = 100	93	Internet hosts per 1,000 pop.	219.3

a 2000

FRANCE

Area	543,965 sq km	Capital	Paris
Arable as % of total land	34	Currency	Euro (€)

People

Population	59.5m	Life expectancy: men	75.2 yrs
Pop. per sq km	105	women	82.8 yrs
Av. ann. growth		Adult literacy	99.0%
in pop. 2000–05	0.47%	Fertility rate (per woman)	1.9
Pop. under 15	18.8%	Urban population	75.5%
Pop. over 60	20.5%		per 1,000 pop.
No. of men per 100 women	95	Crude birth rate	12.3
Human Development Index	92.8	Crude death rate	9.3

The economy

GDP	€1,464bn	GDP per head	$22,030
GDP	$1,310bn	GDP per head in purchasing	
Av. ann. growth in real		power parity (USA=100)	70.2
GDP 1991–2001	1.9%	Economic freedom index	2.55

Origins of GDP[a]		Components of GDP	
	% of total		% of total
Agriculture	3.3	Private consumption	55.0
Industry, of which:	25.7	Public consumption	23.3
manufacturing	...	Investment	20.2
Services	71.0	Exports	28.1
		Imports	-26.3

Structure of employment[a]

	% of total		% of labour force
Agriculture	1	Unemployed 2001	9.1
Industry	25	Av. ann. rate 1995–2001	11.8
Services	74		

Energy

	m TOE		
Total output	130.7	Net energy imports as %	
Total consumption	257.1	of energy use	49
Consumption per head,			
kg oil equivalent	4,366		

Inflation and finance

Consumer price		av. ann. increase 1996–2001	
inflation 2002	1.9%	Euro area:	
Av. ann. inflation 1996–2002	1.3%	Narrow money (M1)	7.6%
Interbank rate, 2001	4.26%	Broad money	5.8%
		Household saving rate	11.4%

Exchange rates

	end 2002		December 2002
			1995 = 100
Euro per $	0.95	Effective rates	
Euro per SDR	1.30	– nominal	94.8
		– real	88.8

Trade

Principal exports	$bn fob	Principal imports	$bn cif
Intermediate goods	90.4	Intermediate goods	92.8
Consumer goods	42.8	Capital goods	68.0
Capital goods	42.1	Consumer goods	47.5
Motor vehicles & other		Energy	34.4
transport equipment	39.5	Motor vehicles & other	
Food & drink	25.1	transport equipment	31.6
Total incl. others	**294.8**	Total incl. others	**299.3**

Main export destinations	% of total	Main origins of imports	% of total
Germany	14.7	Germany	16.7
United Kingdom	9.8	Italy	9.1
Spain	9.6	United States	8.9
Italy	8.8	United Kingdom	7.5
United States	8.7	Belgium & Luxembourg	7.0
EU15	61.3	EU15	58.6

Balance of payments, reserves and aid, $bn

Visible exports fob	291.4	Capital balance	-31.5
Visible imports fob	-288.6	Overall balance	-5.5
Trade balance	2.9	Change in reserves	-5.1
Invisibles inflows	160.0	Level of reserves	
Invisibles outflows	-126.7	end Dec.	58.6
Net transfers	-14.8	No. months of import cover	1.7
Current account balance	21.4	Aid given[b]	4.20
– as % of GDP	1.6	– as % of GDP	0.32

Health and education

Health spending, % of GDP[a]	9.5	Education spending, % of GDP	5.8
Doctors per 1,000 pop.	3.3	Enrolment, %: primary	105
Hospital beds per 1,000 pop.	8.1	secondary	108
Improved-water source access,		tertiary	54
% of pop.	...		

Society

No. of households	24.2m	Colour TVs per 100 households	95.9
Av. no. per household	2.5	Telephone lines per 100 pop.	57.4
Marriages per 1,000 pop.	5.2	Mobile telephone subscribers	
Divorces per 1,000 pop.	2.0	per 100 pop.	60.5
Cost of living, Dec. 2002		Computers per 100 pop.	33.7
New York = 100	103	Internet hosts per 1,000 pop.	36.2

a 2000
b Including aid to French overseas territories.

GERMANY

Area	357,868 sq km	Capital	Berlin
Arable as % of total land	33	Currency	Euro (€)

People

Population	82.0m	Life expectancy: men	75.2 yrs
Pop. per sq km	229	women	81.2 yrs
Av. ann. growth		Adult literacy	99.0%
in pop. 2000–05	0.07%	Fertility rate (per woman)	1.4
Pop. under 15	15.6%	Urban population	87.7%
Pop. over 60	23.2%		per 1,000 pop.
No. of men per 100 women	96	Crude birth rate	8.2
Human Development Index	92.5	Crude death rate	10.6

The economy

GDP	€2,063bn	GDP per head	$22,510
GDP	$1,846bn	GDP per head in purchasing	
Av. ann. growth in real		power parity (USA=100)	73.6
GDP 1991–2001	1.6%	Economic freedom index	2.10

Origins of GDP

	% of total
Agriculture	1.2
Industry, of which:	30.2
manufacturing	...
Services	68.6

Components of GDP

	% of total
Private consumption	59.0
Public consumption	19.1
Investment	20.3
Exports	35.0
Imports	-33.1

Structure of employment

	% of total		% of labour force
Agriculture	3	Unemployed 2001	8.0
Industry	33	Av. ann. rate 1995–2001	9.0
Services	65		

Energy

	m TOE		
Total output	134.3	Net energy imports as %	
Total consumption	339.6	of energy use	60
Consumption per head,			
kg oil equivalent	4,131		

Inflation and finance

Consumer price		av. ann. increase 1996–2001	
inflation 2002	1.3%	Euro area:	
Av. ann. inflation 1996–2002	1.5%	Narrow money (M1)	7.6%
Money market rate, 2002	3.28%	Broad money	5.8%
		Household saving rate	10.1%

Exchange rates

	end 2002		December 2002
Euro per $	0.95	Effective rates	1995 = 100
Euro per SDR	1.30	– nominal	90.3
		– real	82.9

Trade

Principal exports	$bn fob	Principal imports	$bn fob
Road vehicles	104.5	Chemicals	50.2
Machinery	81.5	Road vehicles	46.0
Chemicals	71.0	Machinery	34.1
Telecoms technology	31.3	Telecoms technology	31.4
Electricity devices	28.3	Fuels	30.1
Total incl. others	**571.4**	Total incl. others	**486.0**

Main export destinations	% of total	Main origins of imports	% of total
France	11.1	France	9.4
United States	10.6	Netherlands	8.4
United Kingdom	8.4	United States	8.3
Netherlands	6.2	United Kingdom	6.9
Italy	5.1	Italy	6.5
Belgium	4.9	Belgium	5.2
Spain	4.5	Japan	4.1

Balance of payments, reserves and aid, $bn

Visible exports fob	570.0	Capital balance	-27.1
Visible imports fob	-481.4	Overall balance	-5.5
Trade balance	88.5	Change in reserves	-5.5
Invisibles inflows	192.8	Level of reserves	
Invisibles outflows	-255.1	end Dec.	82.0
Net transfers	-23.8	No. months of import cover	1.3
Current account balance	2.4	Aid given	4.99
– as % of GDP	0.1	– as % of GDP	0.27

Health and education

Health spending, % of GDP	10.7	Education spending, % of GDP	4.6
Doctors per 1,000 pop.	3.6	Enrolment, %: primary	104
Hospital beds per 1,000 pop.[a]	9.1	secondary	99
Improved-water source access,		tertiary[a]	46
% of pop.	...		

Society

No. of households	38.1m	Colour TVs per 100 households	97.1
Av. no. per household	2.2	Telephone lines per 100 pop.	63.5
Marriages per 1,000 pop.	5.2	Mobile telephone subscribers	
Divorces per 1,000 pop.	2.3	per 100 pop.	68.3
Cost of living, Dec. 2002		Computers per 100 pop.	33.6
New York = 100	87	Internet hosts per 1,000 pop.	35.2

a 2000

GREECE

Area	131,957 sq km	Capital	Athens
Arable as % of total land	21	Currency	Euro (€)

People

Population	10.6m	Life expectancy: men	75.7 yrs
Pop. per sq km	80	women	80.9 yrs
Av. ann. growth		Adult literacy	97.3%
in pop. 2000–05	0.14%	Fertility rate (per woman)	1.3
Pop. under 15	15.1%	Urban population	60.3%
Pop. over 60	23.4%		per 1,000 pop.
No. of men per 100 women	97	Crude birth rate	8.9
Human Development Index	88.5	Crude death rate	10.5

The economy

GDP	€131bn	GDP per head	$11,030
GDP	$117.2bn	GDP per head in purchasing	
Av. ann. growth in real		power parity (USA=100)	51.1
GDP 1991–2001	2.5%	Economic freedom index	2.80

Origins of GDP[a]		Components of GDP[a]	
	% of total		% of total
Agriculture	8.5	Private consumption	69.1
Industry, of which:	24.4	Public consumption	14.9
manufacturing & mining	13.4	Investment	23.0
Services	67.1	Exports	19.2
		Imports	-26.8

Structure of employment

	% of total		% of labour force
Agriculture	16	Unemployed 2001	11.0
Industry	23	Av. ann. rate 1995–2001	10.7
Services	61		

Energy

	m TOE		
Total output	10.0	Net energy imports as %	
Total consumption	27.8	of energy use	64
Consumption per head,			
kg oil equivalent	2,635		

Inflation and finance

Consumer price		*av. ann. increase 1996–2001*	
inflation 2002	3.6%	Euro area:	
Av. ann. inflation 1996–2002	3.8%	Narrow money (M1)	7.6%
Treasury bill rate, 2002	3.50%	Broad money	5.8%

Exchange rates

	end 2002		December 2002
Euro per $	0.95	Effective rates	1995 = 100
Euro per SDR	1.30	– nominal	85.5
		– real	106.0

Trade[b]

Principal exports	$bn fob	Principal imports	$bn cif
Food & beverages	1.5	Machinery	5.1
Petroleum products	0.9	Transport equipment	4.2
Chemicals	0.8	Chemicals	3.3
Non-ferrous metals	0.7	Fuels	1.4
Textiles	0.7	Iron & steel	1.0
Total incl. others	**11.6**	Total incl. others	**26.1**

Main export destinations	% of total	Main origins of imports	% of total
Germany	15.9	Italy	15.6
Italy	13.5	Germany	15.0
United Kingdom	6.4	France	9.2
United States	5.7	Netherlands	6.4
EU15	51.6	EU15	66.2

Balance of payments, reserves and debt, $bn

Visible exports fob	10.6	Overall balance	-5.7
Visible imports fob	-29.7	Change in reserves	-8.4
Trade balance	-19.1	Level of reserves	
Invisibles inflows	20.3	end Dec.	6.2
Invisibles outflows	-15.2	No. months of import cover	1.7
Net transfers	3.6	Aid given	0.20
Current account balance	-9.4	– as % of GDP	0.17
– as % of GDP	-8.0		
Capital balance	2.7		

Health and education

Health spending, % of GDP[a]	8.3	Education spending, % of GDP	3.8
Doctors per 1,000 pop.	4.6	Enrolment, %: primary	99
Hospital beds per 1,000 pop.	4.9	secondary	98
Improved-water source access,		tertiary[a]	50
% of pop.	...		

Society

No. of households	3.5m	Colour TVs per 100 households	91.2
Av. no. per household	2.8	Telephone lines per 100 pop.	52.9
Marriages per 1,000 pop.	6.4	Mobile telephone subscribers	
Divorces per 1,000 pop.	0.9	per 100 pop.	75.1
Cost of living, Dec. 2002		Computers per 100 pop.	8.1
New York = 100	72	Internet hosts per 1,000 pop.	19.1

a 2000
b 1999

HONG KONG

Area	1,075 sq km	Capital	Victoria
Arable as % of total land	5	Currency	Hong Kong dollar (HK$)

People

Population	7.0m	Life expectancy: men	77.3 yrs
Pop. per sq km	6,512	women	82.8 yrs
Av. ann. growth		Adult literacy	93.5%
in pop. 2000–05	1.07%	Fertility rate (per woman)	1.0
Pop. under 15	16.6%	Urban population	100.0%
Pop. over 60	14.4%		per 1,000 pop.
No. of men per 100 women	96	Crude birth rate	9.5
Human Development Index	88.8	Crude death rate	5.9

The economy

GDP	HK$1,263bn	GDP per head	$23,260
GDP	$161.9bn	GDP per head in purchasing	
Av. ann. growth in real		power parity (USA=100)	74.6
GDP 1991–2001	4.0%	Economic freedom index	1.45

Origins of GDP		Components of GDP	
	% of total		% of total
Agriculture	0.1	Private consumption	58.3
Manufacturing	5.5	Public consumption	10.2
Other	94.4	Investment	26.5
		Exports	141.0
		Imports	-135.9

Structure of employment

	% of total		% of labour force
Agriculture	0	Unemployed 2001	5.1
Industry	16	Av. ann. rate 1995–2001	4.2
Services	84		

Energy

	m TOE		
Total output	0.05	Net energy imports as %	
Total consumption	15.5	of energy use	100
Consumption per head,			
kg oil equivalent	2,319		

Inflation and finance

Consumer price		av. ann. increase 1996–2001	
inflation 2002	-3.0%	Narrow money (M1)	3.9%
Av. ann. inflation 1996–2002	-0.7%	Broad money	7.4%
Money market rate, 2002	1.50%		

Exchange rates

	end 2002		December 2002
HK$ per $	7.80	Effective rates	1995 = 100
HK$ per SDR	10.61	– nominal	...
HK$ per euro	8.18	– real	...

Trade

Principal exports[a]	$bn fob	Principal imports	$bn cif
Clothing	9.3	Electrical machinery & appliances	33.7
Electrical machinery & apparatus	2.6	Telecommunications & sound equipment	20.3
Textiles	1.1	Office machinery	19.0
Jewellery	1.0	Clothing	16.1
Office machinery	0.6		
Total incl. others	**19.7**	Total incl. others	**201.4**

Main export destinations[b]	% of total	Main origins of imports	% of total
China	36.9	China	43.4
United States	22.3	Japan	11.3
Japan	5.9	Taiwan	6.9
United Kingdom	3.7	United States	6.7

Balance of payments, reserves and debt, $bn

Visible exports fob	190.9	Overall balance	4.7
Visible imports cif	-199.3	Change in reserves	3.6
Trade balance	-8.3	Level of reserves	
Services inflows	89.4	end Dec.	111.2
Services outflows	-67.7	No. months of import cover	5.0
Net transfers	-1.7	Foreign debt	45.9
Current account balance	11.7	– as % of GDP	28
– as % of GDP	7.2	– as % of total exports	16
Capital balance	-6.3	Debt service ratio	3

Health and education

Health spending, % of GDP	7.4	Education spending, % of GDP[c]	2.9
Doctors per 1,000 pop.	1.4	Enrolment, %: primary[c]	94
Hospital beds per 1,000 pop.	5.0	secondary[c]	73
Improved-water source access, % of pop.	98	tertiary[c]	23

Society

No. of households	2.1m	Colour TVs per 100 households	99.2
Av. no. per household	3.3	Telephone lines per 100 pop.	58.1
Marriages per 1,000 pop.	4.5	Mobile telephone subscribers per 100 pop.	84.4
Divorces per 1,000 pop.	1.8		
Cost of living, Dec. 2002		Computers per 100 pop.	38.5
New York = 100	115	Internet hosts per 1,000 pop.	56.8

a Domestic.
b Including re-exports.
c 1997
Note: Hong Kong became a Special Administrative Region of China from July 1 1997.

HUNGARY

Area	93,030 sq km	Capital	Budapest
Arable as % of total land	50	Currency	Forint (Ft)

People

Population	9.9m	Life expectancy:	men	67.7 yrs
Pop. per sq km	106		women	76.0 yrs
Av. ann. growth		Adult literacy		99.3%
in pop. 2000–05	-0.46%	Fertility rate (per woman)		1.2
Pop. under 15	17.0%	Urban population		64.8%
Pop. over 60	19.7%			per 1,000 pop.
No. of men per 100 women	91	Crude birth rate		8.8
Human Development Index	83.5	Crude death rate		13.5

The economy

GDP	Ft14,876bn	GDP per head	$5,240
GDP	$51.9bn	GDP per head in purchasing	
Av. ann. growth in real		power parity (USA=100)	35.0
GDP 1991–2001	1.0%	Economic freedom index	2.65

Origins of GDP[a]

	% of total
Agriculture	4.1
Industry, of which:	33.8
manufacturing	...
Services	62.1

Components of GDP

	% of total
Private consumption	63.9
Public consumption	11.0
Investment	27.2
Exports	60.5
Imports	-62.6

Structure of employment

	% of total		% of labour force
Agriculture	6	Unemployed 2001	5.7
Industry	35	Av. ann. rate 1995–2001	8.0
Services	59		

Energy

	m TOE		
Total output	11.1	Net energy imports as %	
Total consumption	24.8	of energy use	55
Consumption per head,			
kg oil equivalent	2,448		

Inflation and finance

		av. ann. increase 1996–2001	
Consumer price			
inflation 2002	5.3%	Narrow money (M1)	17.5%
Av. ann. inflation 1996–2002	11.1%	Broad money	16.0%
Treasury bill rate, 2002	8.9%		

Exchange rates

	end 2002		December 2002
Ft per $	225.2	Effective rates	1995 = 100
Ft per SDR	306.1	– nominal	72.3
Ft per euro	214.7	– real	139.1

Trade

Principal exports		Principal imports	
	$bn fob		*$bn cif*
Machinery & transport equipment	17.6	Machinery & transport equipment	17.4
Other manufactures	9.5	Other manufactures	11.9
Food & beverages	2.3	Fuels	2.8
Raw materials	0.6	Food & food products	1.0
Total incl. others	**30.5**	Total incl. others	**33.7**

Main export destinations		Main origins of imports	
	% of total		*% of total*
Germany	34.9	Germany	26.4
Austria	8.7	Italy	8.3
Italy	5.9	Austria	7.9
Netherlands	5.6	Russia	6.8

Balance of payments, reserves and debt, $bn

Visible exports fob	28.1	Overall balance	-0.1
Visible imports fob	-30.1	Change in reserves	-0.5
Trade balance	-2.0	Level of reserves	
Invisibles inflows	8.8	end Dec.	10.8
Invisibles outflows	-8.1	No. months of import cover	7.3
Net transfers	0.3	Foreign debt	30.3
Current account balance	-1.1	– as % of GDP	64
– as % of GDP	-2.1	– as % of total exports	93
Capital balance	0.9	Debt service ratio	42

Health and education

Health spending, % of GDP	6.8	Education spending, % of GDP	5.0
Doctors per 1,000 pop.[a]	3.2	Enrolment, %: primary	102
Hospital beds per 1,000 pop.	8.2	secondary	99
Improved-water source access, % of pop.	99	tertiary	40

Society

No. of households	3.7m	Colour TVs per 100 households	90.5
Av. no. per household	2.4	Telephone lines per 100 pop.	37.4
Marriages per 1,000 pop.	4.8	Mobile telephone subscribers	
Divorces per 1,000 pop.	2.5	per 100 pop.	49.8
Cost of living, Dec. 2002		Computers per 100 pop.	10.0
New York = 100	58	Internet hosts per 1,000 pop.	25.6

a 2000

INDIA

Area	3,287,263 sq km	Capital	New Delhi
Arable as % of total land	54	Currency	Indian rupee (Rs)

People

Population	1,025.1m	Life expectancy: men	63.2 yrs
Pop. per sq km	312	women	64.6 yrs
Av. ann. growth		Adult literacy	58.0%
in pop. 2000–05	1.51%	Fertility rate (per woman)	3.0
Pop. under 15	34.1%	Urban population	27.9%
Pop. over 60	7.5%		per 1,000 pop.
No. of men per 100 women	106	Crude birth rate	23.8
Human Development Index	57.7	Crude death rate	8.5

The economy

GDP	Rs22,778bn	GDP per head	$470
GDP	$477.3bn	GDP per head in purchasing	
Av. ann. growth in real		power parity (USA=100)	8.2
GDP 1991–2001	5.4%	Economic freedom index	3.50

Origins of GDP[a]		Components of GDP[a]	
	% of total		% of total
Agriculture	24.3	Private consumption	66.0
Industry, of which:	27.7	Public consumption	12.8
manufacturing	17.6	Investment	23.0
Services	48.0	Exports	14.1
		Imports	-14.9

Structure of employment

	% of total		% of labour force
Agriculture	67	Unemployed 2001	11.6
Industry	12	Av. ann. rate 1995–2001	11.6
Services	21		

Energy

	m TOE		
Total output	421.6	Net energy imports as %	
Total consumption	501.9	of energy use	16
Consumption per head,			
kg oil equivalent	494		

Inflation and finance

Consumer price		av. ann. increase 1996–2001	
inflation 2002	4.3%	Narrow money (M1)	12.3%
Av. ann. inflation 1996–2002	6.1%	Broad money	16.5%
Bank rate, 2002	6.25%		

Exchange rates

	end 2002		December 2002
			1995 = 100
Rs per $	48.03	Effective rates	
Rs per SDR	62.30	– nominal	...
Rs per euro	45.80	– real	...

Trade

Principal exports[a]		**Principal imports**[a]	
	$bn fob		*$bn cif*
Textiles	10.9	Petroleum & products	15.7
Gems & jewellery	7.4	Capital goods	5.5
Engineering goods	7.0	Gems	4.8
Chemicals	5.0	Machine tools	3.7
Total incl. others	**44.0**	Total incl. others	**50.1**

Main export destinations		**Main origins of imports**	
	% of total		*% of total*
United States	21.7	United States	8.3
Germany	5.7	Belgium	6.2
United Kingdom	5.7	Singapore	6.0
Hong Kong	4.9	United Kingdom	5.7
Japan	4.9	Saudi Arabia	5.1

Balance of payments, reserves and debt, $bn

Visible exports fob	44.6	Overall balance	8.7
Visible imports fob	-57.4	Change in reserves	8.0
Trade balance	-12.7	Level of reserves	
Invisibles inflows	23.6	end Dec.	49.1
Invisibles outflows	-23.2	No. months of import cover	7.3
Net transfers	12.3	Foreign debt	97.3
Current account balance	-0.1	– as % of GDP	21
– as % of GDP	-0.0	– as % of total exports	131
Capital balance	8.3	Debt service ratio	12

Health and education

Health spending, % of GDP	5.9	Education spending, % of GDP	4.1
Doctors per 1,000 pop.	0.5	Enrolment, %: primary	102
Hospital beds per 1,000 pop.	1.4	secondary[b]	49
Improved-water source access,		tertiary[b]	11
% of pop.	88		

Society

No. of households	171.3m	Colour TVs per 100 households	31.1
Av. no. per household	5.4	Telephone lines per 100 pop.	3.4
Marriages per 1,000 pop.	...	Mobile telephone subscribers	
Divorces per 1,000 pop.	...	per 100 pop.	0.6
Cost of living, Dec. 2002		Computers per 100 pop.	0.6
New York = 100	41	Internet hosts per 1,000 pop.	0.7

a Year ending March 31, 2001.
b 2000

INDONESIA

Area	1,904,443 sq km	Capital	Jakarta
Arable as % of total land	11	Currency	Rupiah (Rp)

People

Population	214.8m	Life expectancy: men	63.2 yrs
Pop. per sq km	113	women	68.8 yrs
Av. ann. growth		Adult literacy	87.4%
in pop. 2000–05	1.26%	Fertility rate (per woman)	2.4
Pop. under 15	30.9%	Urban population	42.1%
Pop. over 60	7.6%		per 1,000 pop.
No. of men per 100 women	100	Crude birth rate	20.0
Human Development Index	68.4	Crude death rate	7.3

The economy

GDP	Rp1,491trn	GDP per head	$680
GDP	$145.3bn	GDP per head in purchasing	
Av. ann. growth in real		power parity (USA=100)	8.3
GDP 1991–2001	4.1%	Economic freedom index	3.30

Origins of GDP[a]		Components of GDP	
	% of total		% of total
Agriculture	17.0	Private consumption	67.4
Industry, of which:	47.1	Public consumption	7.4
manufacturing	26.2	Investment	16.6
Services	35.9	Exports	41.1
		Imports	-32.6

Structure of employment

	% of total		% of total
Agriculture	45	Unemployed 2001	6.7
Industry	18	Av. ann. rate 1995–2001	5.4
Services	37		

Energy

	m TOE		
Total output	229.5	Net energy imports as %	
Total consumption	145.6	of energy use	-58
Consumption per head,			
kg oil equivalent	706		

Inflation and finance

		av. ann. increase 1996–2001	
Consumer price			
inflation 2002	11.9%	Narrow money (M1)	26.3%
Av. ann. inflation 1996–2002	17.4%	Broad money	24.7%
Money market rate, 2002	13.54%		

Exchange rates

	end 2002		December 2002
Rp per $	8,940	Effective rates	1995 = 100
Rp per SDR	12,154	– nominal	…
Rp per euro	8,525	– real	…

Trade

Principal exports		Principal imports	
	$bn fob		*$bn cif*
Garments & textiles	7.3	Raw materials	23.9
Petroleum & products	6.8	Capital goods	4.8
Natural gas	5.3	Consumer goods	2.3
Total incl. others	**52.1**	Total incl. others	**31.0**

Main export destinations		Main origins of imports	
	% of total		*% of total*
Japan	25.7	Japan	22.5
United States	17.6	Singapore	12.2
Singapore	12.6	South Korea	11.7
South Korea	7.2	United States	8.9

Balance of payments, reserves and debt, $bn

Visible exports fob	57.4	Overall balance	-0.0
Visible imports fob	-34.7	Change in reserves	-1.2
Trade balance	22.7	Level of reserves	
Invisibles inflows	7.5	end Dec.	28.1
Invisibles outflows	-24.8	No. months of import cover	5.7
Net transfers	1.5	Foreign debt	135.7
Current account balance	6.9	– as % of GDP	99
– as % of GDP	4.7	– as % of total exports	205
Capital balance	-7.6	Debt service ratio	23

Health and education

Health spending, % of GDP	1.4	Education spending, % of GDP	1.4
Doctors per 1,000 pop.	0.1	Enrolment, %: primary	110
Hospital beds per 1,000 pop.	0.6	secondary	57
Improved-water source access,		tertiary	15
% of pop.	76		

Society

No. of households	53.2m	Colour TVs per 100 households	47.2
Av. no. per household	4.4	Telephone lines per 100 pop.	3.7
Marriages per 1,000 pop.	...	Mobile telephone subscribers	
Divorces per 1,000 pop.	...	per 100 pop.	2.5
Cost of living, Dec. 2002		Computers per 100 pop.	1.1
New York = 100	68	Internet hosts per 1,000 pop.	0.3

a 2000

IRAN

Area	1,648,000 sq km	Capital	Tehran
Arable as % of total land	9	Currency	Rial (IR)

People

Population	71.4m	Life expectancy: men	68.9 yrs
Pop. per sq km	43	women	71.9 yrs
Av. ann. growth		Adult literacy	77.3%
in pop. 2000–05	1.24%	Fertility rate (per woman)	2.3
Pop. under 15	35.2%	Urban population	64.7%
Pop. over 60	6.4%		per 1,000 pop.
No. of men per 100 women	103	Crude birth rate	22.1
Human Development Index	72.1	Crude death rate	5.3

The economy

GDP	IR664trn	GDP per head	$1,600
GDP	$114.1bn	GDP per head in purchasing	
Av. ann. growth in real		power parity (USA=100)	17.3
GDP 1991–2001	4.2%	Economic freedom index	4.15

Origins of GDP[a]		Components of GDP[a]	
	% of total		% of total
Agriculture	12.9	Private consumption	58.0
Industry, of which:	40.1	Public consumption	10.1
manufacturing	...	Investment	23.8
Services	47.0	Net exports	8.1

Structure of employment[b]

	% of total		% of labour force
Agriculture	23	Unemployed 2001	...
Industry	31	Av. ann. rate 1995–2001	...
Services	45		

Energy

	m TOE		
Total output	242.1	Net energy imports as %	
Total consumption	145.6	of energy use	-115
Consumption per head,			
kg oil equivalent	1,771		

Inflation and finance

Consumer price		av. ann. increase 1996–2001	
inflation 2002	14.3%	Narrow money (M1)	22.3%
Av. ann. inflation 1996–2002	16.2%	Broad money	23.1%

Exchange rates

	end 2002		December 2002
IR per $	7,952	Effective rates	1995 = 100
IR per SDR	10,811	– nominal	84.2
IR per euro	7,583	– real	204.5

Trade

Principal exports[c]

	$bn fob
Oil & gas	16.3
Industrial goods	1.8
Agricultural goods	1.5
Total incl. others	**21.0**

Principal imports[d]

	$bn cif
Transport, machinery & tools	6.3
Chemicals & pharmaceuticals	1.8
Food & animals	1.6
Total incl. others	**14.3**

Main export destinations[e]

	% of total
Japan	17.7
Italy	7.9
France	7.5
United Arab Emirates	7.5
China	5.9

Main origins of imports[e]

	% of total
Germany	9.8
Japan	9.4
Italy	6.2
United Arab Emirates	6.2
China	4.9

Balance of payments[f], reserves and debt, $bn

Visible exports fob	23.7	Overall balance[a]	1.1
Visible imports fob	-18.1	Change in reserves	...
Trade balance	5.6	Level of reserves	
Invisibles inflows[a]	1.8	end Dec.	...
Invisibles outflows[a]	-2.9	No. months of import cover	...
Net transfers[a]	0.5	Foreign debt	7.5
Current account balance	5.3	– as % of GDP	7
– as % of GDP	4.6	– as % of total exports	29
Capital balance[a]	-10.2	Debt service ratio	5

Health and education

Health spending, % of GDP[f]	5.5	Education spending, % of GDP	4.4
Doctors per 1,000 pop.[d]	0.9	Enrolment, %: primary	86
Hospital beds per 1,000 pop.	1.1	secondary	7
Improved-water source access,		tertiary	10
% of pop.	95		

Society

No. of households	12.6m	Colour TVs per 100 households	...
Av. no. per household	5.4	Telephone lines per 100 pop.	15.5
Marriages per 1,000 pop.	8.4	Mobile telephone subscribers	
Divorces per 1,000 pop.	0.7	per 100 pop.	2.3
Cost of living, Dec. 2002		Computers per 100 pop.	7.0
New York = 100	31	Internet hosts per 1,000 pop.	...

a Iranian year ending March 20, 2001.
b 1996
c 1999
d 1998
e 2000
f Iranian year ending March 20, 2002.

IRELAND

Area	70,282 sq km	Capital	Dublin
Arable as % of total land	15	Currency	Euro (€)

People

Population	3.8m	Life expectancy: men	74.4 yrs
Pop. per sq km	54	women	79.6 yrs
Av. ann. growth		Adult literacy	99.0%
in pop. 2000–05	1.12%	Fertility rate (per woman)	1.9
Pop. under 15	21.5%	Urban population	59.3%
Pop. over 60	15.2%		*per 1,000 pop.*
No. of men per 100 women	99	Crude birth rate	15.3
Human Development Index	92.5	Crude death rate	8.3

The economy

GDP	€115.4bn	GDP per head	$26,890
GDP	$103.3bn	GDP per head in purchasing	
Av. ann. growth in real		power parity (USA=100)	79.3
GDP 1991–2001	7.1%	Economic freedom index	1.75

Origins of GDP		**Components of GDP**	
	% of total		*% of total*
Agriculture	5.0	Private consumption	48.2
Industry, of which:	46.1	Public consumption	13.4
manufacturing	...	Investment	23.5
Services	48.9	Exports	98.2
		Imports	-83.4

Structure of employment

	% of total		*% of labour force*
Agriculture	7	Unemployed 2001	3.9
Industry	29	Av. ann. rate 1995–2001	8.0
Services	64		

Energy

	m TOE		
Total output	2.2	Net energy imports as %	
Total consumption	14.6	of energy use	85
Consumption per head,			
kg oil equivalent	3,854		

Inflation and finance

Consumer price		*av. ann. increase 1996–2001*	
inflation 2002	4.7%	Euro area:	
Av. ann. inflation 1996–2002	3.3%	Narrow money (M1)	7.6%
Money market rate, 2002	2.88%	Broad money	5.8%

Exchange rates

	end 2002		*December 2002*
			1995 = 100
Euro per $	0.95	Effective rates	
Euro per SDR	1.30	– nominal	92.8
		– real	...

Trade

Principal exports		Principal imports	
	$bn fob		*$bn cif*
Machinery & transport		Machinery & transport	
equipment	33.9	equipment	26.9
Chemicals	28.8	Chemicals	5.7
Foodstuffs & tobacco	5.2	Manufactured materials	3.9
Manufactured materials	1.8	Food	2.8
		Fuels	2.0
Total incl. others	**83.0**	Total incl. others	**51.3**

Main export destinations		Main origins of imports	
	% of total		*% of total*
United Kingdom	23.9	United Kingdom	35.4
United States	16.9	United States	15.2
Germany	12.6	Germany	6.2
France	6.0	France	4.9
Netherlands	4.6	Japan	3.5
Italy	3.6	Netherlands	3.4
EU15	61.6	EU15	59.0

Balance of payments, reserves and aid, $bn

Visible exports fob	78.4	Capital balance	0.6
Visible imports fob	-48.4	Overall balance	0.4
Trade balance	30.0	Change in reserves	0.2
Invisibles inflows	48.9	Level of reserves	
Invisibles outflows	-80.4	end Dec.	5.6
Net transfers	0.5	No. months of import cover	0.5
Current account balance	-1.0	Aid given	0.29
– as % of GDP	-1.0	– as % of GDP	0.33

Health and education

Health spending, % of GDP	6.7	Education spending, % of GDP	4.4
Doctors per 1,000 pop.	2.4	Enrolment, %: primary	119
Hospital beds per 1,000 pop.	3.4	secondary[a]	109
Improved-water source access,		tertiary	48
% of pop.	...		

Society

No. of households	1.2m	Colour TVs per 100 households	99.2
Av. no. per household	3.1	Telephone lines per 100 pop.	48.5
Marriages per 1,000 pop.	5.1	Mobile telephone subscribers	
Divorces per 1,000 pop.	...	per 100 pop.	72.9
Cost of living, Dec. 2002		Computers per 100 pop.	39.1
New York = 100	85	Internet hosts per 1,000 pop.	25.6

a 2000

ISRAEL

Area	20,770 sq km	Capital	Jerusalem
Arable as % of total land	16	Currency	New Shekel (NIS)

People

Population	6.2m	Life expectancy: men		77.1 yrs
Pop. per sq km	299		women	81.0 yrs
Av. ann. growth		Adult literacy		94.8%
in pop. 2000–05	2.02%	Fertility rate (per woman)		2.7
Pop. under 15	28.3%	Urban population		91.8%
Pop. over 60	13.1%			per 1,000 pop.
No. of men per 100 women	98	Crude birth rate		19.8
Human Development Index	89.6	Crude death rate		6.0

The economy

GDP	NIS456bn	GDP per head	$17,550
GDP	$108.3bn	GDP per head in purchasing	
Av. ann. growth in real		power parity (USA=100)	57.3
GDP 1991–2001	4.6%	Economic freedom index	2.45

Origins of GDP

	% of total
Agriculture	2.6
Industry, of which:	36.2
manufacturing	25.7
Services	61.2

Components of GDP

	% of total
Private consumption	57.8
Public consumption	29.2
Investment	18.7
Exports	35.5
Imports	-43.5

Structure of employment

	% of total		% of labour force
Agriculture	2	Unemployed 2001	9.3
Industry	23	Av. ann. rate 1995–2001	8.1
Services	75		

Energy

	m TOE		
Total output	0.7	Net energy imports as %	
Total consumption	20.2	of energy use	97
Consumption per head,			
kg oil equivalent	3,241		

Inflation and finance

			av. ann. increase 1996–2001
Consumer price			
inflation 2002	5.6%	Narrow money (M1)	13.4%
Av. ann. inflation 1996–2002	4.5%	Broad money	13.4%
Treasury bill rate, 2002	7.4%		

Exchange rates

	end 2002		December 2002
			1995 = 100
NIS per $	4.74	Effective rates	
NIS per SDR	6.44	– nominal	76.9
NIS per euro	4.52	– real	99.4

Trade

Principal exports		Principal imports	
	$bn fob		*$bn fob*
Diamonds	8.5	Diamonds	7.2
Communications, medical &		Investment goods	5.9
scientific equipment	4.3	Machinery & equipment	4.5
Chemicals	4.0	Fuel	3.1
		Chemicals	2.1
Total incl. others	**27.7**	Total incl. others	**30.9**

Main export destinations		Main origins of imports	
	% of total		*% of total*
United States	42.8	United States	23.5
Belgium	7.4	Belgium	10.2
Germany	6.0	Germany	7.9
United Kingdom	4.8	United Kingdom	6.7
Hong Kong	3.6	Switzerland	6.0

Balance of payments, reserves and debt, $bn

Visible exports fob	27.7	Overall balance	0.2
Visible imports fob	-30.9	Change in reserves	0.1
Trade balance	-3.3	Level of reserves	
Invisibles inflows	15.5	end Dec.	23.3
Invisibles outflows	-20.5	No. months of import cover	5.5
Net transfers	6.4	Foreign debt	40.2
Current account balance	-1.9	– as % of GDP	37
– as % of GDP	-1.7	– as % of total exports	145
Capital balance	0.6	Debt service ratio	17

Health and education

Health spending, % of GDP	9.4	Education spending, % of GDP	7.3
Doctors per 1,000 pop.[a]	3.9	Enrolment, %: primary	114
Hospital beds per 1,000 pop.	6.3	secondary	93
Improved-water source access,		tertiary	53
% of pop.	...		

Society

No. of households	1.8m	Colour TVs per 100 households	95.8
Av. no. per household	3.5	Telephone lines per 100 pop.	47.6
Marriages per 1,000 pop.	6.6	Mobile telephone subscribers	
Divorces per 1,000 pop.	2.0	per 100 pop.	80.8
Cost of living, Dec. 2002		Computers per 100 pop.	24.6
New York = 100	85	Internet hosts per 1,000 pop.	37.1

a 2000

ITALY

Area	301,245 sq km	Capital	Rome
Arable as % of total land	27	Currency	Euro (€)

People

Population	57.5m	Life expectancy: men	75.5 yrs
Pop. per sq km	191	women	81.9 yrs
Av. ann. growth		Adult literacy	98.5%
in pop. 2000–05	-0.10%	Fertility rate (per woman)	1.2
Pop. under 15	14.3%	Urban population	67.1%
Pop. over 60	24.1%		per 1,000 pop.
No. of men per 100 women	94	Crude birth rate	8.6
Human Development Index	91.3	Crude death rate	10.9

The economy

GDP	€1,217trn	GDP per head	$18,930
GDP	$1,089bn	GDP per head in purchasing	
Av. ann. growth in real		power parity (USA=100)	71.6
GDP 1991–2001	1.6%	Economic freedom index	2.35

Origins of GDP		Components of GDP	
	% of total		% of total
Agriculture	2.4	Private consumption	59.7
Industry, of which:	30.0	Public consumption	18.9
manufacturing	...	Investment	19.8
Services	67.6	Exports	28.3
		Imports	-26.7

Structure of employment

	% of total		% of labour force
Agriculture	5	Unemployed 2001	10.3
Industry	32	Av. ann. rate 1995–2001	11.2
Services	63		

Energy

	m TOE		
Total output	26.9	Net energy imports as %	
Total consumption	171.6	of energy use	84
Consumption per head,			
kg oil equivalent	2,974		

Inflation and finance

Consumer price		av. ann. increase 1996–2001	
inflation 2002	2.5%	Euro area:	
Av. ann. inflation 1996–2002	2.2%	Narrow money (M1)	7.6%
Money market rate, 2002	3.32%	Broad money	5.8%
		Household saving rate	13.2%

Exchange rates

	end 2002		December 2002
		Effective rates	1995 = 100
Euro per $	0.95	Effective rates	
Euro per SDR	1.30	– nominal	106.7
		– real	113.0

Trade

Principal exports		Principal imports	
	$bn fob		*$bn cif*
Engineering products	91.7	Engineering products	73.8
Textiles & clothing	38.5	Transport equipment	33.4
Transport equipment	26.4	Chemicals	30.2
Chemicals	22.9	Energy products	25.7
Food, drink & tobacco	12.4	Textiles & clothing	18.0
Total incl. others	**244.2**	Total incl. others	**236.1**

Main export destinations		Main origins of imports	
	% of total		*% of total*
Germany	14.5	Germany	17.7
France	12.2	France	11.1
United States	9.7	Netherlands	6.2
United Kingdom	6.7	United Kingdom	5.1
Spain	6.1	United States	4.9
EU15	53.8	EU15	56.5

Balance of payments, reserves and aid, $bn

Visible exports fob	242.4	Capital balance	-2.4
Visible imports fob	-226.6	Overall balance	-0.6
Trade balance	15.9	Change in reserves	-1.0
Invisibles inflows	96.2	Level of reserves	
Invisibles outflows	-106.3	end Dec.	46.2
Net transfers	-6.0	No. months of import cover	1.7
Current account balance	-0.2	Aid given	1.63
– as % of GDP	-0.0	– as % of GDP	0.15

Health and education

Health spending, % of GDP	8.3	Education spending, % of GDP	4.6
Doctors per 1,000 pop.	5.9	Enrolment, %: primary	101
Hospital beds per 1,000 pop.	5.5	secondary	96
Improved-water source access,		tertiary	50
% of pop.	...		

Society

No. of households	22.3m	Colour TVs per 100 households	99.2
Av. no. per household	2.6	Telephone lines per 100 pop.	47.1
Marriages per 1,000 pop.	4.8	Mobile telephone subscribers	
Divorces per 1,000 pop.	0.8	per 100 pop.	83.9
Cost of living, Dec. 2002		Computers per 100 pop.	19.5
New York = 100	79	Internet hosts per 1,000 pop.	67.2

JAPAN

Area	377,727 sq km	Capital	Tokyo
Arable as % of total land	12	Currency	Yen (¥)

People

Population	127.3m	Life expectancy:	men	77.9 yrs
Pop. per sq km	337		women	85.1 yrs
Av. ann. growth		Adult literacy		99.0%
in pop. 2000–05	0.14%	Fertility rate (per woman)		1.3
Pop. under 15	14.6%	Urban population		78.9%
Pop. over 60	23.3%			per 1,000 pop.
No. of men per 100 women	96	Crude birth rate		9.2
Human Development Index	93.3	Crude death rate		8.2

The economy

GDP	¥503trn	GDP per head	$32,520
GDP	$4,141bn	GDP per head in purchasing	
Av. ann. growth in real		power parity (USA=100)	74.5
GDP 1991–2001	1.2%	Economic freedom index	2.50

Origins of GDP		Components of GDP	
	% of total		% of total
Agriculture	1.4	Private consumption	55.2
Industry, of which:	30.4	Public consumption	16.8
manufacturing	20.5	Investment	26.3
Services	68.2	Exports	10.5
		Imports	-8.6

Structure of employment

	% of total		% of labour force
Agriculture	5	Unemployed 2001	5.0
Industry	31	Av. ann. rate 1995–2001	4.1
Services	64		

Energy

	m TOE		
Total output	105.5	Net energy imports as %	
Total consumption	524.7	of energy use	80
Consumption per head,			
kg oil equivalent	4,136		

Inflation and finance

Consumer price		av. ann. increase 1996–2001	
inflation 2002	-1.0%	Narrow money (M1)	8.4%
Av. ann. inflation 1996–2002	-0.1%	Broad money	2.8%
Money market rate, 2002	0.01%	Household saving rate	10.7%

Exchange rates

	end 2002		December 2002
¥ per $	119.9	Effective rates	1995 = 100
¥ per SDR	163.0	– nominal	84.5
¥ per euro	114.3	– real	73.5

Trade

Principal exports

	$bn fob
Electrical machinery	94.5
Transport equipment	91.3
Non-electrical machinery	83.9
Chemicals	30.7
Metals	23.7
Total incl. others	**403.5**

Principal imports

	$bn cif
Machinery & equipment	108.3
Mineral fuels	69.8
Food	43.0
Chemicals	25.4
Raw materials	21.3
Total incl. others	**349.1**

Main export destinations

	% of total
United States	30.1
China	7.7
South Korea	6.3
Taiwan	6.0
Hong Kong	5.8

Main origins of imports

	% of total
United States	18.1
China	16.6
South Korea	4.9
Indonesia	4.3
Taiwan	4.1

Balance of payments, reserves and aid, $bn

Visible exports fob	383.6	Capital balance	-51.0
Visible imports fob	-313.4	Overall balance	40.5
Trade balance	70.2	Change in reserves	40.3
Invisibles inflows	167.4	Level of reserves	
Invisibles outflows	-142.1	end Dec.	402.0
Net transfers	-7.9	No. months of import cover	10.6
Current account balance	87.8	Aid given	9.85
– as % of GDP	2.1	– as % of GDP	0.23

Health and education

Health spending, % of GDP	7.1	Education spending, % of GDP	3.5
Doctors per 1,000 pop.	2.1	Enrolment, %: primary	101
Hospital beds per 1,000 pop.	17.0	secondary	102
Improved-water source access,		tertiary	48
% of pop.	97		

Society

No. of households	47.7m	Colour TVs per 100 households	99.1
Av. no. per household	2.7	Telephone lines per 100 pop.	54.7
Marriages per 1,000 pop.	6.3	Mobile telephone subscribers	
Divorces per 1,000 pop.	1.8	per 100 pop.	57.2
Cost of living, Dec. 2002		Computers per 100 pop.	34.9
New York = 100	139	Internet hosts per 1,000 pop.	72.7

KENYA

Area	582,646 sq km	Capital	Nairobi
Arable as % of total land	7	Currency	Kenyan shilling (KSh)

People

Population	31.3m	Life expectancy: men	43.5 yrs
Pop. per sq km	54	women	45.6 yrs
Av. ann. growth		Adult literacy	83.3%
in pop. 2000–05	1.45%	Fertility rate (per woman)	4.0%
Pop. under 15	43.4%	Urban population	34.4%
Pop. over 60	4.2%		per 1,000 pop.
No. of men per 100 women	98	Crude birth rate	34.1
Human Development Index	51.3	Crude death rate	16.7

The economy

GDP	KSh895bn	GDP per head	$360
GDP	$11.4bn	GDP per head in purchasing	
Av. ann. growth in real		power parity (USA=100)	2.8
GDP 1991–2001	1.6%	Economic freedom index	3.10

Origins of GDP		**Components of GDP**	
	% of total		% of total
Agriculture	24.1	Private consumption	74.2
Industry, of which:	...	Public consumption	17.4
manufacturing	13.0	Investment	16.4
Other	62.9	Exports	28.1
		Imports	-36.1

Structure of employment[a]

	% of total		% of labour force
Agriculture	19	Unemployed 2001	...
Industry	20	Av. ann. rate 1995–2001	...
Services	61		

Energy

	m TOE		
Total output	12.3	Net energy imports as %	
Total consumption	15.5	of energy use	21
Consumption per head,			
kg oil equivalent	515		

Inflation and finance

Consumer price		av. ann. increase 1996–2001	
inflation 2001	5.7%	Narrow money (M1)	9.8%
Av. ann. inflation 1996–2001	7.9%	Broad money	6.7%
Treasury bill rate, 2002	8.95%		

Exchange rates

	end 2002		December 2002
KSh per $	77.1	Effective rates	1995 = 100
KSh per SDR	104.8	– nominal	...
KSh per euro	73.5	– real	...

Trade

Principal exports

	$m fob
Tea	439
Horticultural products	253
Coffee	95
Petroleum products	157
Total incl. others	**1,944**

Principal imports

	$m cif
Crude petroleum	397
Industrial machinery	484
Refined petroleum products	331
Motor vehicles & chassis	185
Total incl. others	**3,192**

Main export destinations

	% of total
Uganda	20.4
United Kingdom	11.1
Tanzania	9.2
Netherlands	6.7

Main origins of imports

	% of total
United Arab Emirates	14.5
United Kingdom	7.5
Japan	5.0
India	4.4

Balance of payments, reserves and debt, $bn

Visible exports fob	1.9	Overall balance	-0.0
Visible imports fob	-3.2	Change in reserves	0.2
Trade balance	-1.3	Level of reserves	
Invisibles inflows	1.1	end Dec.	1.1
Invisibles outflows	-1.0	No. months of import cover	3.0
Net transfers	0.9	Foreign debt	5.8
Current account balance	-0.3	– as % of GDP	55
– as % of GDP	-2.8	– as % of total exports	204
Capital balance	0.2	Debt service ratio	16

Health and education

Health spending, % of GDP	8.3	Education spending, % of GDP	6.4
Doctors per 1,000 pop.[a]	0.1	Enrolment, %: primary	94
Hospital beds per 1,000 pop.	1.2	secondary	31
Improved-water source access,		tertiary	3
% of pop.	49		

Society

No. of households	7.0m	Colour TVs per 100 households	2.1
Av. no. per household	4.6	Telephone lines per 100 pop.	1.0
Marriages per 1,000 pop.	...	Mobile telephone subscribers	
Divorces per 1,000 pop.	...	per 100 pop.	1.6
Cost of living, Dec. 2002		Computers per 100 pop.	0.6
New York = 100	61	Internet hosts per 1,000 pop.	0.2

a 1999

MALAYSIA

Area	332,665 sq km	Capital	Kuala Lumpur
Arable as % of total land	6	Currency Malaysian dollar/ringgit (M$)	

People

Population	22.6m	Life expectancy: men		70.8 yrs
Pop. per sq km	68		women	75.7 yrs
Av. ann. growth		Adult literacy		87.9%
in pop. 2000–05	1.93%	Fertility rate (per woman)		2.9
Pop. under 15	33.7%	Urban population		58.1%
Pop. over 60	6.5%			per 1,000 pop.
No. of men per 100 women	103	Crude birth rate		22.3
Human Development Index	78.2	Crude death rate		4.6

The economy

GDP	M$335bn	GDP per head	$3,890
GDP	$88.0bn	GDP per head in purchasing	
Av. ann. growth in real		power parity (USA=100)	23.1
GDP 1991–2001	6.4%	Economic freedom index	3.00

Origins of GDP		**Components of GDP**	
	% of total		% of total
Agriculture	8.7	Private consumption	45.0
Industry, of which:	39.1	Public consumption	12.8
manufacturing	30.2	Investment	23.8
Services	52.2	Exports	116.3
		Imports	-98.0

Structure of employment

	% of total		% of labour force
Agriculture	17	Unemployed 2001	3.0
Industry	33	Av. ann. rate 1995–2001	3.0
Services	50		

Energy

	m TOE		
Total output	76.8	Net energy imports as %	
Total consumption	49.5	of energy use	-55
Consumption per head,			
kg oil equivalent	2,126		

Inflation and finance

Consumer price		av. ann. increase 1996–2001	
inflation 2002	1.9%	Narrow money (M1)	2.5%
Av. ann. inflation 1996–2002	2.6%	Broad money	8.8%
Money market rate, 2002	2.73%		

Exchange rates

	end 2002		December 2002
M$ per $	3.80	Effective rates	1995 = 100
M$ per SDR	5.17	– nominal	81.9
M$ per euro	3.62	– real	89.0

Trade

Principal exports	$bn fob	Principal imports	$bn cif
Electronics & electrical machinery	52.7	Capital goods & transport equipment	11.5
Petroleum & LNG	5.9	Manufactured goods	7.8
Chemicals & products	3.9	Chemicals	5.5
Palm oil	2.6	Misc. manufactured articles	4.2
Textiles, clothing & footwear	2.4	Mineral fuels & lubricants	3.9
		Food	3.2
Total incl. others	**88.0**	Total incl. others	**73.9**

Main export destinations	% of total	Main origins of imports	% of total
United States	20.5	Japan	19.7
Singapore	17.3	United States	16.2
Japan	13.8	Singapore	13.9
Hong Kong	4.6	China	5.0
Taiwan	4.3	South Korea	5.0
South Korea	3.4	Thailand	3.9

Balance of payments, reserves and debt, $bn

Visible exports fob	88.0	Overall balance	1.0
Visible imports fob	-69.6	Change in reserves	1.0
Trade balance	18.4	Level of reserves	
Invisibles inflows	16.3	end Dec.	30.8
Invisibles outflows	-25.2	No. months of import cover	3.9
Net transfers	-2.2	Foreign debt	43.4
Current account balance	7.3	as % of GDP	56
– as % of GDP	8.3	– as % of total exports	41
Capital balance	-3.9	Debt service ratio	6

Health and education

Health spending, % of GDP	3.0	Education spending, % of GDP	6.3
Doctors per 1,000 pop.	0.8	Enrolment, %: primary	99
Hospital beds per 1,000 pop.	1.6	secondary	70
Improved-water source access, % of pop.	...	tertiary	28

Society

No. of households	5.0m	Colour TVs per 100 households	90.3
Av. no. per household	4.4	Telephone lines per 100 pop.	19.9
Marriages per 1,000 pop.	...	Mobile telephone subscribers per 100 pop.	30.0
Divorces per 1,000 pop.	...	Computers per 100 pop.	12.6
Cost of living, Dec. 2002 New York = 100	63	Internet hosts per 1,000 pop.	3.8

MEXICO

Area	1,972,545 sq km	Capital	Mexico city
Arable as % of total land	13	Currency	Mexican peso (PS)

People

Population	100.4m	Life expectancy: men	70.4 yrs
Pop. per sq km	51	women	76.4 yrs
Av. ann. growth		Adult literacy	91.7%
in pop. 2000–05	1.45%	Fertility rate (per woman)	2.5
Pop. under 15	33.8%	Urban population	74.6%
Pop. over 60	6.9%		per 1,000 pop.
No. of men per 100 women	96	Crude birth rate	22.2
Human Development Index	79.6	Crude death rate	5.0

The economy

GDP	5,772bn pesos	GDP per head	$6,150
GDP	$617.8bn	GDP per head in purchasing	
Av. ann. growth in real		power parity (USA=100)	24.0
GDP 1991–2001	3.1%	Economic freedom index	2.80

Origins of GDP		**Components of GDP**	
	% of total		% of total
Agriculture	5.6	Private consumption	71.6
Industry, of which:	26.1	Public consumption	9.7
manufacturing & mining	22.0	Investment	22.0
Services	68.2	Exports	33.5
		Imports	-36.7

Structure of employment[a]

	% of total		% of labour force
Agriculture	18	Unemployed 2001	1.6
Industry	27	Av. ann. rate 1995–2001	2.6
Services	55		

Energy

	m TOE		
Total output	229.7	Net energy imports as %	
Total consumption	153.5	of energy use	-50
Consumption per head,			
kg oil equivalent	1,567		

Inflation and finance

Consumer price		av. ann. increase 1996–2001	
inflation 2002	5.1%	Narrow money (M1)	20.7%
Av. ann. inflation 1996–2002	12.2%	Broad money	14.0%
Money market rate, 2002	8.17%		

Exchange rates

	end 2002		December 2002
PS per $	10.31	Effective rates	1995 = 100
PS per SDR	14.02	– nominal	...
PS per euro	9.83	– real	...

Trade

Principal exports		Principal imports	
	$bn fob		*$bn fob*
Manufactured products	141.4	Intermediate goods	126.1
Crude oil & products	12.8	Capital goods	22.5
Agricultural products	3.9	Consumer goods	19.8
Total incl. others	**158.4**	Total	**168.4**

Main export destinations		Main origins of imports	
	% of total		*% of total*
United States	88.7	United States	67.7
Canada	1.9	Japan	4.8
Japan	0.4	Canada	2.5
EU15	3.4	EU15	9.7

Balance of payments, reserves and debt, $bn

Visible exports fob	158.4	Overall balance	6.9
Visible imports fob	-168.4	Change in reserves	9.2
Trade balance	-10.0	Level of reserves	
Invisibles inflows	17.8	end Dec.	44.8
Invisibles outflows	-34.9	No. months of import cover	2.6
Net transfers	9.3	Foreign debt	158.3
Current account balance	-17.7	– as % of GDP	29
– as % of gdp	-2.9	– as % of total exports	89
Capital balance	22.3	Debt service ratio	27

Health and education

Health spending, % of GDP	5.3	Education spending, % of GDP	4.4
Doctors per 1,000 pop.	1.3	Enrolment, %: primary	113
Hospital beds per 1,000 pop.	1.1	secondary	75
Improved-water source access,		tertiary	21
% of pop.	86		

Society

No. of households	22.8m	Colour TVs per 100 households	89.4
Av. no. per household	4.3	Telephone lines per 100 pop.	13.5
Marriages per 1,000 pop.	7.6	Mobile telephone subscribers	
Divorces per 1,000 pop.	0.5	per 100 pop.	20.1
Cost of living, Dec. 2002		Computers per 100 pop.	6.7
New York = 100	86	Internet hosts per 1,000 pop.	11.0

a 2000

MOROCCO

Area	446,550 sq km	Capital	Rabat
Arable as % of total land	20	Currency	Dirham (Dh)

People

Population	30.4m	Life expectancy: men		66.8 yrs
Pop. per sq km	68	women		70.5 yrs
Av. ann. growth		Adult literacy		49.8%
in pop. 2000–05	1.62%	Fertility rate (per woman)		2.3
Pop. under 15	32.9%	Urban population		56.1%
Pop. over 60	6.5%		per 1,000 pop.	
No. of men per 100 women	100	Crude birth rate		24.8
Human Development Index	60.2	Crude death rate		6.0

The economy

GDP	Dh387bn	GDP per head	$1,120
GDP	$34.2bn	GDP per head in purchasing	
Av. ann. growth in real		power parity (USA=100)	10.2
GDP 1991–2001	2.6%	Economic freedom index	2.95

Origins of GDP[a]		Components of GDP[a]	
	% of total		% of total
Agriculture	15.2	Private consumption	65.2
Industry, of which:	38.4	Public consumption	18.2
manufacturing	20.8	Investment	22.6
Services	46.4	Exports	25.2
		Imports	-31.2

Structure of employment[b]

	% of total		% of labour force
Agriculture	6	Unemployed 2001	19.0
Industry	33	Av. ann. rate 1995–2001	19.8
Services	61		

Energy

	m TOE		
Total output	0.6	Net energy imports as %	
Total consumption	10.3	of energy use	94
Consumption per head,			
kg oil equivalent	359		

Inflation and finance

		av. ann. increase 1996–2001	
Consumer price			
inflation 2002	3.6%	Narrow money (M1)	11.7%
Av. ann. inflation 1996–2002	1.8%	Broad money	10.9%
Money market rate, 2002	2.99%		

Exchange rates

	end 2002		December 2002
			1995 = 100
Dh per $	10.17	Effective rates	
Dh per SDR	13.82	– nominal	105.4
Dh per euro	9.69	– real	102.5

Trade

Principal exports[a]

	$bn fob
Consumer goods	2.8
Semi-finished goods	1.6
Food, drink & tobacco	1.5
Minerals	0.6
Energy & lubricants	0.3
Total incl. others	**7.4**

Principal imports[a]

	$bn cif
Consumer goods	2.7
Machinery & equipment	2.3
Semi-finished goods	2.2
Energy & lubricants	2.0
Food, drink & tobacco	1.3
Total incl. others	**11.5**

Main export destinations

	% of total
France	24.3
Spain	11.4
United Kingdom	7.0
Italy	5.6

Main origins of imports

	% of total
France	22.3
Spain	11.6
Italy	6.5
Germany	5.4

Balance of payments, reserves and debt, $bn

Visible exports fob	7.1	Overall balance	0.9
Visible imports fob	-10.2	Change in reserves	3.7
Trade balance	-3.0	Level of reserves	
Invisibles inflows	4.4	end Dec.	8.7
Invisibles outflows	-3.3	No. months of import cover	7.7
Net transfers	3.6	Foreign debt	17.0
Current account balance	1.6	– as % of GDP	51
– as % of GDP	4.7	– as % of total exports	126
Capital balance	-1.0	Debt service ratio	11

Health and education

Health spending, % of GDP[a]	4.5	Education spending, % of GDP	5.5
Doctors per 1,000 pop.	0.4	Enrolment, %: primary	94
Hospital beds per 1,000 pop.	0.9	secondary	39
Improved-water source access,		tertiary	10
% of pop.	82		

Society

No. of households	5.4m	Colour TVs per 100 households	44.3
Av. no. per household	5.3	Telephone lines per 100 pop.	3.9
Marriages per 1,000 pop.	...	Mobile telephone subscribers	
Divorces per 1,000 pop.	...	per 100 pop.	15.7
Cost of living, Dec. 2002		Computers per 100 pop.	1.3
New York = 100	64	Internet hosts per 1,000 pop.	...

a 2000
b 1999

NETHERLANDS

Area[a]	41,526 sq km	Capital	Amsterdam
Arable as % of total land	27	Currency	Euro (€)

People

Population	15.9m	Life expectancy: men	75.6 yrs
Pop. per sq km	383	women	81.0 yrs
Av. ann. growth		Adult literacy	99.0%
in pop. 2000–05	0.50%	Fertility rate (per woman)	1.7
Pop. under 15	18.5%	Urban population	89.6%
Pop. over 60	18.2%		per 1,000 pop.
No. of men per 100 women	98	Crude birth rate	10.6
Human Development Index	93.5	Crude death rate	8.9

The economy

GDP	€425bn	GDP per head	$23,860
GDP	$380.1bn	GDP per head in purchasing	
Av. ann. growth in real		power parity (USA=100)	79.9
GDP 1991–2001	2.7%	Economic freedom index	1.90

Origins of GDP		Components of GDP	
	% of total		% of total
Agriculture	3.1	Private consumption	49.6
Industry, of which:	25.7	Public consumption	23.2
manufacturing	...	Investment	21.8
Services	71.2	Exports	65.1
		Imports	-59.7

Structure of employment

	% of total		% of labour force
Agriculture	3	Unemployed 2001	3.0
Industry	17	Av. ann. rate 1995–2001	4.8
Services	80		

Energy

	m TOE		
Total output	57.2	Net energy imports as %	
Total consumption	75.8	of energy use	24
Consumption per head,			
kg oil equivalent	4,762		

Inflation and finance

Consumer price		av. ann. increase 1996–2001	
inflation 2002	3.5%	Euro area:	
Av. ann. inflation 1996–2002	2.8%	Narrow money (M1)	7.6%
Deposit rate, 2002	2.77%	Broad money	5.8%
		Household saving rate	11.2%

Exchange rates

	end 2002		December 2002
Euro per $	0.95	Effective rates	1995 = 100
Euro per SDR	1.30	– nominal	91.4
		– real	97.1

Trade

Principal exports		Principal imports	
	$bn fob		*$bn cif*
Machinery & transport equipment	74.6	Machinery & transport equipment	76.0
Chemicals	33.1	Chemicals	22.2
Food, drink & tobacco	26.1	Fuels	19.9
Fuels	19.9	Food, drink & tobacco	16.4
Total incl. others	**216.1**	Total incl. others	**194.9**

Main export destinations		Main origins of imports	
	% of total		*% of total*
Germany	25.6	Germany	18.4
Belgium	11.8	United States	9.9
United Kingdom	11.1	Belgium	9.2
France	10.3	United Kingdom	8.9
Italy	6.2	France	5.8
EU15	77.6	EU15	54.6

Balance of payments, reserves and aid, $bn

Visible exports fob	202.9	Capital balance	-9.7
Visible imports fob	-183.1	Overall balance	-0.4
Trade balance	19.9	Change in reserves	-0.8
Invisibles inflows	90.9	Level of reserves	
Invisibles outflows	-100.4	end Dec.	16.9
Net transfers	-6.7	No. months of import cover	0.7
Current account balance	3.7	Aid given	3.17
– as % of GDP	1.0	– as % of GDP	0.82

Health and education

Health spending, % of GDP	8.8	Education spending, % of GDP	4.8
Doctors per 1,000 pop.[b]	3.2	Enrolment, %: primary	108
Hospital beds per 1,000 pop.	11.5	secondary	124
Improved-water source access, % of pop.	100	tertiary	55

Society

No. of households	6.9m	Colour TVs per 100 households	98.4
Av. no. per household	2.3	Telephone lines per 100 pop.	62.1
Marriages per 1,000 pop.	5.6	Mobile telephone subscribers	
Divorces per 1,000 pop.	2.0	per 100 pop.	73.9
Cost of living, Dec. 2002		Computers per 100 pop.	42.9
New York = 100	93	Internet hosts per 1,000 pop.	151.9

a Includes water.
b 2000

NEW ZEALAND

Area	270,534 sq km	Capital	Wellington
Arable as % of total land	6	Currency	New Zealand dollar (NZ$)

People

Population	3.8m	Life expectancy: men	75.8 yrs
Pop. per sq km	14	women	80.7 yrs
Av. ann. growth		Adult literacy	99.0%
in pop. 2000–05	0.77%	Fertility rate (per woman)	2.0
Pop. under 15	22.9%	Urban population	85.9%
Pop. over 60	15.7%		per 1,000 pop.
No. of men per 100 women	97	Crude birth rate	13.7
Human Development Index	91.7	Crude death rate	7.6

The economy

GDP	NZ$120bn	GDP per head	$13,240
GDP	$50.4bn	GDP per head in purchasing	
Av. ann. growth in real		power parity (USA=100)	53.2
GDP 1991–2001	2.8%	Economic freedom index	1.70

Origins of GDP		**Components of GDP**	
	% of total		% of total
Agriculture	8.4	Private consumption	58.9
Manufacturing	15.7	Public consumption	18.8
Other	75.9	Investment	19.2
		Exports	36.1
		Imports	-33.0

Structure of employment

	% of total		% of labour force
Agriculture	9	Unemployed 2001	5.3
Industry	23	Av. ann. rate 1995–2001	6.4
Services	68		

Energy

	m TOE		
Total output	15.4	Net energy imports as %	
Total consumption	18.6	of energy use	17
Consumption per head,			
kg oil equivalent	4,864		

Inflation and finance

		av. ann. increase 1996–2001	
Consumer price			
inflation 2002	2.6%	Narrow money (M1)	9.9%
Av. ann. inflation 1996–2002	1.7%	Broad money	4.2%
Money market rate, 2002	5.40%	Household saving rate	2.4%

Exchange rates

	end 2002		December 2002
		Effective rates	1995 = 100
NZ$ per $	1.90		
NZ$ per SDR	2.58	– nominal	93.6
NZ$ per euro	1.81	– real	94.2

Trade

Principal exports	$bn fob	Principal imports	$bn cif
Dairy produce	2.7	Vehicles & aircraft	2.1
Meat	1.7	Machinery	1.8
Forestry products	1.0	Electrical machinery	1.3
Fish	0.6	Mineral fuels	0.7
Total incl. others	**13.9**	**Total incl. others**	**13.7**

Main export destinations	% of total	Main origins of imports	% of total
Australia	18.8	Australia	21.9
United States	14.4	United States	15.9
Japan	12.4	Japan	11.0
United Kingdom	4.8	United Kingdom	3.8

Balance of payments, reserves and aid, $bn

Visible exports fob	13.9	Capital balance	2.4
Visible imports fob	-12.4	Overall balance	-0.2
Trade balance	1.5	Change in reserves	-0.3
Invisibles inflows	4.9	Level of reserves	
Invisibles outflows	-7.9	end Dec.	3.0
Net transfers	0.1	No. months of import cover	1.8
Current account balance	-1.4	Aid given	0.11
– as % of GDP	-2.8	– as % of GDP	0.16

Health and education

Health spending, % of GDP	8.0	Education spending, % of GDP	6.1
Doctors per 1,000 pop.	2.3	Enrolment, %: primary	100
Hospital beds per 1,000 pop.	6.1	secondary	112
Improved-water source access,		tertiary	69
% of pop.	95		

Society

No. of households	1.4m	Colour TVs per 100 households	97.3
Av. no. per household	2.7	Telephone lines per 100 pop.	47.1
Marriages per 1,000 pop.	5.5	Mobile telephone subscribers	
Divorces per 1,000 pop.	3.2	per 100 pop.	62.1
Cost of living, Dec. 2002		Computers per 100 pop.	58.6
New York = 100	69	Internet hosts per 1,000 pop.	113.9

NIGERIA

Area	923,768 sq km	Capital	Abuja
Arable as % of total land	31	Currency	Naira (N)

People

Population	116.9m	Life expectancy: men		51.1 yrs
Pop. per sq km	127		women	51.8 yrs
Av. ann. growth		Adult literacy		65.3%
in pop. 2000–05	2.53%	Fertility rate (per woman)		5.4
Pop. under 15	45.0%	Urban population		44.9%
Pop. over 60	4.8%			per 1,000 pop.
No. of men per 100 women	101	Crude birth rate		39.5
Human Development Index	46.2	Crude death rate		13.7

The economy

GDP	N4,602bn	GDP per head	$350
GDP	$41.4bn	GDP per head in purchasing	
Av. ann. growth in real		power parity (USA=100)	2.3
GDP 1991–2001	2.7%	Economic freedom index	3.85

Origins of GDP		**Components of GDP**	
	% of total		% of total
Agriculture	46.2	Private consumption	59.3
Manufacturing	6.0	Public consumption	14.0
Other	47.8	Investment	6.3
		Exports	26.1
		Imports	-5.8

Structure of employment[a]

	% of total		% of labour force
Agriculture	3	Unemployed 2001	3.9
Industry	22	Av. ann. rate 1995–2001	3.7
Services	75		

Energy

	m TOE		
Total output	197.7	Net energy imports as %	
Total consumption	90.2	of energy use	-119
Consumption per head,			
kg oil equivalent	710		

Inflation and finance

Consumer price		*av. ann. increase 1996–2001*	
inflation 2002	12.9%	Narrow money (M1)	28.2%
Av. ann. inflation 1996–2002	9.6%	Broad money	28.9%
Treasury bill rate 2002	19.03%		

Exchange rates

	end 2002		December 2002
N per $	126.4	Effective rates	1995 = 100
N per SDR	171.8	– nominal	38.8
N per euro	120.5	– real	84.4

Trade

Principal exports		Principal imports	
	$bn fob		$bn cif
Oil	18.7	Manufactured goods	3.3
Non-oil	0.3	Machinery & transport	
		equipment	2.7
		Chemicals	2.6
		Agric products &	
		foodstuffs	1.3
Total	**19.0**	Total incl. others	**11.6**

Main export destinations[b]		Main origins of imports[b]	
	% of total		% of total
United States	47.7	United Kingdom	8.8
Spain	10.0	United States	8.6
India	7.7	Germany	7.9
France	6.1	France	6.8

Balance of payments[c], reserves and debt, $bn

Visible exports fob	12.9	Overall balance	-3.5
Visible imports fob	-8.6	Change in reserves	0.5
Trade balance	4.3	Level of reserves	
Invisibles inflows	1.2	end Dec.	10.6
Invisibles outflows	-6.3	No. months of import cover	6.4
Net transfers	1.3	Foreign debt	31.1
Current account balance	0.5	– as % of GDP	88
– as % of GDP	1.2	– as % of total exports	155
Capital balance	-4.1	Debt service ratio	13

Health and education

Health spending, % of GDP[d]	2.2	Education spending, % of GDP[e]	0.7
Doctors per 1,000 pop.	0.2	Enrolment, %: primary[e]	98
Hospital beds per 1,000 pop.	0.9	secondary[e]	33
Improved-water source access,		tertiary[e]	4
% of pop.	57		

Society

No. of households	22.6m	Colour TVs per 100 households	48.2
Av. no. per household	4.0	Telephone lines per 100 pop.	0.4
Marriages per 1,000 pop.	...	Mobile telephone subscribers	
Divorces per 1,000 pop.	...	per 100 pop.	0.2
Cost of living, Dec. 2002		Computers per 100 pop.	0.7
New York = 100	78	Internet hosts per 1,000 pop.	...

a 1996
b Estimate.
c 1999
d 2000
e 1997

NORWAY

Area	323,878 sq km	Capital	Oslo
Arable as % of total land	3	Currency	Norwegian krone (Nkr)

People

Population	4.5m	Life expectancy: men	76.0 yrs
Pop. per sq km	14	women	81.9 yrs
Av. ann. growth		Adult literacy	99.0%
in pop. 2000–05	0.43%	Fertility rate (per woman)	1.8
Pop. under 15	19.8%	Urban population	75.0%
Pop. over 60	19.5%		per 1,000 pop.
No. of men per 100 women	98	Crude birth rate	11.4
Human Development Index	94.2	Crude death rate	9.9

The economy

GDP	Nkr1,494bn	GDP per head	$37,020
GDP	$166.1bn	GDP per head in purchasing	
Av. ann. growth in real		power parity (USA=100)	85.6
GDP 1991–2001	3.2%	Economic freedom index	2.30

Origins of GDP

	% of total
Agriculture	1.9
Industry, of which:	30.8
manufacturing	...
Services	67.3

Components of GDP

	% of total
Private consumption	43.1
Public consumption	20.3
Investment	19.6
Exports	46.3
Imports	-29.2

Structure of employment

	% of total		% of labour force
Agriculture	4	Unemployed 2001	3.6
Industry	22	Av. ann. rate 1995–2001	3.9
Services	74		

Energy

	m TOE		
Total output	225.0	Net energy imports as %	
Total consumption	25.6	of energy use	-778
Consumption per head,			
kg oil equivalent	5,704		

Inflation and finance

		av. ann. increase 1996–2001	
Consumer price			
inflation 2002	1.3%	Narrow money (M1)	10.9%
Av. ann. inflation 1996–2002	2.4%	Broad money	7.1%
Interbank rate, 2002	6.91%	Household saving rate	4.5%

Exchange rates

	end 2002		December 2002
Nkr per $	6.97	Effective rates	1995 = 100
Nkr per SDR	9.47	– nominal	108.3
Nkr per euro	6.64	– real	144.0

Trade

Principal exports		Principal imports	
	$bn fob		*$bn cif*
Oil, gas & products	34.1	Machinery & equipment	13.4
Manufactured materials	6.6	Misc. manufactures	5.0
Machinery & equipment	5.8	Manufactured materials	4.9
Food, drink & tobacco	3.6	Chemicals	3.1
Total incl. others	**58.0**	Total incl. others	**32.2**

Main export destinations		Main origins of imports	
	% of total		*% of total*
United Kingdom	19.8	Sweden	15.5
France	11.8	Germany	12.8
Germany	11.6	United Kingdom	7.8
Netherlands	10.2	Denmark	7.2
Sweden	7.9	United States	7.1
EU15	76.8	EU15	66.5

Balance of payments, reserves and aid, $bn

Visible exports fob	59.7	Capital balance	-24.0
Visible imports fob	-33.7	Overall balance	-2.1
Trade balance	26.0	Change in reserves	-4.7
Invisibles inflows	25.6	Level of reserves	
Invisibles outflows	-23.9	end Dec.	15.8
Net transfers	-1.7	No. months of import cover	3.3
Current account balance	26.0	Aid given	1.35
– as % of GDP	15.6	– as % of GDP	0.83

Health and education

Health spending, % of GDP[a]	7.8	Education spending, % of GDP	6.9
Doctors per 1,000 pop.	2.8	Enrolment, %: primary	101
Hospital beds per 1,000 pop.	14.0	secondary	115
Improved-water source access,		tertiary	70
% of pop.	100		

Society

No. of households	2.1m	Colour TVs per 100 households	93.0
Av. no. per household	2.2	Telephone lines per 100 pop.	72.0
Marriages per 1,000 pop.	5.6	Mobile telephone subscribers	
Divorces per 1,000 pop.	2.3	per 100 pop.	82.5
Cost of living, Dec. 2002		Computers per 100 pop.	50.8
New York = 100	123	Internet hosts per 1,000 pop.	131.0

a 2000

PAKISTAN

Area	803,940 sq km	Capital	Islamabad
Arable as % of total land	28	Currency	Pakistan rupee (PRs)

People

Population	145.0m	Life expectancy: men	61.2 yrs
Pop. per sq km	180	women	60.9 yrs
Av. ann. growth		Adult literacy	44.1%
in pop. 2000–05	2.44%	Fertility rate (per woman)	5.1
Pop. under 15	42.0%	Urban population	33.4%
Pop. over 60	5.7%		per 1,000 pop.
No. of men per 100 women	105	Crude birth rate	36.3
Human Development Index	49.9	Crude death rate	9.6

The economy

GDP	PRs3,416bn	GDP per head	$400
GDP	$587bn	GDP per head in purchasing	
Av. ann. growth in real		power parity (USA=100)	5.4
GDP 1991–2001	3.8%	Economic freedom index	3.30

Origins of GDP[a]		Components of GDP[a]	
	% of total		% of total
Agriculture	24.7	Private consumption	73.0
Industry, of which:	25.1	Public consumption	9.6
manufacturing	17.4	Investment	13.4
Other	50.2	Exports	16.3
		Imports	-13.8

Structure of employment[b]

	% of total		% of labour force
Agriculture	47	Unemployed 2000	5.9
Industry	17	Av. ann. rate 1995–2000	5.8
Services	36		

Energy

	m TOE		
Total output	47.1	Net energy imports as %	
Total consumption	64.0	of energy use	26
Consumption per head,			
kg oil equivalent	463		

Inflation and finance

Consumer price		av. ann. increase 1996–2001	
inflation 2002	3.6%	Narrow money (M1)	12.8%
Av. ann. inflation 1996–2002	5.4%	Broad money	11.1%
Money market rate, 2002	5.53%		

Exchange rates

	end 2002		December 2002
PRs per $	58.53	Effective rates	1995 = 100
PRs per SDR	79.58	– nominal	65.64
PRs per euro	55.82	– real	87.12

Trade

Principal exports[c]		Principal imports[c]	
	$bn		$bn
Textile yarn & fabrics	2.2	Machinery	2.1
Apparel & clothing accessories	1.4	Chemicals	1.9
Rice	0.6	Minerals, fuels etc	1.5
		Palm oil	0.7
Total incl. others	**8.5**	Total incl. others	**9.3**

Main export destinations		Main origins of imports	
	% of total		% of total
United States	23.9	United Arab Emirates	13.1
United Arab Emirates	7.4	Saudi Arabia	11.3
United Kingdom	6.6	Kuwait	6.7
Germany	5.2	United States	5.8

Balance of payments, reserves and debt, $bn

Visible exports fob	9.1	Overall balance	2.2
Visible imports fob	-9.7	Change in reserves	2.1
Trade balance	-0.6	Level of reserves	
Invisibles inflows	1.6	end Dec.	4.2
Invisibles outflows	-4.5	No. months of import cover	3.5
Net transfers	5.4	Foreign debt	32.0
Current account balance	1.9	– as % of GDP	55
– as % of GDP	3.2	– as % of total exports	299
Capital balance	-0.4	Debt service ratio	28

Health and education

Health spending, % of GDP	3.9	Education spending, % of GDP	1.8
Doctors per 1,000 pop.	0.7	Enrolment, %: primary	74
Hospital beds per 1,000 pop.	0.6	secondary	24
Improved-water source access,		tertiary	4
% of pop.	88		

Society

No. of households	20.8m	Colour TVs per 100 households	34.8
Av. no. per household	6.5	Telephone lines per 100 pop.	2.4
Marriages per 1,000 pop.	...	Mobile telephone subscribers	
Divorces per 1,000 pop.	...	per 100 pop.	0.6
Cost of living, Dec. 2002		Computers per 100 pop.	0.4
New York = 100	45	Internet hosts per 1,000 pop.	...

a Fiscal year ending June 30, 2001.
b 1999
c 1998

PERU

Area	1,285,216 sq km	Capital	Lima
Arable as % of total land	3	Currency	Nuevo Sol (New Sol)

People

Population	26.1m	Life expectancy: men	67.3 yrs
Pop. per sq km	20	women	72.4 yrs
Av. ann. growth		Adult literacy[a]	90.2%
in pop. 2000–05	1.50%	Fertility rate (per woman)	2.3
Pop. under 15	34.5%	Urban population	73.1%
Pop. over 60	7.1%		per 1,000 pop.
No. of men per 100 women	101	Crude birth rate	22.6
Human Development Index	74.7	Crude death rate	6.1

The economy

GDP	New Soles 190bn	GDP per head	$2,070
GDP	$54.0bn	GDP per head in purchasing	
Av. ann. growth in real		power parity (USA=100)	13.0
GDP 1991–2001	3.6%	Economic freedom index	2.80

Origins of GDP		Components of GDP	
	% of total		% of total
Agriculture	9.5	Private consumption	71.9
Industry, of which:	25.7	Public consumption	11.2
manufacturing	14.9	Investment	18.4
Services	64.8	Exports	15.8
		Imports	-17.3

Structure of employment[b]

	% of total		% of labour force
Agriculture	6	Unemployed 2001	7.3
Industry	19	Av. ann. rate 1996–2001	7.5
Services	75		

Energy

	m TOE		
Total output	9.5	Net energy imports as %	
Total consumption	12.7	of energy use	26
Consumption per head,			
kg oil equivalent	463		

Inflation and finance

Consumer price		av. ann. increase 1996–2001	
inflation 2002	0.1%	Narrow money (M1)	19.0%
Av. ann. inflation 1996–2002	4.1%	Broad money	12.3%
Deposit rate, 2002	4.19%		

Exchange rates

	end 2002		December 2002
New Soles per $	3.51	Effective rates	1995 = 100
New Soles per SDR	4.78	– nominal	...
New Soles per Ecu	3.35	– real	...

Trade

Principal exports		Principal imports	
	$bn fob		$bn fob
Gold	1.2	Intermediate goods	3.6
Copper	0.9	Capital goods	1.9
Fish & fish products	0.9	Consumer goods	1.6
Zinc	0.4		
Total incl. others	**7.1**	Total incl. others	**7.2**

Main export destinations		Main origins of imports	
	% of total		% of total
United States	25.4	United States	30.5
United Kingdom	13.5	Spain	8.9
Japan	6.6	Chile	8.1
China	6.1	Colombia	4.1

Balance of payments, reserves and debt, $bn

Visible exports fob	7.1	Overall balance	0.4
Visible imports fob	-7.2	Change in reserves	0.3
Trade balance	-0.1	Level of reserves	
Invisibles inflows	2.1	end Dec.	9.0
Invisibles outflows	-4.1	No. months of import cover	9.5
Net transfers	1.0	Foreign debt	27.5
Current account balance	-1.1	– as % of GDP	53
– as % of GDP	-2.0	– as % of total exports	284
Capital balance	1.0	Debt service ratio	23

Health and education

Health spending, % of GDP[c]	4.8	Education spending, % of GDP	3.4
Doctors per 1,000 pop.	1.0	Enrolment, %: primary	128
Hospital beds per 1,000 pop.	1.7	secondary[c]	81
Improved-water source access,		tertiary[c]	29
% of pop.	77		

Society

No. of households	5.5m	Colour TVs per 100 households	46.4
Av. no. per household	4.7	Telephone lines per 100 pop.	7.8
Marriages per 1,000 pop.	3.2	Mobile telephone subscribers	
Divorces per 1,000 pop.	...	per 100 pop.	5.9
Cost of living, Dec. 2002		Computers per 100 pop.	4.8
New York = 100	61	Internet hosts per 1,000 pop.	0.7

a Excluding indigenous jungle population.
b 1999
c 2000

PHILIPPINES

Area	300,000 sq km	Capital	Manila
Arable as % of total land	19	Currency	Philippine peso (P)

People

Population	77.1m	Life expectancy:	men	68.0 yrs
Pop. per sq km	257		women	72.0 yrs
Av. ann. growth		Adult literacy		95.5%
in pop. 2000–05	1.79%	Fertility rate (per woman)		3.2
Pop. under 15	37.5%	Urban population		59.4%
Pop. over 60	5.5%			per 1,000 pop.
No. of men per 100 women	101	Crude birth rate		26.0
Human Development Index	75.4	Crude death rate		5.1

The economy

GDP	P3,643bn	GDP per head	$930
GDP	$71.4bn	GDP per head in purchasing	
Av. ann. growth in real		power parity (USA=100)	11.9
GDP 1991–2001	2.9%	Economic freedom index	2.85

Origins of GDP

	% of total
Agriculture	15.1
Industry, of which:	31.6
manufacturing	22.8
Services	53.3

Components of GDP

	% of total
Private consumption	70.5
Public consumption	12.8
Investment	17.6
Exports	48.5
Imports	-47.0

Structure of employment

	% of total		% of labour force
Agriculture	38	Unemployed 2001	10.3
Industry	16	Av. ann. rate 1995–2001	9.0
Services	40		

Energy

	m TOE		
Total output	20.9	Net energy imports as %	
Total consumption	42.4	of energy use	51
Consumption per head,			
kg oil equivalent	554		

Inflation and finance

		av. ann. increase 1996–2001	
Consumer price			
inflation 2002	3.1%	Narrow money (M1)	11.0%
Av. ann. inflation 1996–2002	6.0%	Broad money	11.8%
Treasury bill rate, 2002	5.49%		

Exchange rates

	end 2002		December 2002
			1995 = 100
P per $	53.10	Effective rates	
P per SDR	72.19	– nominal	58.9
P per euro	50.63	– real	80.9

Trade

Principal exports		**Principal imports**	
	$bn fob		*$bn fob*
Electrical & electronic		Semi-processed raw	
equipment	16.7	materials	10.1
Machinery & transport		Telecom & electrical machinery	6.1
equipment	6.1	Electrical equipment parts	3.8
Clothing	2.4	Crude petroleum	2.7
Coconut products	0.5	Chemicals	2.5
Fish	0.3		
Total incl. others	**32.7**	Total incl. others	**31.4**

Main export destinations		**Main origins of imports**	
	% of total		*% of total*
United States	27.9	Japan	20.6
Japan	15.7	United States	16.9
Netherlands	9.3	South Korea	6.6
Singapore	7.2	Singapore	6.1
Hong Kong	5.0	Taiwan	5.4
EU15	19.3	EU15	9.3

Balance of payments, reserves and debt, $bn

Visible exports fob	31.2	Overall balance	-0.7
Visible imports fob	-28.5	Change in reserves	0.6
Trade balance	2.7	Level of reserves	
Invisibles inflows	10.5	end Dec.	15.6
Invisibles outflows	-9.2	No. months of import cover	5.0
Net transfers	0.4	Foreign debt	52.4
Current account balance	4.5	– as % of GDP	67
– as % of GDP	6.3	– as % of total exports	114
Capital balance	-4.2	Debt service ratio	17

Health and education

Health spending, % of GDP	3.6	Education spending, % of GDP	4.2
Doctors per 1,000 pop.[a]	1.2	Enrolment, %: primary	113
Hospital beds per 1,000 pop.	1.1	secondary	77
Improved-water source access,		tertiary	31
% of pop.	87		

Society

No. of households	15.7m	Colour TVs per 100 households	64.1
Av. no. per household	4.9	Telephone lines per 100 pop.	4.0
Marriages per 1,000 pop.	7.3	Mobile telephone subscribers	
Divorces per 1,000 pop.	...	per 100 pop.	13.7
Cost of living, Dec. 2002		Computers per 100 pop.	2.2
New York = 100	42	Internet hosts per 1,000 pop.	0.5

a 2000

POLAND

Area	312,683 sq km	Capital	Warsaw
Arable as % of total land	46	Currency	Zloty (Zl)

People

Population	38.6m	Life expectancy: men	69.8 yrs
Pop. per sq km	123	women	78.0 yrs
Av. ann. growth		Adult literacy	99.7%
in pop. 2000–05	-0.08%	Fertility rate (per woman)	1.3
Pop. under 15	19.2%	Urban population	62.5%
Pop. over 60	16.6%		per 1,000 pop.
No. of men per 100 women	94	Crude birth rate	9.5
Human Development Index	83.3	Crude death rate	10.0

The economy

GDP	Zl722bn	GDP per head	$4,570
GDP	$176.3bn	GDP per head in purchasing	
Av. ann. growth in real		power parity (USA=100)	27.3
GDP 1991–2001	3.4%	Economic freedom index	2.90

Origins of GDP		Components of GDP	
	% of total		% of total
Agriculture	3.8	Private consumption	64.9
Industry, of which:	31.4	Public consumption	17.8
manufacturing	...	Investment	21.1
Services	64.8	Exports	28.1
		Imports	-31.8

Structure of employment

	% of total		% of labour force
Agriculture	19	Unemployed 2001	18.3
Industry	31	Av. ann. rate 1995–2001	13.6
Services	50		

Energy

	m TOE		
Total output	79.0	Net energy imports as %	
Total consumption	90.0	of energy use	12
Consumption per head,			
kg oil equivalent	2,328		

Inflation and finance

Consumer price		av. ann. increase 1996–2001	
inflation 2002	1.9%	Narrow money (M1)	12.5%
Av. ann. inflation 1996–2002	8.6%	Broad money	19.9%
Money market rate, 2002	9.4%		

Exchange rates

	end 2002		December 2002
Zl per $	3.84	Effective rates	1995 = 100
Zl per SDR	5.22	– nominal	80.9
Zl per euro	3.66	– real	130.3

Trade

Principal exports

	$bn fob
Machinery & transport equipment	13.1
Semi-manufactured goods	8.6
Other manufactured goods	6.3
Agric. products & foodstuffs	2.7
Total incl. others	**36.1**

Principal imports

	$bn cif
Machinery & transport equipment	18.3
Semi-manufactured goods	10.3
Chemicals	7.3
Mineral fuels	5.1
Total incl. others	**50.3**

Main export destinations

	% of total
Germany	34.4
France	5.4
Italy	5.4
United Kingdom	5.0

Main origins of imports

	% of total
Germany	23.9
Russia	8.8
Italy	8.2
France	6.8

Balance of payments, reserves and debt, $bn

Visible exports fob	41.7	Overall balance	-0.4
Visible imports fob	-49.3	Change in reserves	-0.9
Trade balance	-7.7	Level of reserves	
Invisibles inflows	12.4	end Dec.	26.6
Invisibles outflows	-13.0	No. months of import cover	5.1
Net transfers	2.9	Foreign debt	62.4
Current account balance	-5.4	– as % of GDP	39
– as % of GDP	-3.0	– as % of total exports	129
Capital balance	3.2	Debt service ratio	32

Health and education

Health spending, % of GDP	5.8	Education spending, % of GDP	5.0
Doctors per 1,000 pop.	2.3	Enrolment, %: primary	100
Hospital beds per 1,000 pop.	5.1	secondary	101
Improved-water source access, % of pop.	…	tertiary	56

Society

No. of households	13.6m	Colour TVs per 100 households	82.6
Av. no. per household	2.8	Telephone lines per 100 pop.	29.5
Marriages per 1,000 pop.	5.5	Mobile telephone subscribers	
Divorces per 1,000 pop.	1.1	per 100 pop.	26.0
Cost of living, Dec. 2002		Computers per 100 pop.	8.5
New York = 100	65	Internet hosts per 1,000 pop.	21.8

PORTUGAL

Area	88,940 sq km	Capital	Lisbon
Arable as % of total land	22	Currency	Euro (€)

People

Population	10.0m	Life expectancy: men	72.6 yrs
Pop. per sq km	112	women	79.6 yrs
Av. ann. growth		Adult literacy	92.6%
in pop. 2000–05	0.13%	Fertility rate (per woman)	1.5
Pop. under 15	16.7%	Urban population	65.8%
Pop. over 60	20.8%		per 1,000 pop.
No. of men per 100 women	93	Crude birth rate	11.0
Human Development Index	88.0	Crude death rate	10.8

The economy

GDP	€123bn	GDP per head	$10,940
GDP	$109.8bn	GDP per head in purchasing	
Av. ann. growth in real		power parity (USA=100)	51.7
GDP 1991–2001	2.7%	Economic freedom index	2.40

Origins of GDP

	% of total
Agriculture	3.6
Industry, of which:	28.6
manufacturing	...
Services	67.7

Components of GDP

	% of total
Private consumption	60.9
Public consumption	20.5
Investment	28.2
Exports	31.6
Imports	-41.2

Structure of employment

	% of total		% of labour force
Agriculture	13	Unemployed 2001	3.9
Industry	35	Av. ann. rate 1995–2001	5.5
Services	52		

Energy

	m TOE		
Total output	3.1	Net energy imports as %	
Total consumption	24.6	of energy use	87
Consumption per head,			
kg oil equivalent	2,459		

Inflation and finance

Consumer price			av. ann. increase 1996–2001
inflation 2002	3.6%	Euro area:	
Av. ann. inflation 1996–2002	3.0%	Narrow money (M1)	7.6%
Interbank rate, 2001	4.26%	Broad money	5.8%
		Household saving rate	10.3%

Exchange rates

	end 2002		December 2002
			1995 = 100
Euro per $	0.95	Effective rates	
Euro per SDR	1.30	– nominal	95.2
		– real	103.1

Trade

Principal exports

	$bn fob
Consumer goods	8.8
Capital goods	7.5
Raw materials & semi-manufactures	7.1
Energy products	0.4
Total incl. others	**23.9**

Principal imports

	$bn cif
Capital goods	13.5
Raw materials & semi-manufactures	11.9
Consumer goods	8.8
Energy products	3.7
Total incl. others	**37.9**

Main export destinations

	% of total
Germany	19.2
Spain	18.6
France	12.6
United Kingdom	10.3
United States	5.8

Main origins of imports

	% of total
Spain	26.5
Germany	13.9
France	10.3
Italy	6.7
United Kingdom	5.0

Balance of payments, reserves and debt, $bn

Visible exports fob	25.8	Overall balance	0.9
Visible imports fob	-38.8	Change in reserves	0.8
Trade balance	-13.0	Level of reserves	
Invisibles inflows	13.9	end Dec.	15.1
Invisibles outflows	-14.4	No. months of import cover	3.4
Net transfers	3.5	Aid given	0.27
Current account balance	-10.0	– as % of GDP	0.25
– as % of GDP	-9.1		
Capital balance	11.5		

Health and education

Health spending, % of GDP	7.7	Education spending, % of GDP	5.8
Doctors per 1,000 pop.	3.3	Enrolment, %: primary	121
Hospital beds per 1,000 pop.	4.0	secondary[a]	114
Improved-water source access, % of pop.	...	tertiary	45

Society

No. of households	3.7m	Colour TVs per 100 households	97.6
Av. no. per household	2.7	Telephone lines per 100 pop.	42.9
Marriages per 1,000 pop.	6.4	Mobile telephone subscribers	
Divorces per 1,000 pop.	1.6	per 100 pop.	77.4
Cost of living, Dec. 2002		Computers per 100 pop.	11.7
New York = 100	71	Internet hosts per 1,000 pop.	29.1

a Includes training for unemployed.

ROMANIA

Area	237,500 sq km	Capital	Bucharest
Arable as % of total land	41	Currency	Leu (L)

People

Population	22.4m	Life expectancy: men	67.0 yrs
Pop. per sq km	94	women	74.2 yrs
Av. ann. growth		Adult literacy	98.2%
in pop. 2000–05	-0.23%	Fertility rate (per woman)	1.3
Pop. under 15	18.2%	Urban population	55.2%
Pop. over 60	18.9%		per 1,000 pop.
No. of men per 100 women	95	Crude birth rate	10.4
Human Development Index	77.5	Crude death rate	12.5

The economy

GDP	L1,154trn	GDP per head	$1,730
GDP	$38.7bn	GDP per head in purchasing	
Av. ann. growth in real		power parity (USA=100)	16.9
GDP 1991–2001	-1.2%	Economic freedom index	3.75

Origins of GDP		**Components of GDP**	
	% of total		% of total
Agriculture	15.0	Private consumption	79.9
Industry, of which:	34.6	Public consumption	6.3
manufacturing	...	Investment	21.9
Services	50.4	Exports	33.5
		Imports	-41.6

Structure of employment[a]

	% of total		% of labour force
Agriculture	42	Unemployed 2001	6.6
Industry	28	Av. ann. rate 1995–2001	6.8
Services	30		

Energy

	m TOE		
Total output	28.3	Net energy imports as %	
Total consumption	36.3	of energy use	22
Consumption per head,			
kg oil equivalent	1,619		

Inflation and finance

		av. ann. increase 1996–2001	
Consumer price			
inflation 2002	22.5%	Narrow money (M1)	41.8%
Av. ann. inflation 1996–2002	55.6%	Broad money	54.9%
Treasury bill rate, 2002	27.0%		

Exchange rates

	end 2002		December 2002
			1995 = 100
L per $	33,500	Effective rates	
L per SDR	45,544	– nominal	0.10
L per euro	31,944	– real	111.7

Trade

Principal exports

	$bn fob
Textiles	3.0
Machinery & equipment	1.7
Basic metals & products	1.5
Footwear	1.0
Minerals & fuels	0.7
Total incl. others	**11.4**

Principal imports

	$bn cif
Machinery & equipment	3.5
Textiles & footwear	2.5
Fuels & minerals	2.2
Chemicals	1.2
Total incl. others	**15.6**

Main export destinations

	% of total
Italy	25.0
Germany	15.6
France	8.1
EU15	67.8

Main origins of imports

	% of total
Italy	19.9
Germany	15.2
Russia	7.6
EU15	57.3

Balance of payments, reserves and debt, $bn

Visible exports fob	11.4	Overall balance	1.5
Visible imports fob	-14.4	Change in reserves	1.5
Trade balance	-3.0	Level of reserves	
Invisibles inflows	2.5	end Dec.	6.4
Invisibles outflows	-2.9	No. months of import cover	4.4
Net transfers	1.1	Foreign debt	11.7
Current account balance	-2.3	– as % of GDP	31
– as % of GDP	-6.0	– as % of total exports	96
Capital balance	3.0	Debt service ratio	22

Health and education

Health spending, % of GDP	7.0	Education spending, % of GDP	3.5
Doctors per 1,000 pop.	2.0	Enrolment, %: primary	99
Hospital beds per 1,000 pop.	7.7	secondary	82
Improved-water source access,		tertiary	27
% of pop.	58		

Society

No. of households	7.6m	Colour TVs per 100 households	51.0
Av. no. per household	2.9	Telephone lines per 100 pop.	18.3
Marriages per 1,000 pop.	6.1	Mobile telephone subscribers	
Divorces per 1,000 pop.	2.0	per 100 pop.	17.2
Cost of living, Dec. 2002		Computers per 100 pop.	3.6
New York = 100	49	Internet hosts per 1,000 pop.	4.1

a 1999

RUSSIA

Area	17,075,400 sq km	Capital	Moscow
Arable as % of total land	7	Currency	Rouble (Rb)

People

Population	144.7m	Life expectancy: men	60.8 yrs
Pop. per sq km	8	women	73.1 yrs
Av. ann. growth		Adult literacy	99.6%
in pop. 2000–05	-0.57%	Fertility rate (per woman)	1.1
Pop. under 15	18.0%	Urban population	72.9%
Pop. over 60	18.5%		per 1,000 pop.
No. of men per 100 women	88	Crude birth rate	8.6
Human Development Index	78.1	Crude death rate	14.6

The economy

GDP	Rb9,041bn	GDP per head	$2,140
GDP	$310bn	GDP per head in purchasing	
Av. ann. growth in real		power parity (USA=100)	20.1
GDP 1991–2001	-3.3%	Economic freedom index	3.70

Origins of GDP

	% of total
Agriculture	7.2
Industry, of which:	39.4
manufacturing	...
Services	53.4

Components of GDP

	% of total
Private consumption	50.9
Public consumption	14.3
Investment	22.1
Net exports	13.0

Structure of employment[a]

	% of total		% of labour force
Agriculture	12	Unemployed 2001	10.2
Industry	29	Av. ann. rate 1995–2001	11.2
Services	59		

Energy

	m TOE		
Total output	966.5	Net energy imports as %	
Total consumption	614.0	of energy use	-57
Consumption per head,			
kg oil equivalent	4,218		

Inflation and finance

		av. ann. increase 1996–2001	
Consumer price			
inflation 2002	15.8%	Narrow money (M1)	44.0%
Av. ann. inflation 1996–2002	29.1%	Broad money	42.8%
Money market rate, 2002	8.19%		

Exchange rates

	end 2002		December 2002
			1995 = 100
Rb per $	31.78	Effective rates	
Rb per SDR	43.21	– nominal	32.95
Rb per euro	30.31	– real	109.05

Trade

Principal exports		Principal imports	
	$bn fob		*$bn fob*
Mineral products	53.6	Machinery & equipment	14.1
Metals	14.6	Food products	9.1
Machinery & equipment	10.4	Chemicals	7.5
Chemicals	7.4	Metals	3.0
Total incl. others	**103.1**	Total incl. others	**59.0**

Main export destinations		Main origins of imports	
	% of total		*% of total*
Germany	9.2	Germany	13.8
United States	8.2	Belarus	9.6
Italy	7.4	Ukraine	9.3
China	5.6	United States	7.6
Belarus	5.2	Kazakhstan	4.8
Ukraine	5.2	Italy	4.1

Balance of payments, reserves and debt, $bn

Visible exports fob	101.6	Overall balance	11.3
Visible imports fob	-53.8	Change in reserves	8.6
Trade balance	47.8	Level of reserves	
Invisibles inflows	17.7	end Dec.	36.3
Invisibles outflows	-30.2	No. months of import cover	5.2
Net transfers	-0.8	Foreign debt	152.6
Current account balance	34.6	– as % of GDP	63
– as % of GDP	11.2	– as % of total exports	140
Capital balance	-13.5	Debt service ratio	16

Health and education

Health spending, % of GDP	6.1	Education spending, % of GDP	4.4
Doctors per 1,000 pop.	4.4	Enrolment, %: primary	107
Hospital beds per 1,000 pop.	13.1	secondary	83
Improved-water source access,		tertiary	64
% of pop.	99		

Society

No. of households	51.8m	Colour TVs per 100 households	78.4
Av. no. per household	2.8	Telephone lines per 100 pop.	24.3
Marriages per 1,000 pop.	6.2	Mobile telephone subscribers	
Divorces per 1,000 pop.	3.0	per 100 pop.	3.8
Cost of living, Dec. 2002		Computers per 100 pop.	5.0
New York = 100	84	Internet hosts per 1,000 pop.	3.3

a 1999

SAUDI ARABIA

Area	2,200,000 sq km	Capital	Riyadh
Arable as % of total land	2	Currency	Riyal (SR)

People

Population	21.0m	Life expectancy:	men	71.1 yrs
Pop. per sq km	10		women	73.7 yrs
Av. ann. growth		Adult literacy		77.1%
in pop. 2000–05	2.92%	Fertility rate (per woman)		4.5
Pop. under 15	39.7%	Urban population		86.7%
Pop. over 60	4.1%			per 1,000 pop.
No. of men per 100 women	116	Crude birth rate		33.8
Human Development Index	75.9	Crude death rate		3.7

The economy

GDP	SR698bn	GDP per head	$8,870
GDP	$186.5bn	GDP per head in purchasing	
Av. ann. growth in real		power parity (USA=100)	38.8
GDP 1991–2001	2.1%	Economic freedom index	2.95

Origins of GDP

	% of total
Agriculture	5.2
Industry, of which:	51.2
manufacturing	10.5
Services	43.6

Components of GDP

	% of total
Private consumption	36.6
Public consumption	27.0
Investment	18.1
Exports	41.9
Imports	-24.4

Structure of employment

	% of total		% of labour force
Agriculture	5	Unemployed 2001	4.0
Industry	26	Av. ann. rate 1995–2001	4.0
Services	69		

Energy

	m TOE		
Total output	487.9	Net energy imports as %	
Total consumption	105.3	of energy use	-363
Consumption per head,			
kg oil equivalent	5,081		

Inflation and finance

		av. ann. increase 1996-2001	
Consumer price			
inflation 2002	-0.5%	Narrow money (M1)	6.2%
Av. ann. inflation 1996–2002	-0.6%	Broad money	5.0%

Exchange rates

	end 2002		December 2002
			1995 = 100
SR per $	3.75	Effective rates	
SR per SDR	5.09	– nominal	100.0
SR per euro	3.57	– real	120.3

Trade

Principal exports		Principal imports	
	$bn fob		*$bn cif*
Crude oil & refined petroleum	51.0	Machinery & transport equipment	12.0
Oil products	11.7	Chemical products	5.4
Total incl. others	**68.1**	Total incl. others	**31.2**

Main export destinations		Main origins of imports	
	% of total		*% of total*
United States	18.3	United States	17.7
Japan	17.4	Japan	10.4
South Korea	10.2	Germany	7.9
Singapore	5.4	United Kingdom	6.5

Balance of payments, reserves and aid, $bn

Visible exports fob	73.0	Overall balance	-1.9
Visible imports fob	-28.6	Change in reserves	-2.0
Trade balance	44.4	Level of reserves	
Invisibles inflows	9.3	end Dec.	18.9
Invisibles outflows	-24.0	No. months of import cover	4.3
Net transfers	-15.2	Aid given	0.49
Current account balance	14.5	– as % of GDP	0.35
– as % of GDP	7.8		
Capital balance	-16.4		

Health and education

Health spending, % of GDP	11.0	Education spending, % of GDP	9.5
Doctors per 1,000 pop.	0.2	Enrolment, %: primary	68
Hospital beds per 1,000 pop.	0.2	secondary	68
Improved-water source access, % of pop.	95	tertiary	22

Society

No. of households	2.8m	Colour TVs per 100 households	99.4
Av. no. per household	7.8	Telephone lines per 100 pop.	19.5
Marriages per 1,000 pop.	3.2	Mobile telephone subscribers	
Divorces per 1,000 pop.	...	per 100 pop.	11.3
Cost of living, Dec. 2002		Computers per 100 pop.	6.3
New York = 100	72	Internet hosts per 1,000 pop.	0.5

SINGAPORE

Area	639 sq km	Capital	Singapore
Arable as % of total land	2	Currency	Singapore dollar (S$)

People

Population	4.1m	Life expectancy: men		75.9 yrs
Pop. per sq km	6,416	women		80.3 yrs
Av. ann. growth		Adult literacy		92.6%
in pop. 2000–05	1.69%	Fertility rate (per woman)		1.4
Pop. under 15	21.8%	Urban population		100.0%
Pop. over 60	10.5%			per 1,000 pop.
No. of men per 100 women	101	Crude birth rate		10.8
Human Development Index	88.5	Crude death rate		5.2

The economy

GDP	S$153bn	GDP per head	$20,850
GDP	$85.6bn	GDP per head in purchasing	
Av. ann. growth in real		power parity (USA=100)	66.7
GDP 1991–2001	6.9%	Economic freedom index	1.50

Origins of GDP		Components of GDP	
	% of total		% of total
Agriculture	0.2	Private consumption	44.7
Industry, of which:	32.3	Public consumption	12.7
manufacturing	23.6	Investment	24.3
Services	67.5	Exports	173.6
		Imports	-151.8

Structure of employment

	% of total		% of labour force
Agriculture	0	Unemployed 2001	4.3
Industry	26	Av. ann. rate 1995–2001	3.5
Services	74		

Energy

	m TOE		
Total output	0.06	Net energy imports as %	
Total consumption	24.6	of energy use	100
Consumption per head,			
kg oil equivalent	6,120		

Inflation and finance

Consumer price		av. ann. increase 1996–2001	
inflation 2002	-0.4%	Narrow money (M1)	5.9%
Av. ann. inflation 1996–2002	0.7%	Broad money	10.1%
Money market rate, 2002	0.96%		

Exchange rates

	end 2002		December 2002
S$ per $	1.74	Effective rates	1995 = 100
S$ per SDR	2.36	– nominal	101.8
S$ per euro	1.66	– real	93.3

Trade

Principal exports	$bn fob	Principal imports	$bn cif
Machinery & equipment	78.6	Machinery & equipment	69.2
Mineral fuels	12.6	Mineral fuels	14.6
Chemicals	9.9	Manufactured products	8.5
Manufactured products	5.3	Chemicals	6.8
Food	2.6	Food	4.0
Total incl. others	**121.8**	**Total incl. others**	**116.0**

Main export destinations	% of total	Main origins of imports	% of total
Malaysia	17.3	Malaysia	17.3
United States	15.4	United States	16.4
Hong Kong	8.9	Japan	13.9
Japan	7.7	China	6.2
Taiwan	5.1	Thailand	4.5
China	4.4	Taiwan	4.3
Thailand	4.3	Saudi Arabia	3.6

Balance of payments, reserves and debt, $bn

Visible exports fob	122.5	Overall balance	-0.9
Visible imports fob	-109.5	Change in reserves	-4.8
Trade balance	12.9	Level of reserves	
Invisibles inflows	41.1	end Dec.	75.4
Invisibles outflows	-34.7	No. months of import cover	6.3
Net transfers	-1.4	Foreign debt	9.8
Current account balance	17.9	– as % of GDP	11.5
– as % of GDP	20.9	– as % of total exports	6
Capital balance	-18.9	Debt service ratio	2

Health and education

Health spending, % of GDP	3.3	Education spending, % of GDP	3.7
Doctors per 1,000 pop.	1.4	Enrolment, %: primary[a]	92
Hospital beds per 1,000 pop.	3.6	secondary[a]	67
Improved-water source access,		tertiary[b]	39
% of pop.	100		

Society

No. of households	1.0m	Colour TVs per 100 households	98.5
Av. no. per household	3.5	Telephone lines per 100 pop.	47.2
Marriages per 1,000 pop.	5.5	Mobile telephone subscribers	
Divorces per 1,000 pop.	1.8	per 100 pop.	69.2
Cost of living, Dec. 2002		Computers per 100 pop.	50.8
New York = 100	99	Internet hosts per 1,000 pop.	82.5

a 2000
b 1997

SLOVAKIA

Area	49,035 sq km	Capital	Bratislava
Arable as % of total land	30	Currency	Koruna (Kc)

People

Population	5.4m	Life expectancy: men	69.8 yrs
Pop. per sq km	110	women	77.6 yrs
Av. ann. growth		Adult literacy	99.0%
in pop. 2000–05	0.08%	Fertility rate (per woman)	1.3
Pop. under 15	19.5%	Urban population	57.6%
Pop. over 60	15.4%		per 1,000 pop.
No. of men per 100 women	94	Crude birth rate	10.2
Human Development Index	83.5	Crude death rate	9.8

The economy

GDP	Kc989bn	GDP per head	$3,790
GDP	$20.5bn	GDP per head in purchasing	
Av. ann. growth in real		power parity (USA=100)	34.4
GDP 1991–2001	0.6%	Economic freedom index	2.90

Origins of GDP[a]

Components of GDP

	% of total		% of total
Agriculture	4.3	Private consumption	56.6
Industry, of which:	35.2	Public consumption	20.0
manufacturing	...	Investment	32.0
Services	60.5	Exports	74.0
		Imports	-82.5

Structure of employment

	% of total		% of labour force
Agriculture	6	Unemployed 2001	19.0
Industry	37	Av. ann. rate 1995–2001	14.6
Services	57		

Energy

	m TOE		
Total output	6.0	Net energy imports as %	
Total consumption	17.5	of energy use	66
Consumption per head,			
kg oil equivalent	3,234		

Inflation and finance

Consumer price		av. ann. increase 1996–2001	
inflation 2002	3.3%	Narrow money (M1)	5.4%
Av. ann. inflation 1996–2002	7.6%	Broad money	10.4%
Money market rate, 2002	6.33%		

Exchange rates

	end 2002		December 2002
Kc per $	40.04	Effective rates	1995 = 100
Kc per SDR	54.43	– nominal	89.83
Kc per euro	38.18	– real	111.38

Trade

Principal exports		Principal imports	
	$bn fob		*$bn fob*
Machinery & transport equipment	4.9	Machinery & transport equipment	5.6
Intermediate manufactured goods	3.4	Fuels	2.7
Other manufactured goods	1.7	Intermediate manufactured goods	2.2
Chemicals	0.9	Chemicals	1.5
Fuels	0.8	Other manufactured goods	1.4
Total incl. others	**12.6**	Total incl. others	**15.5**

Main export destinations		Main origins of imports	
	% of total		*% of total*
Germany	26.9	Germany	22.7
Czech Republic	18.0	Czech Republic	13.3
Italy	7.9	Russia	13.0
Austria	7.3	Italy	6.4
EU15	59.9	EU15	49.8

Balance of payments, reserves and debt, $bn

Visible exports fob	12.6	Overall balance[a]	0.9
Visible imports fob	-14.8	Change in reserves	0.1
Trade balance	-2.1	Level of reserves	
Invisibles inflows	2.8	end Dec.	4.4
Invisibles outflows	-2.6	No. months of import cover	3.1
Net transfers	0.2	Foreign debt	11.1
Current account balance	-1.8	– as % of GDP	56
– as % of GDP	-8.8	– as % of total exports	79
Capital balance[a]	1.6	Debt service ratio	19.0

Health and education

Health spending, % of GDP	5.4	Education spending, % of GDP	4.2
Doctors per 1,000 pop.	4.7	Enrolment, %: primary	103
Hospital beds per 1,000 pop.	7.2	secondary	87
Improved-water source access, % of pop.	100	tertiary	30

Society

No. of households	2.0m	Colour TVs per 100 households	86.0
Av. no. per household	2.7	Telephone lines per 100 pop.	28.8
Marriages per 1,000 pop.	4.8	Mobile telephone subscribers per 100 pop.	39.7
Divorces per 1,000 pop.	1.6		
Cost of living, Dec. 2002 New York = 100	...	Computers per 100 pop.	14.8
		Internet hosts per 1,000 pop.	14.9

a 2000

SLOVENIA

Area	20,253 sq km	Capital	Ljubljana
Arable as % of total land	9	Currency	Tolars (SIT)

People

Population	2.0m	Life expectancy: men	72.6 yrs
Pop. per sq km	99	women	79.8 yrs
Av. ann. growth		Adult literacy	99.6%
in pop. 2000–05	-0.11%	Fertility rate (per woman)	1.1
Pop. under 15	15.9%	Urban population	49.1%
Pop. over 60	19.2%		per 1,000 pop.
No. of men per 100 women	95	Crude birth rate	8.2
Human Development Index	87.9	Crude death rate	9.8

The economy

GDP	SIT4,566bn	GDP per head	$9,480
GDP	$18.8bn	GDP per head in purchasing	
Av. ann. growth in real		power parity (USA=100)	49.8
GDP 1991–2001	2.0%	Economic freedom index	2.85

Origins of GDP

	% of total
Agriculture	3.2
Industry, of which:	34.7
manufacturing	25.8
Services	62.1

Components of GDP

	% of total
Private consumption	53.9
Public consumption	21.0
Investment	26.2
Exports	59.8
Imports	-61.0

Structure of employment

	% of total		% of labour force
Agriculture	10	Unemployed 2001	5.9
Industry	38	Av. ann. rate 1995–2001	7.1
Services	52		

Energy

	m TOE		
Total output	3.1	Net energy imports as %	
Total consumption	6.5	of energy use	53
Consumption per head,			
kg oil equivalent	3,288		

Inflation and finance

		av. ann. increase 1996–2001	
Consumer price			
inflation 2002	7.5%	Narrow money (M1)	18.9%
Av. ann. inflation 1996–2002	8.7%	Broad money	21.2%
Money market rate, 2002	4.93%		

Exchange rates

	end 2002		December 2002
SIT per $	221.1	Effective rates	1995 = 100
SIT per SDR	300.6	– nominal	...
SIT per euro	210.8	– real	...

Trade

Principal exports	$bn fob	Principal imports	$bn fob
Manufactures	4.1	Machinery & transport	
Machinery & transport		equipment	3.4
equipment	3.3	Manufactures	3.4
Chemicals	1.1	Chemicals	1.3
Food & live animals	0.2	Mineral fuels	0.8
Total incl. others	**9.3**	Total incl. others	**10.1**

Main export destinations	% of total	Main origins of imports	% of total
Germany	26.0	Germany	19.2
Italy	12.4	Italy	17.7
Croatia	8.6	France	10.6
Austria	7.4	Austria	8.3
France	6.7	Croatia	4.0
EU15	61.6	EU15	67.6

Balance of payments, reserves and debt, $bn

Visible exports fob	9.3	Overall balance	1.3
Visible imports fob	-10.0	Change in reserves	1.2
Trade balance	-0.6	Level of reserves	
Invisibles inflows	2.4	end Dec.	4.4
Invisibles outflows	-1.9	No. months of import cover	4.4
Net transfers	0.1	Foreign debt	6.7
Current account balance	0.0	– as % of GDP	34
– as % of GDP	0.2	– as % of total exports	57
Capital balance	1.2	Debt service ratio	14

Health and education

Health spending, % of GDP	7.6	Education spending, % of GDP	5.8
Doctors per 1,000 pop.	2.3	Enrolment, %: primary	100
Hospital beds per 1,000 pop.	5.3	secondary[a]	99
Improved-water source access,		tertiary	61
% of pop.	100		

Society

No. of households	0.6m	Colour TVs per 100 households	90.6
Av. no. per household	3.0	Telephone lines per 100 pop.	40.1
Marriages per 1,000 pop.	3.9	Mobile telephone subscribers	
Divorces per 1,000 pop.	1.0	per 100 pop.	76.0
Cost of living, Dec. 2002		Computers per 100 pop.	27.6
New York = 100	...	Internet hosts per 1,000 pop.	15.0

a 2000

SOUTH AFRICA

Area	1,225,815 sq km	Capital	Pretoria
Arable as % of total land	12	Currency	Rand (R)

People

Population	43.8m	Life expectancy: men	45.1 yrs
Pop. per sq km	36	women	50.7 yrs
Av. ann. growth		Adult literacy	85.6%
in pop. 2000–05	0.59%	Fertility rate (per woman)	2.6
Pop. under 15	34.0%	Urban population	57.7%
Pop. over 60	5.9%		per 1,000 pop.
No. of men per 100 women	96	Crude birth rate	24.6
Human Development Index	69.5	Crude death rate	16.9

The economy

GDP	R975bn	GDP per head	$2,590
GDP	$113.3bn	GDP per head in purchasing	
Av. ann. growth in real		power parity (USA=100)	31.8
GDP 1991–2001	1.8%	Economic freedom index	2.65

Origins of GDP

Components of GDP

	% of total		% of total
Agriculture	4.4	Private consumption	63.3
Industry, of which:	32.3	Public consumption	16.6
manufacturing	20.0	Investment	15.2
Services	63.3	Exports	26.1
		Imports	-21.9

Structure of employment

	% of total		% of labour force
Agriculture	6	Unemployed 2001	23.8
Industry	24	Av. ann. rate 1995–2001	22.1
Services	70		

Energy

	m TOE		
Total output	144.5	Net energy imports as %	
Total consumption	107.6	of energy use	-34
Consumption per head,			
kg oil equivalent	2,514		

Inflation and finance

		av. ann. increase 1996–2001	
Consumer price			
inflation 2002	10.6%	Narrow money (M1)	16.2%
Av. ann. inflation 1996–2002	6.6%	Broad money	13.2%
Money market rate, 2002	10.59%		

Exchange rates

	end 2002		December 2002
R per $	8.64	Effective rates	1995 = 100
R per SDR	11.75	– nominal	49.5
R per euro	8.24	– real	74.3

Trade

Principal exports[a]	$bn fob	Principal imports[a]	$bn cif
Metals & metal products	6.3	Machinery & appliances	8.9
Gold	5.6	Mineral products	3.7
Diamonds	2.9	Chemicals	3.4
Machinery & transport		Transport & equipment	1.7
equipment	2.6		
Total incl. others	**31.0**	Total incl. others	**32.9**

Main export destinations	% of total	Main origins of imports	% of total
United States	13.0	Germany	15.2
United Kingdom	12.4	United States	11.4
Germany	9.2	United Kingdom	8.6
Japan	6.9	Japan	5.8
Italy	6.4		

Balance of payments, reserves and debt, $bn

Visible exports fob	30.6	Overall balance	2.2
Visible imports fob	-25.7	Change in reserves	-0.1
Trade balance	5.0	Level of reserves	
Invisibles inflows	6.8	end Dec.	7.6
Invisibles outflows	-11.2	No. months of import cover	2.5
Net transfers	-0.7	Foreign debt	24.1
Current account balance	-0.2	– as % of GDP	50
– as % of GDP	-0.1	– as % of total exports	65
Capital balance	0.5	Debt service ratio	12

Health and education

Health spending, % of GDP	7.5	Education spending, % of GDP	5.5
Doctors per 1,000 pop.	0.7	Enrolment, %: primary	111
Hospital beds per 1,000 pop.	3.1	secondary	87
Improved-water source access,		tertiary	15
% of pop.	86		

Society

No. of households	10.0m	Colour TVs per 100 households	63.9
Av. no. per household	4.3	Telephone lines per 100 pop.	11.4
Marriages per 1,000 pop.	3.5	Mobile telephone subscribers	
Divorces per 1,000 pop.	0.9	per 100 pop.	21.0
Cost of living, Dec. 2002		Computers per 100 pop.	6.7
New York = 100	45	Internet hosts per 1,000 pop.	4.5

a 1997

SOUTH KOREA

Area	99,274 sq km	Capital	Seoul
Arable as % of total land	17	Currency	Won (W)

People

Population	47.1m	Life expectancy: men	71.8 yrs
Pop. per sq km	474	women	79.3 yrs
Av. ann. growth		Adult literacy	97.2%
in pop. 2000–05	0.57%	Fertility rate (per woman)	2.0
Pop. under 15	20.9%	Urban population	82.5%
Pop. over 60	11.0%		per 1,000 pop.
No. of men per 100 women	101	Crude birth rate	12.8
Human Development Index	88.2	Crude death rate	5.9

The economy

GDP	W545trn	GDP per head	$8,970
GDP	$422.2bn	GDP per head in purchasing	
Av. ann. growth in real		power parity (USA=100)	43.9
GDP 1991–2001	5.9%	Economic freedom index	2.70

Origins of GDP

	% of total
Agriculture	4.6
Industry, of which:	42.8
manufacturing	30.0
Services	52.6

Components of GDP

	% of total
Private consumption	59.4
Public consumption	10.4
Investment	26.9
Exports	43.1
Imports	-40.5

Structure of employment

	% of total		% of labour force
Agriculture	10	Unemployed 2001	3.7
Industry	28	Av. ann. rate 1995–2001	3.9
Services	62		

Energy

	m TOE		
Total output	33.6	Net energy imports as %	
Total consumption	193.6	of energy use	83
Consumption per head,			
kg oil equivalent	4,119		

Inflation and finance

		av. ann. increase 1996–2001	
Consumer price			
inflation 2002	2.8%	Narrow money (M1)	6.2%
Av. ann. inflation 1996–2002	3.7%	Broad money	21.3%
Money market rate, 2002	4.2%	Household saving rate	10.0%

Exchange rates

	end 2002		December 2002
			1995 = 100
W per $	1,186	Effective rates	
W per SDR	1,613	– nominal	...
W per euro	1,131	– real	...

Trade

Principal exports		Principal imports	
	$bn fob		*$bn cif*
Electronic products	47.4	Electrical machinery	33.8
Machinery	11.6	Crude petroleum	21.4
Motor vehicles	11.5	Machinery & equipment	15.3
Chemicals	10.8	Chemicals	11.3
Metal goods	10.0	Iron & steel products	5.0
Total incl. others	**150.4**	Total incl. others	**141.1**

Main export destinations		Main origins of imports	
	% of total		*% of total*
United States	20.7	Japan	18.9
Japan	11.0	United States	15.9
China	12.1	China	9.4
Hong Kong	6.3	Saudi Arabia	5.7
Taiwan	3.9	Australia	3.9

Balance of payments, reserves and debt, $bn

Visible exports fob	151.4	Overall balance	13.4
Visible imports fob	-138.0	Change in reserves	6.6
Trade balance	13.4	Level of reserves	
Invisibles inflows	36.6	end Dec.	102.9
Invisibles outflows	-41.1	No. months of import cover	6.9
Net transfers	-0.4	Foreign debt	108.2
Current account balance	8.6	– as % of GDP	25
– as % of GDP	2.0	– as % of total exports	58
Capital balance	2.1	Debt service ratio	12

Health and education

Health spending, % of GDP	6.0	Education spending, % of GDP	3.8
Doctors per 1,000 pop.	1.6	Enrolment, %: primary	101
Hospital beds per 1,000 pop.	5.9	secondary	94
Improved-water source access,		tertiary	78
% of pop.	92		

Society

No. of households	14.4m	Colour TVs per 100 households	93.0
Av. no. per household	3.3	Telephone lines per 100 pop.	47.6
Marriages per 1,000 pop.	7.7	Mobile telephone subscribers	
Divorces per 1,000 pop.	1.5	per 100 pop.	60.8
Cost of living, Dec. 2002		Computers per 100 pop.	25.1
New York = 100	97	Internet hosts per 1,000 pop.	8.6

SPAIN

Area	504,782 sq km	Capital	Madrid
Arable as % of total land	27	Currency	Euro (€)

People

Population	39.9m	Life expectancy: men	75.9 yrs
Pop. per sq km	79	women	82.8 yrs
Av. ann. growth		Adult literacy	97.7%
in pop. 2000–05	0.21%	Fertility rate (per woman)	1.2
Pop. under 15	14.6%	Urban population	77.8%
Pop. over 60	21.2%		per 1,000 pop.
No. of men per 100 women	96	Crude birth rate	8.9
Human Development Index	91.3	Crude death rate	9.1

The economy

GDP	€650bn	GDP per head	$14,570
GDP	$581.8bn	GDP per head in purchasing	
Av. ann. growth in real		power parity (USA=100)	57.9
GDP 1991–2001	2.7%	Economic freedom index	2.35

Origins of GDP		**Components of GDP**	
	% of total		% of total
Agriculture	3.6	Private consumption	58.7
Industry, of which:	30.2	Public consumption	17.3
manufacturing	...	Investment	25.5
Services	66.2	Exports	29.9
		Imports	-31.4

Structure of employment[a]

	% of total		% of labour force
Agriculture	7	Unemployed 2001	13.1
Industry	31	Av. ann. rate 1995–2001	18.3
Services	62		

Energy

	m TOE		
Total output	31.9	Net energy imports as %	
Total consumption	124.9	of energy use	74
Consumption per head,			
kg oil equivalent	3,084		

Inflation and finance

Consumer price		av. ann. increase 1996–2001	
inflation 2002	3.1%	Euro area:	
Av. ann. inflation 1996–2002	2.7%	Narrow money (M1)	7.6%
Money market rate, 2002	3.28%	Broad money	5.8%
		Household saving rate	10.3%

Exchange rates

	end 2002		December 2002
Euro per $	0.95	Effective rates	1995 = 100
Euro per SDR	1.30	– nominal	93.8
		– real	108.0

Trade

Principal exports		Principal imports	
	$bn fob		*$bn cif*
Raw materials & intermediate products	51.2	Raw materials & intermediate products (excl. fuels)	70.0
Consumer goods	46.7	Consumer goods	40.5
Capital goods	14.0	Capital goods	25.8
Energy products	3.3	Energy products	17.1
Total incl. others	**115.2**	Total incl. others	**153.6**

Main export destinations		Main origins of imports	
	% of total		*% of total*
France	19.5	France	16.8
Germany	11.8	Germany	15.5
Portugal	10.0	Italy	9.1
Italy	9.0	Benelux	7.3
United Kingdom	8.9	United Kingdom	7.0
EU15	71.3	EU15	63.9

Balance of payments, reserves and aid, $bn

Visible exports fob	117.6	Capital balance	20.8
Visible imports fob	-149.1	Overall balance	-1.3
Trade balance	-31.5	Change in reserves	-1.4
Invisibles inflows	77.6	Level of reserves	
Invisibles outflows	-62.9	end Dec.	34.2
Net transfers	1.7	No. months of import cover	1.9
Current account balance	-15.1	Aid given	1.74
– as % of GDP	-2.6	– as % of GDP	0.30

Health and education

Health spending, % of GDP	7.0	Education spending, % of GDP	4.5
Doctors per 1,000 pop.	4.6	Enrolment, %: primary	105
Hospital beds per 1,000 pop.	3.6	secondary	116
Improved-water source access, % of pop.	...	tertiary	59

Society

No. of households	12.5m	Colour TVs per 100 households	98.3
Av. no. per household	3.2	Telephone lines per 100 pop.	43.1
Marriages per 1,000 pop.	5.1	Mobile telephone subscribers	
Divorces per 1,000 pop.	0.8	per 100 pop.	65.5
Cost of living, Dec. 2002		Computers per 100 pop.	16.8
New York = 100	78	Internet hosts per 1,000 pop.	42.5

a 2000

SWEDEN

Area	449,964 sq km	Capital	Stockholm
Arable as % of total land	7	Currency	Swedish krona (Skr)

People

Population	8.8m	Life expectancy: men	77.6 yrs
Pop. per sq km	20	women	82.6 yrs
Av. ann. growth		Adult literacy	99.0%
in pop. 2000–05	0.09%	Fertility rate (per woman)	1.6
Pop. under 15	18.3%	Urban population	83.3%
Pop. over 60	22.3%		per 1,000 pop.
No. of men per 100 women	98	Crude birth rate	8.2
Human Development Index	94.1	Crude death rate	10.6

The economy

GDP	Skr2,167bn	GDP per head	$23,750
GDP	$209.8bn	GDP per head in purchasing	
Av. ann. growth in real		power parity (USA=100)	69.4
GDP 1991–2001	1.7%	Economic freedom index	1.90

Origins of GDP

	% of total
Agriculture	2.0
Industry, of which:	29.0
manufacturing	...
Services	69.0

Components of GDP

	% of total
Private consumption	48.8
Public consumption	27.3
Investment	18.2
Exports	45.2
Imports	-39.5

Structure of employment

	% of total		% of labour force
Agriculture	2	Unemployed 2001	4.0
Industry	24	Av. ann. rate 1995–2001	6.4
Services	74		

Energy

	m TOE		
Total output	30.7	Net energy imports as %	
Total consumption	47.5	of energy use	35
Consumption per head,			
kg oil equivalent	5,354		

Inflation and finance

		av. ann. increase 1996–2000	
Consumer price			
inflation 2002	2.2%	Narrow money (M1)	...
Av. ann. inflation 1996–2002	1.2%	Broad money	3.8%
Money market rate, 2001	4.08%	Household saving rate	4.9%

Exchange rates

	end 2002		December 2002
			1995 = 100
Skr per $	8.83	Effective rates	
Skr per SDR	12.00	– nominal	96.7
Skr per euro	8.42	– real	99.1

Trade

Principal exports		Principal imports	
	$bn fob		$bn cif
Machinery & transport equipment	34.2	Machinery & transport equipment	25.8
Manufactured goods	16.3	Manufactured goods	9.2
Chemicals	8.3	Miscellaneous manufactures	8.8
Crude materials	4.4	Chemicals	6.8
Total incl. others	**75.8**	Total incl. others	**63.5**

Main export destinations		Main origins of imports	
	% of total		% of total
Germany	10.6	Germany	17.8
United States	10.5	United Kingdom	8.7
United Kingdom	8.8	Norway	8.5
Norway	8.6	Denmark	8.2
Denmark	6.1	United States	6.9
EU15	54.6	EU15	66.3

Balance of payments, reserves and aid, $bn

Visible exports fob	76.2	Capital balance	2.3
Visible imports fob	-62.4	Overall balance	-1.0
Trade balance	13.8	Change in reserves	-0.9
Invisibles inflows	39.9	Level of reserves	
Invisibles outflows	-43.8	end Dec.	15.6
Net transfers	-3.3	No. months of import cover	1.8
Current account balance	6.7	Aid given	1.67
– as % of GDP	3.2	– as % of GDP	0.81

Health and education

Health spending, % of GDP	7.9	Education spending, % of GDP	7.8
Doctors per 1,000 pop.	3.3	Enrolment, %: primary	110
Hospital beds per 1,000 pop.	3.5	secondary	149
Improved-water source access,		tertiary	70
% of pop.	100		

Society

No. of households	4.4m	Colour TVs per 100 households	97.3
Av. no. per household	2.0	Telephone lines per 100 pop.	73.9
Marriages per 1,000 pop.	4.5	Mobile telephone subscribers	
Divorces per 1,000 pop.	2.2	per 100 pop.	77.1
Cost of living, Dec. 2002		Computers per 100 pop.	56.1
New York = 100	89	Internet hosts per 1,000 pop.	137.4

SWITZERLAND

Area	41,293 sq km	Capital	Berne
Arable as % of total land	10	Currency	Swiss franc (SFr)

People

Population	7.2m	Life expectancy: men	75.9 yrs
Pop. per sq km	174	women	82.3 yrs
Av. ann. growth		Adult literacy	99.0%
in pop. 2000–05	-0.05%	Fertility rate (per woman)	1.4
Pop. under 15	16.7%	Urban population	67.3%
Pop. over 60	21.3%		per 1,000 pop.
No. of men per 100 women	98	Crude birth rate	8.6
Human Development Index	92.8	Crude death rate	9.8

The economy

GDP	SFr417bn	GDP per head	$34,460
GDP	$247.1bn	GDP per head in purchasing	
Av. ann. growth in real		power parity (USA=100)	90.3
GDP 1991–2001	0.9%	Economic freedom index	1.95

Origins of GDP[a]		Components of GDP	
	% of total		% of total
Agriculture	1.6	Private consumption	60.0
Industry, of which:	33.8	Public consumption	14.2
manufacturing	...	Investment	20.3
Services	64.6	Exports	43.9
		Imports	-38.3

Structure of employment

	% of total		% of labour force
Agriculture	4	Unemployed 2001	2.5
Industry	26	Av. ann. rate 1995–2001	3.3
Services	70		

Energy

	m TOE		
Total output	11.8	Net energy imports as %	
Total consumption	27.0	of energy use	56
Consumption per head,			
kg oil equivalent	3,704		

Inflation and finance

Consumer price		av. ann. increase 1996–2001	
inflation 2002	0.7%	Narrow money (M1)	6.3%
Av. ann. inflation 1996–2002	0.8%	Broad money	1.8%
Money market rate, 2002	0.44%	Household saving rate	8.7%

Exchange rates

	end 2002		December 2002
SFr per $	1.39	Effective rates	1995 = 100
SFr per SDR	1.89	– nominal	101.4
SFr per euro	1.32	– real	115.3

Trade

Principal exports		Principal imports	
	$bn		$bn
Chemicals	24.8	Machinery	17.5
Machinery	21.3	Chemicals	15.5
Watches & jewellery	6.3	Motor vehicles	8.4
Metals & metal manufactures	6.1	Textiles	5.3
Precision instruments	5.0	Precision instruments	4.8
Total incl. others	**78.1**	Total incl. others	**77.1**

Main export destinations		Main origins of imports	
	% of total		% of total
Germany	22.2	Germany	32.2
United States	10.6	France	11.0
France	9.0	Italy	10.2
Italy	8.0	Netherlands	5.9
United Kingdom	5.3	United States	5.3
Japan	3.9	United Kingdom	4.6
EU15	61.0	EU15	79.9

Balance of payments, reserves and aid, $bn

Visible exports fob	95.8	Capital balance	-30.5
Visible imports fob	-94.3	Overall balance	0.6
Trade balance	1.6	Change in reserves	-2.1
Invisibles inflows	77.5	Level of reserves	
Invisibles outflows	-52.3	end Dec.	51.5
Net transfers	-4.1	No. months of import cover	4.2
Current account balance	22.6	Aid given	0.91
– as % of GDP	9.2	– as % of GDP	0.34

Health and education

Health spending, % of GDP	10.8	Education spending, % of GDP	5.5
Doctors per 1,000 pop.[b]	3.5	Enrolment, %: primary	107
Hospital beds per 1,000 pop.	17.9	secondary	100
Improved-water source access,		tertiary	42
% of pop.	100		

Society

No. of households	3.2m	Colour TVs per 100 households	97.4
Av. no. per household	2.2	Telephone lines per 100 pop.	71.8
Marriages per 1,000 pop.	4.9	Mobile telephone subscribers	
Divorces per 1,000 pop.	2.7	per 100 pop.	72.4
Cost of living, Dec. 2002		Computers per 100 pop.	50.0
New York = 100	112	Internet hosts per 1,000 pop.	100.5

a 1998
b 2000

TAIWAN

Area	36,179 sq km	Capital	Taipei
Arable as % of total land	25	Currency	Taiwan dollar (T$)

People

Population	22.3m	Life expectancy:[a] men	74.0
Pop. per sq km	617	women	79.7
Av. ann. growth		Adult literacy	96.1
in pop. 1995–98	0.87%	Fertility rate (per woman)	1.8
Pop. under 15	22.0%	Urban population	...
Pop. over 65	8.6%		per 1,000 pop.
No. of men per 100 women	105.2	Crude birth rate	12.9
Human Development Index	...	Crude death rate[a]	6.1

The economy

GDP	T$9,542bn	GDP per head	$12,660
GDP	$282.3bn	GDP per head in purchasing	
Av. ann. growth in real		power parity (USA=100)	50.2
GDP 1991–2001	5.6%	Economic freedom index	2.30

Origins of GDP

	% of total
Agriculture	1.9
Industry, of which:	30.4
manufacturing	25.3
Services	67.7

Components of GDP

	% of total
Private consumption	63.6
Public consumption	13.0
Investment	17.7
Exports	50.9
Imports	-45.2

Structure of employment

	% of total		% of labour force
Agriculture	8	Unemployed 2001	2.9
Industry	36	Av. ann. rate 1995–2001	2.6
Services	56		

Energy

	m TOE		
Total output	...	Net energy imports as %	
Total consumption	...	of energy use	...
Consumption per head,			
kg oil equivalent	...		

Inflation and finance

		av. ann. increase 1996–2001	
Consumer price			
inflation 2002	-0.2%	Narrow money (M1)	8.0%
Av. ann. inflation 1996–2002	0.6%	Broad money	7.1%
Deposit rate, 2002	2.2%		

Exchange rates

	end 2002		December 2002
			1995 = 100
T$ per $	34.8	Effective rates	
T$ per SDR	47.3	– nominal	...
T$ per euro	36.5	– real	...

Trade

Principal exports		Principal imports	
	$bn fob		$bn cif
Machinery & electrical equipment	66.9	Machinery & electrical equipment	47.5
Textiles & clothing	13.9	Minerals	11.8
Base metals & manufactures	11.3	Chemicals	10.2
Plastics and rubber products	8.0	Metals	7.8
Vehicles, aircraft & ships	4.4	Precision instruments, clocks & watches	6.2
Total incl. others	**122.7**	Total incl. others	**107.3**

Main export destinations		Main origins of imports	
	% of total		% of total
United States	22.5	Japan	24.1
Hong Kong	22.0	United States	17.0
Japan	10.4	South Korea	6.2
Germany	3.6	Malaysia	3.9

Balance of payments, reserves and debt, $bn

Visible exports fob	122.1	Overall balance	17.4
Visible imports fob	-101.8	Change in reserves	15.5
Trade balance	20.3	Level of reserves	
Invisibles inflows	30.0	end Dec.	122.2
Invisibles outflows	-28.6	No. months of import cover	11.2
Net transfers	-2.7	Foreign debt	19.1
Current account balance	19.0	– as % of GDP	7
– as % of GDP	6.7	– as % of total exports	13
Capital balance	-1.0	Debt service ratio	3

Health and education

Health spending, % of GDP	0.4	Education spending, % of GDP	...
Doctors per 1,000 pop.	1.6	Enrolment, %: primary[b]	89
Hospital beds per 1,000 pop.	5.3	secondary[b]	59
Improved-water source access, % of pop.	...	tertiary[b]	21

Society

No. of households	6.7m	Colour TVs per 100 households	99.4
Av. no. per household	3.3	Telephone lines per 100 pop.	57.3
Marriages per 1,000 pop.	7.7	Mobile telephone subscribers	
Divorces per 1,000 pop.	1.8	per 100 pop.	96.6
Cost of living, Dec. 2002		Computers per 100 pop.	22.3
New York = 100	92	Internet hosts per 1,000 pop.	97.3

a 2002 estimate.
b 1997

THAILAND

Area	513,115 sq km	Capital	Bangkok
Arable as % of total land	29	Currency	Baht (Bt)

People

Population	63.6m	Life expectancy: men	65.3 yrs
Pop. per sq km	124	women	73.5 yrs
Av. ann. growth		Adult literacy	95.7%
in pop. 2000–05	1.01%	Fertility rate (per woman)	1.9
Pop. under 15	26.3%	Urban population	20.0%
Pop. over 60	8.4%		per 1,000 pop.
No. of men per 100 women	96	Crude birth rate	17.8
Human Development Index	76.2	Crude death rate	7.1

The economy

GDP	Bt5,101bn	GDP per head	$1,800
GDP	$114.7bn	GDP per head in purchasing	
Av. ann. growth in real		power parity (USA=100)	18.2
GDP 1991–2001	4.2%	Economic freedom index	2.55

Origins of GDP		Components of GDP	
	% of total		% of total
Agriculture	10.0	Private consumption	56.9
Industry, of which:	44.2	Public consumption	11.6
manufacturing	36.3	Investment	24.0
Services	45.8	Exports	66.3
		Imports	-60.2

Structure of employment

	% of total		% of labour force
Agriculture	44	Unemployed 2001	3.5
Industry	22	Av. ann. rate 1995–2001	2.2
Services	34		

Energy

	m TOE		
Total output	41.1	Net energy imports as %	
Total consumption	73.6	of energy use	44
Consumption per head,			
kg oil equivalent	1,212		

Inflation and finance

Consumer price		av. ann. increase 1996–2001	
inflation 2002	0.6%	Narrow money (M1)	9.0%
Av. ann. inflation 1996–2002	2.9%	Broad money	7.4%
Money market rate, 2002	1.76%		

Exchange rates

	end 2002		December 2002
Bt per $	43.15	Effective rates	1995 = 100
Bt per SDR	58.67	– nominal	...
Bt per euro	41.15	– real	...

Trade

Principal exports		**Principal imports**	
	$bn fob		*$bn cif*
Machinery & mech. appliances	9.4	Capital goods	29.5
Integrated circuits	7.9	Raw materials & intermediates	15.8
Computer parts	7.7	Petroleum & products	7.1
Electrical appliance	4.9	Consumer goods	6.2
Total incl. others	**65.1**	Total incl. others	**62.1**

Main export destinations		**Main origins of imports**	
	% of total		*% of total*
United States	20.3	Japan	16.0
Japan	15.3	United States	11.6
Singapore	8.1	China	6.0
Hong Kong	5.1	Singapore	6.0
Malaysia	4.2	Malaysia	5.0

Balance of payments, reserves and debt, $bn

Visible exports fob	63.2	Overall balance	2.5
Visible imports fob	-54.6	Change in reserves	0.4
Trade balance	8.6	Level of reserves	
Invisibles inflows	16.9	end Dec.	33.0
Invisibles outflows	-19.8	No. months of import cover	5.3
Net transfers	0.6	Foreign debt	67.4
Current account balance	6.2	– as % of GDP	58
– as % of GDP	5.4	– as % of total exports	84
Capital balance	-3.9	Debt service ratio	25

Health and education

Health spending, % of GDP	6.8	Education spending, % of GDP	5.4
Doctors per 1,000 pop.	0.3	Enrolment, %: primary	95
Hospital beds per 1,000 pop.	5.9	secondary	82
Improved-water source access,		tertiary	35
% of pop.	80		

Society

No. of households	15.7m	Colour TVs per 100 households	81.7
Av. no. per household	3.8	Telephone lines per 100 pop.	9.4
Marriages per 1,000 pop.	5.8	Mobile telephone subscribers	
Divorces per 1,000 pop.	1.0	per 100 pop.	11.9
Cost of living, Dec. 2002		Computers per 100 pop.	2.7
New York = 100	59	Internet hosts per 1,000 pop.	1.6

TURKEY

Area	779,452 sq km	Capital	Ankara
Arable as % of total land	31	Currency	Turkish Lira (L)

People

Population	67.6m	Life expectancy: men		68.0 yrs
Pop. per sq km	87		women	73.2 yrs
Av. ann. growth		Adult literacy		85.6%
in pop. 2000–05	1.42%	Fertility rate (per woman)		2.4
Pop. under 15	31.7%	Urban population		66.2%
Pop. over 60	8.0%			per 1,000 pop.
No. of men per 100 women	102	Crude birth rate		20.1
Human Development Index	74.2	Crude death rate		6.0

The economy

GDP	L181,408trn	GDP per head	$2,180
GDP	$147.7bn	GDP per head in purchasing	
Av. ann. growth in real		power parity (USA=100)	17.0
GDP 1991–2001	2.5%	Economic freedom index	3.50

Origins of GDP		**Components of GDP**	
	% of total		% of total
Agriculture	12.9	Private consumption	72.3
Industry, of which:	30.4	Public consumption	14.1
manufacturing	...	Investment	16.5
Services	59.5	Exports	33.2
		Imports	-30.8

Structure of employment[a]

	% of total		% of labour force
Agriculture	46	Unemployed 2001	7.6
Industry	20	Av. ann. rate 1995–2001	6.8
Services	34		

Energy

	m TOE		
Total output	26.2	Net energy imports as %	
Total consumption	77.1	of energy use	66
Consumption per head,			
kg oil equivalent	1,181		

Inflation and finance

			av. ann. increase 1996–2001
Consumer price			
inflation 2002	45.0%	Narrow money (M1)	65.2%
Av. ann. inflation 1996–2002	64.2%	Broad money	81.4%
Money market rate, 2002	49.5%		

Exchange rates

	end 2002		December 2002
L per $	1,643,699	Effective rates	1995 = 100
L per SDR	2,234,642	– nominal	...
L per euro	1,567,368	– real	...

Trade

Principal exports		Principal imports	
	$bn fob		*$bn cif*
Clothing & textiles	10.3	Chemicals & products	6.8
Metals	2.9	Crude oil & gas	6.1
Vehicles & parts	2.7	Machinery & equipment	5.1
Agricultural products	2.2	Metals	3.6
Food	1.8	Vehicles & parts	2.2
Total incl. others	**31.3**	Total incl. others	**41.4**

Main export destinations		Main origins of imports	
	% of total		*% of total*
Germany	17.2	Germany	12.9
United States	10.0	Italy	8.4
Italy	7.5	Russia	8.3
United Kingdom	6.9	United States	7.9
France	6.0	France	5.5
EU15	51.4	EU15	44.2

Balance of payments, reserves and debt, $bn

Visible exports fob	34.4	Overall balance	-12.9
Visible imports fob	-38.9	Change in reserves	-3.6
Trade balance	-4.5	Level of reserves	
Invisibles inflows	18.8	end Dec.	19.9
Invisibles outflows	-14.7	No. months of import cover	4.5
Net transfers	3.8	Foreign debt	115.1
Current account balance	3.4	– as % of GDP	65
– as % of GDP	2.3	– as % of total exports	207
Capital balance	-14.2	Debt service ratio	40

Health and education

Health spending, % of GDP	5.0	Education spending, % of GDP	3.5
Doctors per 1,000 pop.	1.3	Enrolment, %: primary	101
Hospital beds per 1,000 pop.	2.6	secondary[b]	58
Improved-water source access,		tertiary[b]	15
% of pop.	83		

Society

No. of households	16.0m	Colour TVs per 100 households	67.3
Av. no. per household	4.0	Telephone lines per 100 pop.	28.5
Marriages per 1,000 pop.	7.7	Mobile telephone subscribers	
Divorces per 1,000 pop.	0.6	per 100 pop.	30.2
Cost of living, Dec. 2002		Computers per 100 pop.	4.1
New York = 100	61	Internet hosts per 1,000 pop.	2.9

a 1999
b 2000

UKRAINE

Area	603,700 sq km	Capital	Kiev
Arable as % of total land	56	Currency	Hryvnya (UAH)

People

Population	49.1m	Life expectancy: men		64.7 yrs
Pop. per sq km	81	women		74.7 yrs
Av. ann. growth		Adult literacy		99.6%
in pop. 2000–05	-0.78%	Fertility rate (per woman)		1.2
Pop. under 15	17.8%	Urban population		68.0%
Pop. over 60	20.6%			per 1,000 pop.
No. of men per 100 women	87	Crude birth rate		8.1
Human Development Index	74.8	Crude death rate		14.2

The economy

GDP	UAH202bn	GDP per head	$770
GDP	$37.6bn	GDP per head in purchasing	
Av. ann. growth in real		power parity (USA=100)	12.5
GDP 1991–2001	-6.6%	Economic freedom index	3.65

Origins of GDP		Components of GDP[a]	
	% of total		% of total
Agriculture	23.4	Private consumption	60.2
Industry, of which:	41.5	Public consumption	19.0
manufacturing	...	Investment	19.8
Services	35.1	Exports	52.6
		Imports	-51.5

Structure of employment[a]

	% of total		% of labour force
Agriculture	26	Unemployed 2001	11.8
Industry	26	Av. ann. rate 1995–2001	9.8
Services	48		

Energy

	m TOE		
Total output	26.2	Net energy imports as %	
Total consumption	140.0	of energy use	41
Consumption per head,			
kg oil equivalent	2,820		

Inflation and finance

		av. ann. increase 1996–2001	
Consumer price			
inflation 2002	0.8%	Narrow money (M1)	36.4%
Av. ann. inflation 1996–2002	14.7%	Broad money	37.0%
Money market rate, 2002	5.50%		

Exchange rates

	end 2002		December 2002
UAH per $	5.33	Effective rates	1995 = 100
UAH per SDR	7.25	– nominal	129.1
UAH per euro	5.08	– real	109.0

Trade

Principal exports		Principal imports	
	$bn fob		$bn cif
Metals	6.7	Fuels, mineral products	6.5
Machinery & transport		Machinery & transport	
equipment	2.3	equipment	3.4
Chemicals	1.9	Chemicals	2.0
Food & agricultural produce	1.8	Food & agricultural produce	1.1
Total incl. others	**17.1**	Total incl. others	**16.9**

Main export destinations		Main origins of imports	
	% of total		% of total
Russia	21.5	Russia	34.4
Turkey	5.9	Turkmenistan	9.8
Italy	4.9	Germany	8.2
Germany	4.2	Belarus	2.4
United States	3.3	Italy	2.4

Balance of payments, reserves and debt, $bn

Visible exports fob	17.1	Overall balance	1.0
Visible imports fob	-16.9	Change in reserves	1.6
Trade balance	0.2	Level of reserves	
Invisibles inflows	4.2	end Dec.	3.1
Invisibles outflows	-4.4	No. months of import cover	1.7
Net transfers	1.5	Foreign debt	12.8
Current account balance	1.4	– as % of GDP	39
– as % of GDP	3.7	– as % of total exports	66
Capital balance	-0.2	Debt service ratio	12

Health and education

Health spending, % of GDP	3.3	Education spending, % of GDP	4.5
Doctors per 1,000 pop.	4.6	Enrolment, %: primary[a]	78
Hospital beds per 1,000 pop.	9.2	secondary[a]	105
Improved-water source access,		tertiary[a]	43
% of pop.	...		

Society

No. of households	18.7m	Colour TVs per 100 households	73.6
Av. no. per household	2.5	Telephone lines per 100 pop.	21.2
Marriages per 1,000 pop.	6.2	Mobile telephone subscribers	
Divorces per 1,000 pop.	3.4	per 100 pop.	4.4
Cost of living, Dec. 2002		Computers per 100 pop.	1.8
New York = 100	65	Internet hosts per 1,000 pop.	1.3

a 1999

UNITED KINGDOM

Area	242,534 sq km	Capital	London
Arable as % of total land	24	Currency	Pound (£)

People

Population	59.5m	Life expectancy: men	75.7 yrs
Pop. per sq km	245	women	80.7 yrs
Av. ann. growth		Adult literacy	99.0%
in pop. 2000–05	0.31%	Fertility rate (per woman)	1.6
Pop. under 15	19.1%	Urban population	89.5%
Pop. over 60	20.7%		per 1,000 pop.
No. of men per 100 women	95	Crude birth rate	10.6
Human Development Index	92.8	Crude death rate	10.4

The economy

GDP	£989bn	GDP per head	$23,920
GDP	$1,424bn	GDP per head in purchasing	
Av. ann. growth in real		power parity (USA=100)	71.0
GDP 1991–2001	2.7%	Economic freedom index	1.85

Origins of GDP

	% of total	**Components of GDP**	% of total
Agriculture	0.9	Private consumption	65.8
Industry, of which:	27.6	Public consumption	19.2
manufacturing	17.5	Investment	17.2
Services	71.4	Exports	27.1
		Imports	-29.3

Structure of employment

	% of total		% of labour force
Agriculture	1	Unemployed 2001	4.4
Industry	25	Av. ann. rate 1995–2001	6.6
Services	74		

Energy

	m TOE		
Total output	272.3	Net energy imports as %	
Total consumption	232.6	of energy use	-17
Consumption per head,			
kg oil equivalent	3,962		

Inflation and finance

		av. ann. increase 1996–2001	
Consumer price			
inflation 2002	1.6%	Narrow money (M0)	7.4%
Av. ann. inflation 1996–2002	2.4%	Broad money	6.7%
Money market rate, 2002	3.89%	Household saving rate	6.1%

Exchange rates

	end 2002		December 2002
£ per $	0.62	Effective rates	1995 = 100
£ per SDR	0.54	– nominal	124.4
£ per euro	0.59	– real	143.8

Trade

Principal exports		Principal imports	
	$bn fob		*$bn fob*
Finished manufactured		Finished manufactured	
products	159.4	products	193.2
Semi-manufactured products	73.4	Semi-manufactured products	77.1
Fuels	23.7	Food, beverages & tobacco	27.0
Food, beverages & tobacco	14.0	Fuels	15.5
Basic materials	3.0	Basic materials	9.3
Total incl. others	**275.6**	Total incl. others	**321.0**

Main export destinations		Main origins of imports	
	% of total		*% of total*
United States	15.4	United States	13.2
Germany	12.5	Germany	12.7
France	10.2	France	8.6
Netherlands	7.7	Netherlands	6.7
Ireland	7.3		
EU15	58.1	EU15	51.7

Balance of payments, reserves and aid, $bn

Visible exports fob	273.7	Capital balance	16.8
Visible imports fob	-322.0	Overall balance	-4.5
Trade balance	-48.4	Change in reserves	-7.8
Invisibles inflows	317.2	Level of reserves	
Invisibles outflows	-282.8	end Dec.	40.4
Net transfers	-9.6	No. months of import cover	0.8
Current account balance	-23.5	Aid given	4.58
– as % of GDP	-1.6	– as % of GDP	0.32

Health and education

Health spending, % of GDP	7.3	Education spending, % of GDP	4.5
Doctors per 1,000 pop.	1.8	Enrolment, %: primary	99
Hospital beds per 1,000 pop.	3.9	secondary	156
Improved-water source access,		tertiary	60
% of pop.	100		

Society

No. of households	24.6m	Colour TVs per 100 households	98.6
Av. no. per household	2.3	Telephone lines per 100 pop.	57.8
Marriages per 1,000 pop.	5.1	Mobile telephone subscribers	
Divorces per 1,000 pop.	2.6	per 100 pop.	78.3
Cost of living, Dec. 2002		Computers per 100 pop.	36.6
New York = 100	108	Internet hosts per 1,000 pop.	43.4

UNITED STATES

Area	9,372,610 sq km	Capital	Washington DC
Arable as % of total land	19	Currency	US dollar ($)

People

Population	285.9m	Life expectancy:	men	74.3 yrs
Pop. per sq km	30		women	79.9 yrs
Av. ann. growth		Adult literacy		99.0%
in pop. 2000–05	1.03%	Fertility rate (per woman)		2.1
Pop. under 15	21.8%	Urban population		77.4%
Pop. over 60	16.1%			per 1,000 pop.
No. of men per 100 women	97	Crude birth rate		13.1
Human Development Index	93.9	Crude death rate		8.3

The economy

GDP	$10,065bn	GDP per head	$35,200
Av. ann. growth in real		GDP per head in purchasing	
GDP 1991–2001	3.3%	power parity (USA=100)	100
		Economic freedom index	1.80

Origins of GDP		**Components of GDP**	
	% of total		% of total
Agriculture	1.4	Private consumption	69.2
Industry, of which:	20.3	Public consumption	18.0
manufacturing	14.1	Investment	16.0
Services[a]	78.3	Exports	10.3
		Imports	-13.7

Structure of employment

	% of total		% of labour force
Agriculture	2	Unemployed 2001	4.7
Industry	23	Av. ann. rate 1995–2001	4.8
Services	75		

Energy

	m TOE		
Total output	1,675.8	Net energy imports as %	
Total consumption	2,299.7	of energy use	27
Consumption per head, kg oil equivalent	8,148		

Inflation and finance

		av. ann. increase 1996–2001	
Consumer price inflation 2002	1.5%	Narrow money (M1)	5.3%
Av. ann. inflation 1996–2002	2.3%	Broad money	9.1%
Treasury bill rate, 2002	1.61%	Household saving rate	2.3%

Exchange rates

	end 2002		December 2002
$ per SDR	1.36	Effective rates	1995 = 100
$ per euro	0.95	– nominal	122.5
		– real	129.2

Trade

Principal exports		**Principal imports**	
	$bn fob		*$bn fob*
Capital goods, excl. vehicles	321.7	Capital goods, excl. vehicles	298.0
Industrial supplies	160.1	Industrial supplies	284.3
Consumer goods, excl. vehicles	88.3	Consumer goods, excl. vehicles	273.9
Vehicles & products	75.4	Vehicles & products	189.8
Food & beverages	49.4	Food & beverages	46.4
Total incl. others	**729.1**	Total incl. others	**1,141.0**

Main export destinations		**Main origins of imports**	
	% of total		*% of total*
Canada	22.4	Canada	19.0
Mexico	13.9	Mexico	11.5
Japan	7.9	Japan	11.1
United Kingdom	5.6	China	8.9
Germany	4.1	Germany	5.2
EU15	21.2	EU15	19.2

Balance of payments, reserves and aid, $bn

Visible exports fob	721.8	Capital balance	387.6
Visible imports fob	-1,146.0	Overall balance	4.9
Trade balance	-424.2	Change in reserves	1.7
Invisibles inflows	560.0	Level of reserves	
Invisibles outflows	-479.7	end Dec.	130.1
Net transfers	-49.4	No. months of import cover	1.0
Current account balance	-393.4	Aid given	11.43
– as % of GDP	-3.9	– as % of GDP	0.13

Health and education

Health spending, % of GDP	13.0	Education spending, % of GDP	4.9
Doctors per 1,000 pop.	2.8	Enrolment, %: primary	101
Hospital beds per 1,000 pop.	3.5	secondary	95
Improved-water source access,		tertiary	73
% of pop.	100		

Society

No. of households	105.0m	Colour TVs per 100 households	99.5
Av. no. per household	2.5	Telephone lines per 100 pop.	66.5
Marriages per 1,000 pop.	8.2	Mobile telephone subscribers	
Divorces per 1,000 pop.	4.3	per 100 pop.	44.4
Cost of living, Dec. 2002		Computers per 100 pop.	62.3
New York = 100	100	Internet hosts per 1,000 pop.[b]	375.1

a Including utilities.
b Includes all hosts ending ".com", ".net" and ".org" which exaggerates the numbers.

VENEZUELA

Area	912,050 sq km	Capital	Caracas
Arable as % of total land	3	Currency	Bolivar (Bs)

People

Population	24.6m	Life expectancy:	men	70.9 yrs
Pop. per sq km	27		women	76.7 yrs
Av. ann. growth		Adult literacy		92.9%
in pop. 2000–05	1.86%	Fertility rate (per woman)		2.7
Pop. under 15	34.0%	Urban population		87.2%
Pop. over 60	6.6%			per 1,000 pop.
No. of men per 100 women	101	Crude birth rate		22.8
Human Development Index	77.0	Crude death rate		4.6

The economy

GDP	Bs90,421bn	GDP per head	$5,070
GDP	$124.9bn	GDP per head in purchasing	
Av. ann. growth in real		power parity (USA=100)	16.3
GDP 1991–2001	1.3%	Economic freedom index	3.50

Origins of GDP		Components of GDP	
	% of total		% of total
Agriculture	4.9	Private consumption	68.2
Industry, of which:	46.3	Public consumption	8.0
manufacturing	14.3	Investment	18.7
Services	48.9	Exports	22.7
		Imports	-17.6

Structure of employment[a]

	% of total		% of labour force
Agriculture	11	Unemployed 2001	14.1
Industry	24	Av. ann. rate 1995–2001	12.6
Services	65		

Energy

	m TOE		
Total output	225.5	Net energy imports as %	
Total consumption	59.3	of energy use	-280
Consumption per head,			
kg oil equivalent	2,452		

Inflation and finance

Consumer price		av. ann. increase 1996–2001	
inflation 2002	22.4%	Narrow money (M1)	27.3%
Av. ann. inflation 1996–2002	26.1%	Broad money	26.1%
Money market rate, 2002	27.33%		

Exchange rates

	end 2002		December 2002
Bs per $	1,401	Effective rates	1995 = 100
Bs per SDR	1,905	– nominal	16.3
Bs per euro	1,336	– real	...

Trade

Principal exports		Principal imports	
	$bn fob		*$bn fob*
Oil	21.3	Non-oil	10.9
Non-oil	4.9	Oil	1.3
Total incl. others	**27.4**	Total incl. others	**18.0**

Main export destinations		Main origins of imports	
	% of total		*% of total*
United States	57.4	United States	34.1
Brazil	4.7	Colombia	10.4
Canada	3.4	Italy	4.6
Spain	3.4	Brazil	4.5
Colombia	2.8	Germany	3.1

Balance of payments, reserves and debt, $bn

Visible exports fob	26.7	Overall balance	-2.1
Visible imports fob	-17.4	Change in reserves	-3.6
Trade balance	9.3	Level of reserves	
Invisibles inflows	3.8	end Dec.	12.3
Invisibles outflows	-8.6	No. months of import cover	5.7
Net transfers	-0.6	Foreign debt	34.7
Current account balance	3.9	– as % of GDP	30
– as % of GDP	3.1	– as % of total exports	113
Capital balance	-0.8	Debt service ratio	25

Health and education

Health spending, % of GDP[a]	4.2	Education spending, % of GDP[a]	5.2
Doctors per 1,000 pop.	2.4	Enrolment, %: primary	102
Hospital beds per 1,000 pop.	2.0	secondary	59
Improved-water source access,		tertiary	29
% of pop.	84		

Society

No. of households	5.2m	Colour TVs per 100 households	91.5
Av. no. per household	4.6	Telephone lines per 100 pop.	11.2
Marriages per 1,000 pop.	3.8	Mobile telephone subscribers	
Divorces per 1,000 pop.	0.9	per 100 pop.	26.4
Cost of living, Dec. 2002		Computers per 100 pop.	5.3
New York = 100	56	Internet hosts per 1,000 pop.	1.0

a 2000

VIETNAM

Area	331,114 sq km	Capital	Hanoi
Arable as % of total land	18	Currency	Dong (D)

People

Population	79.2m	Life expectancy:	men	66.9 yrs
Pop. per sq km	239		women	71.6 yrs
Av. ann. growth		Adult literacy		93.6%
in pop. 2000–05	1.35%	Fertility rate (per woman)		2.3
Pop. under 15	33.4%	Urban population		24.5%
Pop. over 60	7.5%			per 1,000 pop.
No. of men per 100 women	99	Crude birth rate		19.7
Human Development Index	68.8	Crude death rate		6.4

The economy

GDP	D484trn	GDP per head	$410
GDP	$32.7bn	GDP per head in purchasing	
Av. ann. growth in real		power parity (USA=100)	6.0
GDP 1991–2001	7.7%	Economic freedom index	3.70

Origins of GDP		**Components of GDP**	
	% of total		% of total
Agriculture	23.6	Private consumption	65.0
Industry, of which:	37.8	Public consumption	6.2
manufacturing	...	Investment	28.9
Services	38.6	Exports	55.3
		Imports	-57.3

Structure of employment[a]

	% of total		% of labour force
Agriculture	70	Unemployed 2001	...
Industry	13	Av. ann. rate 1995–2001	...
Services	17		

Energy

	m TOE		
Total output	46.3	Net energy imports as %	
Total consumption	40.0	of energy use	-25
Consumption per head,			
kg oil equivalent	471		

Inflation and finance

		av. ann. increase 1996–2001	
Consumer price			
inflation 2002	3.9%	Narrow money (M1)	27.4
Av. ann. inflation 1996–2002	2.8%	Broad money	34.5
Treasury bill rate, 2002	5.92%		

Exchange rates

	end 2002		December 2002
D per $	15,403	Effective rates	1995 = 100
D per SDR	20,941	– nominal	...
D per euro	14,688	– real	...

Trade

Principal exports		Principal imports	
	$bn fob		*$bn cif*
Crude oil	3.2	Petroleum products	1.9
Textiles & garments	2.0	Textiles	1.6
Fisheries products	1.8	Computers & electronic goods	0.7
Footwear	1.5	Steel	0.9
Rice	0.6	Motorcycles	0.6
Total incl. others	**15.1**	Total incl. others	**16.0**

Main export destinations		Main origins of imports	
	% of total		*% of total*
Japan	17.1	Singapore	13.6
Australia	7.6	China	11.9
China	7.5	Japan	11.6
Germany	6.9	South Korea	11.2
Singapore	5.4	Thailand	5.1
United States	5.2	Hong Kong	3.5

Balance of payments, reserves and debt, $bn

Visible exports fob	15.0	Overall balance	0.2
Visible imports fob	-14.5	Change in reserves	0.3
Trade balance	0.5	Level of reserves	
Invisibles inflows	3.1	end Dec.	3.8
Invisibles outflows	-4.2	No. months of import cover	2.4
Net transfers	1.3	Foreign debt	12.6
Current account balance	0.7	– as % of GDP	41
– as % of GDP	2.1	– as % of total exports	76
Capital balance	0.4	Debt service ratio	7

Health and education

Health spending, % of GDP	4.5	Education spending, % of GDP[b]	3.0
Doctors per 1,000 pop.	0.5	Enrolment, %: primary	106
Hospital beds per 1,000 pop.	2.5	secondary	67
Improved-water source access,		tertiary	10
% of pop.	56		

Society

No. of households	15.5m	Colour TVs per 100 households	37.6
Av. no. per household	4.8	Telephone lines per 100 pop.	3.8
Marriages per 1,000 pop.	...	Mobile telephone subscribers	
Divorces per 1,000 pop.	...	per 100 pop.	1.5
Cost of living, Dec. 2002		Computers per 100 pop.	1.0
New York = 100	69	Internet hosts per 1,000 pop.	...

a 1995
b 1997

ZIMBABWE

Area	390,759 sq km	Capital	Harare
Arable as % of total land	8	Currency	Zimbabwe dollar (Z$)

People

Population	12.9m	Life expectancy:	men	33.7 yrs
Pop. per sq km	33		women	32.6 yrs
Av. ann. growth		Adult literacy		89.3%
in pop. 2000–05	0.49%	Fertility rate (per woman)		3.9
Pop. under 15	43.9%	Urban population		36.0%
Pop. over 60	4.9%			per 1,000 pop.
No. of men per 100 women	99	Crude birth rate		35.1
Human Development Index	54.8	Crude death rate		27.0

The economy

GDP	Z$499bn	GDP per head	$700
GDP	$9.1bn	GDP per head in purchasing	
Av. ann. growth in real		power parity (USA=100)	6.5
GDP 1991–2001	0.1%	Economic freedom index	4.40

Origins of GDP[a]		Components of GDP[a]	
	% of total		% of total
Agriculture	25.1	Private consumption	71.7
Manufacturing	14.0	Public consumption	15.4
Other	60.9	Investment	13.5
		Net exports	-0.6

Structure of employment[b]

	% of total		% of labour force
Agriculture	26	Unemployed 1999	6
Industry	28	Av. ann. rate 1995–99	6.5
Services	46		

Energy

	m TOE		
Total output	8.7	Net energy imports as %	
Total consumption	10.2	of energy use	15
Consumption per head,			
kg oil equivalent	809		

Inflation and finance

		av. ann. increase 1996–2001	
Consumer price			
inflation 2002	134.5%	Narrow money (M1)	56.9%
Av. ann. inflation 1996–2002	58.4%	Broad money	52.5%
Money market rate, 2002	32.35%		

Exchange rates

	end 2002		December 2002
			1995 = 100
Z$ per $	5.49	Effective rates	
Z$ per SDR	7.46	– nominal	...
Z$ per euro	5.24	– real	...

Trade

Principal exports[a]	$m fob	Principal imports[a]	$m cif
Tobacco	609	Machinery & transport equipment	544
Food	265	Manufactured products	312
Textiles & cotton	245	Chemicals	310
Iron & steel	175	Petroleum products & electricity	207
Nickel	108		
Total incl. others	**1,925**	**Total incl. others**	**1,869**

Main export destinations	% of total	Main origins of imports	% of total
South Africa	14.1	South Africa	44.5
Japan	6.6	Mozambique	4.6
Netherlands	6.6	United Kingdom	4.1
Germany	6.5	Germany	3.5
United Kingdom	6.0	United States	3.4

Balance of payments, reserves and debt, $bn

Visible exports fob	1.7	Overall balance	-0.5
Visible imports fob	-1.5	Change in reserves	-0.2
Trade balance	0.3	Level of reserves	
Net invisibles outflows	-0.5	end Dec.	0.1
Net transfers	0.2	No. months of import cover	0.7
Current account balance	-0.1	Foreign debt	3.8
– as % of GDP	-0.9	– as % of GDP	54
Capital balance	-0.1	– as % of total exports	174
		Debt service ratio	6

Health and education

Health spending, % of GDP[a]	7.3	Education spending, % of GDP	10.4
Doctors per 1,000 pop.	0.1	Enrolment, %: primary	95
Hospital beds per 1,000 pop.[a]	0.5	secondary	44
Improved-water source access, % of pop.	85	tertiary	4

Society

No. of households	3.2m	Colour TVs per 100 households	3.0
Av. no. per household	3.7	Telephone lines per 100 pop.[a]	1.9
Marriages per 1,000 pop.	...	Mobile telephone subscribers	
Divorces per 1,000 pop.	...	per 100 pop.	2.4
Cost of living, Dec. 2002		Computers per 100 pop.	1.2
New York = 100	30	Internet hosts per 1,000 pop.	0.2

a 2000
b 1994

EURO AREA[a]

Area	2,365,000 sq km	Capital	–
Arable as % of total land	26.6	Currency	Euro (€)

People

Population	303.2m	Life expectancy: men		75.3 yrs
Pop. per sq km	128	women		81.8 yrs
Av. ann. growth		Adult literacy		98.3%
in pop. 2000–05	0.35%	Fertility rate (per woman)		1.5
Pop. under 15	16.2%	Urban population		77.4%
Pop. over 60	21.9%			per 1,000 pop.
No. of men per 100 women	95.9	Crude birth rate		10.3
Human Development Index	92.0	Crude death rate[b]		10.0

The economy

GDP	€6,810bn	GDP per head	$20,100
GDP	$6,094bn	GDP per head in purchasing	
Av. ann. growth in real		power parity (USA=100)	69.4
GDP 1991–2001	2.2%	Economic freedom index	2.28

Origins of GDP		Components of GDP	
	% of total		% of total
Agriculture	2	Private consumption	57
Industry, of which:	29	Public consumption	20
manufacturing	22	Investment	21
Services	69	Exports	37
		Imports	-35

Structure of employment

	% of total		% of labour force
Agriculture	4.8	Unemployed 2001	9.8
Industry	30.5	Av. ann. rate 1995–2001	10.7
Services	64.7		

Energy

	m TOE		
Total output	434.4	Net energy imports as %	
Total consumption	1,160.7	of energy use	63
Consumption per head,			
kg oil equivalent	3,824		

Inflation and finance

Consumer price		av. ann. increase 1996–2001	
inflation 2002	2.3%	Narrow money (M1)	7.6%
Av. ann. inflation 1996–2002	1.8%	Broad money	5.8%
Money market rate, 2002	3.32%		

Exchange rates

	end 2002		December 2002
€ per $	0.95	Effective rates	1995 = 100
€ per SDR	1.30	– nominal	85.0
		– real	77.4

Trade[b]

Principal exports

	$bn fob
Machinery & transport equip.	411
Manufactures	235
Chemicals	125
Food, drink & tobacco	46
Fuels & raw materials	38
Total incl. others	**1,186**

Principal imports

	$bn fob
Machinery & transport equip.	337
Manufactures	254
Fuels & raw materials	172
Chemicals	68
Food, drink & tobacco	52
Total incl. others	**920**

Main export destinations

	% of total
United States	24.4
Switzerland	7.6
Japan	4.6
Poland	3.6
China	3.1
Russia	2.8

Main origins of imports

	% of total
United States	19.1
China	7.4
Japan	7.4
Switzerland	5.9
Russia	4.6
Norway	4.4
Poland	2.6

Balance of payments, reserves and aid, $bn

Visible exports fob	924.6	Capital balance	-43.2
Visible imports fob	-857.0	Overall balance	-16.9
Trade balance	67.6	Change in reserves	-6.4
Invisibles inflows	539.9	Level of reserves	
Invisibles outflows	-574.8	end Dec.	345.6
Net transfers	-45.1	No. months of import cover	2.9
Current account balance	-12.3	Aid given	18.41
– as % of GDP	-0.2	– as % of GDP	0.25

Health and education

Health spending, % of GDP	9.3	Education spending, % of GDP	4.81
Doctors per 1,000 pop.	3.8	Enrolment, %: primary	106
Hospital beds per 1,000 pop.	7.1	secondary	104
Improved-water source access,		tertiary	50
% of pop.	...		

Society

No. of households	122.4m	Colour TVs per 100 households	96.6
Av. no. per household	2.48	Telephone lines per 100 pop.	50.1
Marriages per 1,000 pop.	5.1	Mobile telephone subscribers	
Divorces per 1,000 pop.	1.7	per 100 pop.	64.1
Cost of living, Dec. 2002		Computers per 100 pop.	26.4
New York = 100	...	Internet hosts per 1,000 pop.	54.9

a Data refer to EU12. Where necessary, population-weighted averages have been
  calculated.
b EU15 data.

WORLD

Area	148,698,382 sq km	Capital	...
Arable as % of total land	11	Currency	...

People

Population	6,134.1m	Life expectancy: men	63.3 yrs
Pop. per sq km	41	women	67.6 yrs
Av. ann. growth		Adult literacy	79.0%
in pop. 2000–05	1.22%	Fertility rate (per woman)	2.69
Pop. under 15	30.1%	Urban population	47.7%
Pop. over 60	10.0%		per 1,000 pop.
No. of men per 100 women	101	Crude birth rate	21.3
Human Development Index	72.2	Crude death rate	9.1

The economy

GDP	$31.1trn	GDP per head	$5,060
Av. ann. growth in real		GDP per head in purchasing	
GDP 1991–2001	2.6%	power parity (USA=100)	21.5
		Economic freedom index	3.20

Origins of GDP		**Components of GDP**	
	% of total		% of total
Agriculture	4	Private consumption	58
Industry, of which:	30	Public consumption	18
manufacturing	20	Investment	22
Services	66	Exports	30
		Imports	-28

Structure of employment[a]

	% of total		% of labour force
Agriculture	7	Unemployed 2001	6.5
Industry	27	Av. ann. rate 1995–2001	6.8
Services	66		

Energy

	m TOE		
Total output	10,010.0	Net energy imports as %	
Total consumption	9,886.1	of energy use	-1
Consumption per head,			
kg oil equivalent	1,694		

Inflation and finance[a]

Consumer price		av. ann. increase 1996–2001	
inflation 2002	2.0%	Narrow money (M0)	9.7%
Av. ann. inflation 1996–2002	3.0%	Broad money	11.2%
LIBOR rate, 3-month, 2002	1.79%	Household saving rate	6.7%

Trade
World exports

	$bn fob		$bn fob
Machinery & transport equip.	2,584	Food, drink & tobacco	388
Manufactured products	1,634	Raw materials	213
Fuels	596		
Chemicals	567	Total incl. others	**6,180**

Main export destinations

	% of total
United States	18.1
Germany	7.9
United Kingdom	5.5
Japan	5.2
France	5.1

Main origins of imports

	% of total
United States	12.4
Germany	8.9
Japan	7.1
China	6.6
France	4.8

Balance of payments, reserves and aid, $bn

Visible exports fob	6,069	Capital balance	107
Visible imports fob	-6,060	Overall balance	0
Trade balance	9	Change in reserves	-141.2
Invisibles inflows	2,842	Level of reserves	
Invisibles outflows	-2,942	end Dec.	2,140.2
Net transfers	-27	No. months of import cover	3
Current account balance	-117	Aid given[b]	53.51
– as % of GDP	-0.4	– as % of GDP[b]	0.17

Health and education

Health spending, % of GDP	9	Education spending, % of GDP	4.5
Doctors per 1,000 pop.	1.4	Enrolment, %: primary	104
Hospital beds per 1,000 pop.	3.2	secondary	60
Improved-water source access,		tertiary	...
% of pop.	80		

Society

No. of households	...	TVs per 100 households	24
Av. no. per household	...	Telephone lines per 100 pop.	17
Marriages per 1,000 pop.	...	Mobile telephone subscribers	
Divorces per 1,000 pop.	...	per 100 pop.	16
Cost of living, Dec. 2002		Computers per 100 pop.	9
New York = 100	...	Internet hosts per 1,000 pop.	27.9

a OECD countries.
b OECD and Middle East countries.

Glossary

Balance of payments The record of a country's transactions with the rest of the world. The **current account** of the balance of payments consists of: visible trade (goods); "invisible" trade (services and income); private transfer payments (eg, remittances from those working abroad); official transfers (eg, payments to international organisations, famine relief). Visible imports and exports are normally compiled on rather different definitions to those used in the trade statistics (shown in principal imports and exports) and therefore the statistics do not match. The **capital account** consists of long- and short-term transactions relating to a country's assets and liabilities (eg, loans and borrowings). Adding the current to the capital account gives the **overall balance**. This is compensated by net monetary movements and changes in reserves. In practice methods of statistical recording are neither complete nor accurate and an errors and omissions item, sometimes quite large, will appear. In the country pages of this book this item is included in the overall balance. **Changes in reserves** exclude revaluation effects and are shown without the practice often followed in balance of payments presentations of reversing the sign.

CFA Communauté Financière Africaine. Its members, most of the francophone African nations, share a common currency, the CFA franc, which used to be pegged to the French franc but is now pegged to the euro.

Cif/fob Measures of the value of merchandise trade. Imports include the cost of "carriage, insurance and freight" (cif) from the exporting country to the importing. The value of exports does not include these elements and is recorded "free on board" (fob). Balance of payments statistics are generally adjusted so that both exports and imports are shown fob; the cif elements are included in invisibles.

Commonwealth of Independent States All former Soviet Union Republics, excluding Estonia, Latvia and Lithuania. It was established January 1 1992; Azerbaijan joined in September 1993 and Georgia in December 1993.

Crude birth rate The number of live births in a year per 1,000 population. The crude rate will automatically be relatively high if a large proportion of the population is of childbearing age.

Crude death rate The number of deaths in a year per 1,000 population. Also affected by the population's age structure.

Debt, foreign Financial obligations owed by a country to the rest of the world and repayable in foreign currency. **The debt service ratio** is debt service (principal repayments plus interest payments) expressed as a percentage of the country's earnings from exports of goods and services.

EU European Union. Members are: Austria, Belgium, Denmark, Finland, France, Germany, Greece, Ireland, Italy, Luxembourg, Netherlands, Portugal, Spain, Sweden and the United Kingdom.

Effective exchange rate The nominal index measures a currency's depreciation (figures below 100) or appreciation (figures over 100) from a base date against a trade weighted basket of the currencies of the country's main trading partners. The real effective exchange rate reflects adjustments for relative movements in prices or costs.

Euro Replaced the ecu (European currency unit), on a one-to-one basis on January 1 1999. The currencies of the 12 euro area members have irrevocably fixed conversion rates for the euro. Notes and coins went into circulation on January 1 2002.

Euro area Members are those of the EU

except Denmark, Sweden and the United Kingdom.

Fertility rate The average number of children born to a woman who completes her childbearing years.

GDP Gross domestic product. The sum of all output produced by economic activity within a country. GNP (gross national product) and GNI (gross national income) include net income from abroad eg, rent, profits.

Household saving rate Household savings as % of disposable household income.

Import cover The number of months of imports covered by reserves, ie reserves ÷ ¹⁄₁₂ annual imports (visibles and invisibles).

Inflation The annual rate at which prices are increasing. The most common measure and the one shown here is the increase in the consumer price index.

Internet hosts Websites and other computers that sit permanently on the internet.

Life expectancy The average length of time a baby born today can expect to live.

Literacy is defined by UNESCO as the ability to read and write a simple sentence, but definitions can vary from country to country.

Median age Divides the age distribution into two halves. Half of the population is above and half below the median age.

Money supply A measure of the "money" available to buy goods and services. Various definitions exist. The measures shown here are based on definitions used by the IMF and may differ from measures used nationally. Narrow money (M1) consists of cash in circulation and demand deposits (bank deposits that can be withdrawn on demand). "Quasi-money" (time, savings and foreign currency deposits) is added to this to create broad money.

OECD Organisation for Economic Co-operation and Development. The "rich countries" club was established in 1961 to promote economic growth and the expansion of world trade. It is based in Paris and now has 30 members.

Opec Organisation of Petroleum Exporting Countries. Set up in 1960 and based in Vienna, Opec is mainly concerned with oil pricing and production issues. Members are; Algeria, Indonesia, Iran, Iraq, Kuwait, Libya, Nigeria, Qatar, Saudi Arabia, United Arab Emirates and Venezuela.

PPP Purchasing power parity. PPP statistics adjust for cost of living differences by replacing normal exchange rates with rates designed to equalise the prices of a standard "basket" of goods and services. These are used to obtain PPP estimates of GDP per head. PPP estimates are shown on an index, taking the United States as 100.

Real terms Figures adjusted to exclude the effect of inflation.

Reserves The stock of gold and foreign currency held by a country to finance any calls that may be made for the settlement of foreign debt.

SDR Special drawing right. The reserve currency, introduced by the IMF in 1970, was intended to replace gold and national currencies in settling international transactions. The IMF uses SDRs for book-keeping purposes and issues them to member countries. Their value is based on a basket of the US dollar (with a weight of 45%), the euro (29%), the Japanese yen (15%) and the pound sterling (11%).

List of countries

Whenever data is available, the world rankings consider 177 countries: all those which had (in 2001) or have recently had a population of at least 1m or a GDP of at least $1bn. Here is a list of them.

	Population	GDP	GDP per head	Area	Median age
	m	*$bn*	*$PPP*	*'000 sq km*	*years*
Afghanistan	22.5	21.0[ac]	930[ac]	652	18.1
Albania	3.1	4.1	3,810	29	26.7
Algeria	30.8	54.7	5,910	2,382	21.7
Andorra	0.1	1.3[ac]	14,440[ac]	0.4	37.0
Angola	13.5	9.5	1,690	1,247	16.3
Argentina	37.5	268.6	10,980	2,767	27.9
Armenia	3.8	2.1	2,730	30	30.7
Aruba	0.1	1.9	28,000[ac]	0.2	34.0
Australia	19.3	368.7	24,630	7,682	35.2
Austria	8.1	188.5	26,380	84	38.3
Azerbaijan	8.1	5.6	2,890	87	25.6
Bahamas	0.3	4.8[c]	15,680[c]	14	26.1
Bahrain	0.6	7.9	15,390	1	26.9
Bangladesh	140.4	46.7	1,600	144	20.0
Barbados	0.3	2.8	15,110	0.4	32.6
Belarus	10.1	12.2	7,630	208	36.5
Belgium	10.3	229.6	26,150	31	39.1
Benin	6.1	2.4	970	113	16.6
Bermuda	0.1	2.2[a]	34,800[a]	1	36.0
Bhutan	2.1	0.5	1,530	47	18.3
Bolivia	8.5	8.0	2,240	1,099	20.1
Bosnia	4.1	4.8	6,250	51	35.1
Botswana	1.6	5.2	7,410	581	19.1
Brazil	172.6	502.5	7,070	8,512	25.4
Brunei	0.3	6.2[a]	18,000[a]	6	25.0
Bulgaria	7.9	13.6	6,740	111	39.1
Burkina Faso	11.9	2.5	1,120	274	15.5
Burundi	6.5	0.7	680	28	15.8
Cambodia	13.4	3.4	1,790	181	17.5
Cameroon	15.2	8.5	1,580	475	18.1
Canada	31.0	694.5	26,530	9,971	36.9
Central African Rep	3.8	1.0	1,300	622	18.3
Chad	8.1	1.6	1,060	1,284	16.7
Chile	15.4	66.5	8,840	757	28.3
China	1285.0	1,159.0	3,950	9,561	30.0
Colombia	42.8	82.4	6,790	1,142	24.0
Congo-Kinshasa	52.5	5.2	630	2,345	16.5
Congo-Brazzaville	3.1	2.8	680	342	16.7
Costa Rica	4.1	16.1	9,260	51	24.5
Côte d'Ivoire	16.3	10.4	1,400	322	18.1
Croatia	4.7	20.3	8,930	57	38.9
Cuba	11.2	25.5[a]	2,280[a]	111	33.0
Cyprus	0.8	9.1	21,110	9	33.4
Czech Republic	10.3	56.8	14,320	79	37.6

	Population	GDP	GDP per head	Area	Median age
	m	*$bn*	*$PPP*	*'000 sq km*	*years*
Denmark	5.3	161.5	28,490	43	38.7
Dominican Republic	8.5	21.2	6,650	48	23.1
Ecuador	12.9	18.0	2,960	272	22.7
Egypt	69.1	98.5	3,560	1,000	21.3
El Salvador	6.4	13.7	5,160	21	21.8
Eritrea	3.8	0.7	1,030	117	16.9
Estonia	1.4	5.5	9,650	45	37.9
Ethiopia	64.5	6.2	800	1,134	16.9
Fiji	0.8	1.7	4,920	18	23.1
Finland	5.2	120.9	24,030	338	39.4
France	59.5	1309.8[b]	24,080	544	37.6
French Polynesia	0.2	3.9[c]	28,020[c]	3	25.1
Gabon	1.3	4.3	5,190	268	18.9
Gambia, The	1.4	0.4	2,010	11	19.4
Georgia	5.2	3.1	2,580	70	34.8
Germany	82.0	1,846.1	25,240	358	39.9
Ghana	19.7	5.3	2,170	239	18.8
Greece	10.6	117.2	17,520	132	39.1
Guadeloupe	0.4	5.3[c]	12,000[c]	2	31.8
Guam	0.2	3.2[ac]	21,000[ac]	1	27.4
Guatemala	11.7	20.5	4,380	109	17.8
Guinea	8.3	3.0	1,900	246	17.6
Guinea-Bissau	1.2	0.2	890	36	16.6
Haiti	8.3	3.7	1,870	28	18.9
Honduras	6.6	6.4	2,760	112	18.7
Hong Kong	7.0	161.9	25,560	1	36.1
Hungary	9.9	51.9	11,990	93	38.1
Iceland	0.3	7.7	28,850	103	32.9
India	1025.1	477.3	2,820	3,287	23.4
Indonesia	214.8	145.3	2,830	1,904	24.6
Iran	71.4	114.1	5,940	1,648	20.6
Iraq	23.6	27.9[a]	1,180[ad]	438	18.7
Ireland	3.8	103.3	27,170	70	31.9
Israel	6.2	108.3	19,630	21	27.9
Italy	57.5	1,088.8	24,530	301	40.2
Jamaica	2.6	7.8	3,490	11	24.1
Japan	127.3	4,141.4	25,550	378	41.3
Jordan	5.1	8.8	3,880	89	20.1
Kazakhstan	16.1	22.4	6,150	2,717	27.9
Kenya	31.3	11.4	970	583	17.7
Kirgizstan	5.0	1.5	2,630	583	23.2
Kuwait	2.0	32.8	21,530	18	28.6
Laos	5.4	1.8	1,540	237	18.5
Latvia	2.4	7.5	7,760	64	37.8
Lebanon	3.6	16.7	4,400	10	25.2
Lesotho	2.1	0.8	2,980	30	18.8
Liberia	3.1	0.5	1,100[a]	111	16.6

	Population	GDP	GDP per head	Area	Median age
	m	$bn	$PPP	'000 sq km	years
Libya	5.4	34.1[c]	7,600[a]	1,760	21.8
Lithuania	3.7	12.0	8,350	65	36.0
Luxembourg	0.4	18.5	48,560	3	37.0
Macau	0.5	6.2	21,630	0.02	33.5
Macedonia	2.0	3.4	6,040	26	32.3
Madagascar	16.4	4.6	820	587	17.5
Malawi	11.6	1.7	560	118	17.1
Malaysia	22.6	88.0	7,910	333	23.6
Mali	11.7	2.6	770	1,240	15.4
Malta	0.4	3.6	13,140	0.3	36.5
Martinique	0.4	5.5[c]	14,030[c]	1	33.8
Mauritania	2.7	1.0	1,940	1,031	18.2
Mauritius	1.2	4.5	9,860	2	28.9
Mexico	100.4	617.8	8,240	1,973	22.9
Moldova	4.3	1.5	2,300	34	31.7
Mongolia	2.6	1.0	1,710	1,565	21.8
Morocco	30.4	34.2	3,500	447	23.0
Mozambique	18.6	3.6	1,050	799	17.8
Myanmar	48.4	4.7[a]	1,500[a]	677	23.4
Namibia	1.8	3.1	7,410	824	18.4
Nepal	23.6	5.6	1,360	147	19.5
Netherlands	15.9	380.1	27,390	42	37.6
Netherlands Antilles	0.2	2.4[ac]	11,400[ac]	1	32.0
New Caledonia	0.2	3.1	25,200[c]	19	26.9
New Zealand	3.8	50.4	19,130	271	34.5
Nicaragua	5.2	2.5[a]	2,500[a]	130	18.1
Niger	11.2	2.0	880	1,267	15.1
Nigeria	116.9	41.4	790	924	17.3
North Korea	22.4	22.0[a]	1,000[a]	121	29.4
Norway	4.5	166.1	29,340	324	37.2
Oman	2.6	19.9	10,720[c]	310	21.2
Pakistan	145.0	58.7	1,860	804	18.8
Panama	2.9	10.2	5,440	77	24.8
Papua New Guinea	4.9	3.0	2,450	463	19.1
Paraguay	5.6	7.2	5,180	407	19.7
Peru	26.1	54.0	4,470	1,285	22.7
Philippines	77.1	71.4	4,070	300	20.9
Poland	38.6	176.3	9,370	313	35.2
Portugal	10.0	109.8	17,710	89	37.0
Puerto Rico	4.0	67.9	18,090	9	31.8
Qatar	0.8	16.2	21,200[a]	11	31.0
Réunion	0.7	7.8[c]	10,500[c]	3	28.3
Romania	22.4	38.7	5,780	238	34.7
Russia	144.7	310.0	6,880	17,075	36.8
Rwanda	7.9	1.7	1,240	26	17.0
Saudi Arabia	21.0	186.5	13,290	2,200	20.6
Senegal	9.7	4.6	1,480	197	17.6

	Population	GDP	GDP per head	Area	Median age
	m	*$bn*	*$PPP*	*'000 sq km*	*years*
Serbia & Montenegro	10.5	10.9	2,370[a]	102	35.4
Sierra Leone	4.6	0.7	460	72	17.9
Singapore	4.1	85.6	22,850	1	34.5
Slovakia	5.4	20.5	11,780	49	34.0
Slovenia	2.0	18.8	17,060	20	38.1
Somalia	9.2	4.1[a]	550[a]	638	16.0
South Africa	43.8	113.3	10,910	1,226	22.6
South Korea	47.1	422.2	15,060	99	31.8
Spain	39.9	581.8	20,150	505	37.4
Sri Lanka	19.1	15.9	3,260	66	28.1
Sudan	31.8	12.5	1,750	2,506	19.7
Suriname	0.4	0.8	3,310	164	23.5
Swaziland	1.1	1.3	4,430	17	17.4
Sweden	8.8	209.8	23,800	450	39.6
Switzerland	7.2	247.1	30,970	41	40.2
Syria	16.6	19.5	3,160	185	19.0
Taiwan	22.3	282.3	17,200[a]	36	31.0
Tajikistan	6.1	1.1	1,140	143	19.9
Tanzania	36.0	9.3	520	945	16.8
Thailand	63.6	114.7	5,230	513	27.5
Togo	4.7	1.3	1,620	57	17.7
Trinidad & Tobago	1.3	8.8	8,620	5	27.6
Tunisia	9.6	20.0	6,090	164	24.4
Turkey	67.6	147.7	5,830	779	24.2
Turkmenistan	4.8	6.0	4,240	488	21.6
Uganda	24.0	5.7	1,460	241	15.1
Ukraine	49.1	37.6	4,270	604	37.3
United Arab Emirates	2.7	67.6	21,100[a]	84	29.6
United Kingdom	59.5	1,424.1	24,340	243	37.7
United States	285.9	10,065.3	34,280	9,373	35.2
Uruguay	3.4	18.7	8,250	176	31.4
Uzbekistan	25.3	11.3	2,410	447	21.5
Venezuela	24.6	124.9	5,590	912	23.1
Vietnam	79.2	32.7	2,070	331	23.1
Virgin Islands	0.1	1.8[ac]	15,000[ac]	0.4	31.4
West Bank and Gaza	3.3	4.0	1,000[a]	6	16.8
Yemen	19.1	9.3	730	528	15.4
Zambia	10.6	3.6	750	753	16.7
Zimbabwe	12.9	9.1	2,340	391	17.5
Euro area (12)	303.2	6,094.4	23,800	2,497	38.7

a Estimate.
b Including French Guiana, Guadeloupe, Martinique and Réunion.
c 2000
d At market exchange rates.

Sources

Airports Council International, *Worldwide Airport Traffic Report*

BP, *Statistical Review of World Energy*

British Mountaineering Council

Centre for International Earth Science Information Network, Columbia University

Commission for Distilled Spirits, World Drink Trends

Corporate Resources Group, *Quality of Living Report*

Council of Europe

Demographia

Economist Intelligence Unit, *Business Operating Costs*; *Cost of Living Survey*; *Country Forecasts*; *Country Reports*; *Global Outlook – Business Environment Rankings*

ERC Statistics International, *World Cigarette Report*

Euromonitor, *International Marketing Data and Statistics*; *European Marketing Data and Statistics*

Europa Publications, *The Europa World Yearbook*

European Bank for Reconstruction and Development, *Transition Report*

Eurostat, *Statistics in Focus*

FAO, *FAOSTAT database*; *State of the World's Forests*

Financial Times Business Information, *The Banker*

The Heritage Foundation, *The 2001 Index of Economic Freedom*

IMD, *World Competitiveness Yearbook*

IMF, *Direction of Trade*; *International Financial Statistics*; *World Economic Outlook*

International Cocoa Organisation, *Quarterly Bulletin of Cocoa Statistics*

International Civil Aviation Organisation, *Civil Aviation Statistics of the World*

International Coffee Organisation

International Cotton Advisory Committee, *Bulletin*

International Criminal Police Organisation (Interpol), *International Crime Statistics*

International Road Federation, *World Road Statistics*

International Rubber Study Group, *Rubber Statistical Bulletin*

International Federation of the Phonographic Industry

International Grains Council, *The Grain Market Report*

International Sugar Organisation, *Sugar Yearbook*

International Tea Committee, *Annual Bulletin of Statistics*

International Telecommunication Union, *ITU Indicators*

International Wool Textile Organisation

Inter-Parliamentary Union

ISTA Mielke, *Oil World*

Johnson Matthey

Lloyd's Register, *Statistical Tables*

William M. Mercer Limited

National statistics offices

Network Wizards

Nobel Foundation

OECD, *Development Assistance Committee Report*; *Environmental Data*; *Main Economic Indicators*

Standard & Poor's *Emerging Stock Markets Factbook*

Swiss Re, *sigma*

Taiwan Statistical Data Book

The Times, *Atlas of the World*

Time Inc Magazines, *Fortune International*

Transparency International

UN, *Demographic Yearbook, Global Refugee Trends*; *State of World Population Report*; *Statistical Chart on World Families*; *World Population*; *World Population Prospects*; *World Urbanisation Prospects*

UN Development Programme, *Human Development Report*

Unicef *Global Database of Fertility and Contraceptive Use*

UNESCO, website: unescostat. unesco.org

Union Internationale des Chemins de Fer, *Statistiques Internationales des Chemins de Fer*

US Department of Agriculture, *Rice Report*

University of Michigan, Windows to the Universe website

WHO, *Mortability Database*; *Weekly Epidemiological Record*; *World Health Statistics Annual*; *World Report on Violence and Health*

World Bank, *Global Development Finance*; *Little Green Data Book*; *World Development Indicators*; *World Development Report*

World Bureau of Metal Statistics, *World Metal Statistics*

World Economic Forum/Harvard University, *Global Competitiveness Yearbook*

World Resources Institute, *World Resources*

World Tourist Organisation, *Yearbook of Tourism Statistics*

World Trade Organisation, *Annual Report*

World Water Council

World Wide Fund for Nature